THE MIND POSSESSED

THE MIND POSSESSED

A Physiology of Possession,
Mysticism and Faith Healing

WILLIAM SARGANT

J. B. Lippincott Company

Philadelphia and New York

1974

U.S. Library of Congress Cataloging in Publication Data

Sargant, William Walters.
  The mind possessed.

  Bibliography: p.
  1. Psychology, Religious. 2. Spirit possession.
3. Demoniac possession. I. Title.
BL53.S27   1974   248'.2   73-15627
ISBN-0-397-01011-7

Contents

List of Illustrations

Between pages 116–117

'And something moved in John's body, which was not John. He was invaded, set at nought, possessed. This power had struck John . . . in a moment, wholly, filling him with an anguish he could never in his life have imagined, that he surely could not endure, that even now he could not believe . . . had ripped him and felled him in a moment, so that John . . . lay here, now, helpless, screaming, at the very bottom of darkness.

*　　*　　*

Then John saw the Lord—for a moment only; and the darkness, for a moment only, was filled with a light he could not bear. Then, in a moment, he was set free . . . his heart, like a fountain of waters, burst.

*　　*　　*

Yes, the night had passed, the powers of darkness had been beaten back. He moved among the saints . . . he scarcely knew how he moved, for his hands were new, and his feet were new, and he moved in a new and Heaven-bright air.'

Go Tell It on the Mountain
James Baldwin

Michael Joseph, 1954

Preface

Brought up in a large middle-class Methodist family, it was still possible, when young, to meet those, including members of my own family, who had been suddenly and spiritually changed, as it were in the twinkling of an eye. Their whole life had been altered and the change was permanent rather than transitory. Such happenings were thought to be due to the intervention of the Holy Ghost.

These alterations of thought and behaviour were forgotten during my medical and psychiatric training, and my interest was only re-aroused later on when I started to see what seemed to me to be basically similar sorts of phenomena in a non-religious setting with the introduction of the new shock treatments in psychiatry, and particularly during the intensive use of the emotionally arousing drug abreactive techniques in the Second World War.

In 1957 in *Battle for the Mind*,[1] I tried to link abreactive and shock treatments with the physiology of sudden religious conversion and brain washing. This book has had very large and continuing sales, and an acceptance which has encouraged me to continue this research, alongside my main work of teaching medical students, and trying to learn better how to help patients, mostly along the new physical and mechanistic lines.

I have fortunately been able to travel frequently and in many parts of the world, studying, photographing and filming examples of religious and non-religious possession, healing and trance. Despite their tremendous importance—for a man's whole life can be so easily changed when such things happen to him—such investigations earned no official research grants or help. Too often I was straying outside my own psychiatric territory and into that of other disciplines. Fortunately, book sales and frequent invitations to lecture abroad have made it possible to continue this work over many years.

Battle for the Mind correctly anticipated the recently ever-increasing interest in matters mystical and how life can be given —if so desired—a more philosophical and less materialistic purpose. In my Maudsley Lecture in 1967 on the Physiology of Faith I also discussed physical aids to the attainment of spiritual grace and do so again here, including dancing, drugs and sex which are being so much more used now for this purpose.

If at the end of this research, I come to the conclusion that many of the happenings examined and recorded are man-made, rather than originating from co-existing spiritual worlds, this makes it all the more important that man's thoughts are somehow more continually directed towards good rather than evil ends; often most effectively, it also seems, by the mechanistic methods discussed here.

Man himself may well be our most approachable god; and so man must sooner or later start to behave as a beneficent deity rather than so often as the devil incarnate. With his increasingly godlike powers, he has, for instance, used these to kill no less than 60,000,000 of his fellow men in the last forty years and could now destroy all life on earth. Our prayers should constantly include ourselves and be about ourselves and our actions.

In *Battle for the Mind* and *The Unquiet Mind*,[2] I was fortunate in having Robert Graves to help in the final rewriting and to provide additional factual information. This time, Richard Cavendish, formerly editor of *Man, Myth and Magic*, has been very helpful in both these same respects. Dr Alexander Walk has been as knowledgeable and helpful in his proof corrections and suggestions in this book, as in previous ones. I have to thank several research secretaries at St Thomas's Hospital for help with the script and also my former secretary Miss M. English. My wife's help has been invaluable in many respects, especially in the collection of sound, photographic and film recordings under sometimes strange circumstances.

London, 1973   William Sargant

NOTES

1 W. Sargant, *Battle for the Mind*. Heinemann, 1957.
2 W. Sargant, *The Unquiet Mind*. Heinemann, 1967.

PART ONE

The Mind Under Stress

The origin of this book dates back to the Second World War and the treatment of battle neuroses—psychological disorders stemming from horrifying and mentally overwhelming experiences of war. Soldiers who had broken down, in combat or afterwards, sometimes became totally preoccupied by their memories of what had happened to them. In other cases, these memories had been repressed into the subconscious mind but were causing feelings of depression, fatigue, irritability, irrational fears or nightmares.

Experiments were made with various drugs which enabled previously 'normal' people, suffering from recent battle neuroses, to relive emotionally, or to 'abreact' as it is called, experiences which had led to breakdown. We would inject a drug intravenously or give ether on a mask to the patient. Then we would suggest to him, in his drug-disinhibited state, that he was back in the situation of terror and stress which was troubling him. If his best friend's head had been blown off into his lap, or he had been trapped in a burning tank or buried alive by an exploding shell, he was made to put himself back into the experience and live through it again. If successful, the effect was to stir up intense nervous excitement which produced violent outbursts of emotion.

As we increased the crescendo of the patient's excitement, he might suddenly collapse and fall back inert on the couch. At first we thought this collapse might be caused by the drug, but it later became clear that it was an *emotional* collapse, brought about by the excitement aroused during abreaction. After the patient had come round, he might burst into tears or shake his head and smile, and then report that all his previous fears and abnormal preoccupations had suddenly left him, that his mind was functioning more normally again, that he felt more like his old self, that memories which had obsessed and terrified him could now be thought of without fear or anxiety. This could happen after weeks or months of illness, and the failure of other treatments. But it was only a really intense abreactive experience, followed by a phase of collapse, which was likely to produce such a dramatic relief of symptoms.

Our method of treatment, supposedly new, was in fact of time-honoured antiquity. Alcohol had earlier been used to bring about states of sudden and violent abreactive emotional release, and hypnosis had been used extensively in the First World War, and was still sometimes employed in the Second, to induce a patient to relive traumatic battle experiences. But more significantly, as this book will show, our method of treatment was markedly similar to techniques which men have employed for thousands of years all over the world in their dealings with the abnormal: not only in terms of mental illness, but in relation to 'supernormal' or 'supernatural' agencies—gods, spirits and demons.[1]

We found that traumatic events had to be relived in the *present tense*. It was of little value if the patient merely described what had happened to him in a dull recital of events in the past tense and without renewed emotion. We tried to put him mentally right back into the horrifying situation, to make him live through it afresh, feeling, remembering and describing the whole experience in words. It was this verbalizing and emotional re-creation of a harrowing past experience which both Freud and Breuer, one of Freud's early co-workers, had insisted was the essential curative agent of the abreactive process. For it enabled repressed and highly traumatic memories to flood back into the patient's normal stream of consciousness, instead of being isolated and shut off from it, perhaps even totally forgotten, but still existing in the patient's subconscious mind and causing disabling symptoms.

Towards the end of the war we started to use more powerfully excitatory types of drug, such as ether and methedrine (an amphetamine), instead of the more sedative intravenous barbiturates, such as pentothal or sodium amytal. We now began to find that it was not always the reliving of specific traumatic incidents in the past that produced the most beneficial effects, but the release by one means or another of states of really intense emotional excitement, anger or fear. These states might be created around incidents which were comparatively trivial and unimportant. We even found on occasion that the release of great anger or fear could be more effectively produced around incidents which were entirely imaginary and had never happened to the patient at all, and such abreactions of imaginary events could have remarkably beneficial effects. In fact, in dealing with people whose minds had only *just recently* broken down under stresses and strains, it might only be necessary to produce a state of severe emotional excitement centred about almost anything, to break up a recently implanted abnormal pattern of behaviour; and this would help to return the nervous system to its more normal functioning. Though many soldiers still remained 'scarred' and sensitized in a variety of ways because of their sudden breakdown.[2]

We found that the two emotions which it was most helpful to arouse, to break up recently implanted abnormal patterns of behaviour and thought, were feelings of great anger and aggression, or of intense fear and anxiety. The release of feelings of depression did not bring any real benefit, and laughter was not a sufficiently powerful emotion for the purpose. Laughter is more useful in preventing a person from becoming too emotionally involved, angry and fearful in the first place, and helps to avoid breakdown rather than to relieve it later on.

When we could not provoke an overwhelming release of emotion around terrifying incidents in the patient's past, we might still rouse him to intense fear or anger by getting him to release all the repressed emotions he felt about some authority figure, a bullying sergeant-major perhaps, who had disciplined and terrorized him during the months before his breakdown. For a sergeant-major and the repressive discipline he imposed might have just as traumatic and disruptive effects on the nervous stability of some soldiers in the long run as the sudden acute stresses of a highly unpleasant battle experience.

We found that if a patient had always been chronically neurotic and unstable, long before the events leading up to his breakdown, our treatment usually had little lasting effect. Furthermore, if the patient was deeply depressed or melancholic, rather than anxious and hysterical, it was generally impossible to make him release intense anger or fear during the abreaction, and so no improvement resulted. It seemed that in this type of case the brain was too inhibited, in its deeply depressed state, to be able to release enough emotion to break up the depressive condition. Similarly, schizophrenics often became much more chaotic in their minds when too intense a release of emotion was encouraged in them. In fact, we soon gave up trying to treat seriously mentally ill patients by abreactive methods, which were far more useful in treating recent *neurotic* illnesses in previously *normal* people.

However, it is significant that since the introduction of electrical shock therapy and insulin-coma therapy, even deeply depressed and schizophrenic patients, with previously stable and conscientious personalities, can be helped by what is basically the same method. Electrical shock therapy creates states of intense brain excitement, leading on to the same phase of temporary inhibition and collapse which we induced through drugs. The same thing could happen when the blood sugar was lowered in the insulin shock treatment of schizophrenia. A series of these physiological shock treatments often brings a patient who is depressed, deluded, hallucinated, perhaps totally mentally disorganized, back to his old more normal self again.

In my earlier book, *Battle for the Mind*, I described how, towards the end of the war and while we were dealing with casualties from the Normandy beach-head in 1944, I went to visit my father at his house in Highgate and casually took down from a bookshelf the second volume of John Wesley's *Journal*, covering the year 1739 and the early 1740s.[3] And suddenly I saw accounts of excitatory and abreactive happenings, leading on to states of sudden religious conversion, which were strikingly similar to the reactions we had seen in patients under drug abreactive treatment. Wesley was a powerful and moving preacher, and it was an essential part of his message to put his audience vividly in mind of the eternity of agonized suffering in the flames of hell which awaited them, if they did not sincerely repent and resolve to lead a changed life. Some of those who heard this message were terror-stricken and 'pierced to the heart'. They groaned and cried out, writhing, shuddering, pouring with sweat, struggling in agony of mind for hour after hour in some cases, until they collapsed. They would then come round with a profound sense of release and change. They said that their old sinful ways had somehow lost their hold on them, that they now saw things in an entirely new light and were ready to lead a new life, to adopt values and standards quite different from, and indeed diametrically opposed to, their previous values. Not only had their old patterns of thinking been violently disrupted, but they had evidently become far more suggestible and open to persuasion about the new patterns which should take place.

There is a clear parallel between these experiences at Wesley's meetings and the artificially induced states of intense emotional excitement, leading to a collapse and followed by a sense of release and sudden change, experienced in the drug abreactive treatment of neurosis. It is worth comparing a doctor's reported observation from Wesley's *Journal* for 1739 with an account by two doctors of drug abreactions in North Africa in 1942, to emphasize the similarity. Wesley on this occasion was preaching in Newgate Prison to condemned felons who were soon to be hanged, which no doubt, as Johnson said, 'concentrated their minds wonderfully' and made them particularly sensitive to Wesley's alternatives of hell-fire or repentance and salvation. 'We understand,' Wesley wrote on 30 April 1739, 'that many were offended at the cries of those on whom the power of God came; among whom was a physician, who was much afraid there might be fraud or imposture in the case. Today one whom he had known many years was the first who broke out "into strong cries and tears." He could hardly believe his own eyes and ears. He went and stood close to her, and observed every symptom, till great drops of sweat ran down her face and all her bones shook. He then knew not what to think, being clearly convinced it was not fraud nor yet any natural disorder. But when both her soul and body were healed in a moment, he acknowledged the finger of God.'

Some two hundred years later, Grinker and Spiegel, reporting on the use of intravenous pentothal in the treatment of battle neuroses, wrote: 'The terror exhibited . . . is electrifying to watch. The body becomes increasingly tense and rigid; the eyes widen and the pupils dilate, while the skin becomes covered with a fine perspiration. The hands move convulsively . . . Breathing becomes incredibly rapid or shallow. The intensity of the emotion sometimes becomes more than they can bear; and frequently at the height of the reaction, there is a collapse and the patient falls back in the bed and remains quiet for a few minutes . . .'[4]

The same phenomena are explained very differently in different intellectual climates. Experiences of this sort were described for hundreds of years in Europe, and are still described in many societies (and by a good many people in Europe, for that matter) in terms of 'spirit possession' or 'demonic possession', the entry into a man's mind and body of some supernatural intelligence which controls him. Wesley himself put what was happening down to the intervention of the Holy Ghost. Later the effects of his preaching were sometimes so bizarre and disturbing that he thought the devil himself must have a hand in them. Charles Wesley was particularly inclined to this view and the Wesleys in fact helped to revive the decaying belief in a personal devil. Grinker and Spiegel, on the other hand, interpreted their results in terms of Freud's theories of the subconscious mind. We ourselves were initially more concerned to observe exactly what was happening than to theorize about it, for very little was known, or still is known, about how the brain actually works, and this may remain the case for many years to come.

However, it was fortunate that, at the time, I had just been recommended to read Pavlov's last series of lectures, which he gave around the age of eighty, based upon his years of experience in the conditioning and deconditioning of dogs, and his attempts, towards the end of his life, to apply the lessons he had learned from animals to problems of human behaviour. His lectures on *Conditioned Reflexes and Psychiatry*[5] were translated by Horsley Gantt and published in 1941, but most of the copies had been destroyed in the London Blitz, and I was fortunate to obtain a copy from Major Howard Fabing, who was over in England at the time with the United States Armed Forces, and was himself interested in the treatment of battle neuroses and allied psychiatric states. He had been struck by the similarity of the final breakdown in normal soldiers under stress to behaviour reported in animals, and in some of Pavlov's fascinating comparisons between the two.

In Pavlov's account of the behaviour of his animals under stress there was one experience which seemed to provide a clue to what might be happening in the drug abreaction of our military casualties. Some of Pavlov's dogs were accidentally trapped in their cages when the Neva River flooded Leningrad in 1924. The water entered Pavlov's laboratory and reached nearly to the top of the cages containing his dogs. Towards the end, when they were swimming around the very tops of their cages, they were dramatically rescued by a laboratory attendant, who brought the dogs out under the water to safety.

All the dogs had met the frightening experience with initial fear and excitement. But after their rescue some were in a state of severe inhibition, stupor and collapse. The strain on the nervous system had been so intense that the fearful excitement aroused had resulted in a final emotional collapse, just as had happened when we produced artificial states of excitement in soldiers through the use of amytal, ether or methedrine. Other dogs met the situation with mounting excitement, but this had not led to a total emotional collapse at the time of their rescue.

Pavlov was most excited when he found that in all those dogs which had experienced the collapse, all their recently implanted conditioned reflexes had been abolished. It was as if the recently printed brain-slate had been suddenly wiped clean, and Pavlov was able to imprint on it new conditioned patterns of behaviour. Those dogs which had been intensely excited but had not collapsed, had not suffered this dramatic wiping clean of the brain-slate. But all the dogs had become highly sensitized by their terrifying experience. Years later, if a trickle of water was allowed to run in under the door of the laboratory, they all still showed signs of anxious sensitivity.

I came to the conclusion that we were probably seeing, in the drug abreaction of war neuroses—when soldiers suddenly collapsed and lay inert on the couch and then woke up saying that their recent fears and past horrors had suddenly lost their hold on them—similar reactions to those experienced by some of Pavlov's dogs. And it was then that we started not to bother so much about the actual incidents which produced states of intense excitement in our soldiers, but to try to find the best chemical or psychological means of bringing on the maximum degree of non-specific brain excitement and collapse as a powerful treatment in its own right, somewhat similar to a psychologically induced shock treatment.

For instance, at the height of an ether abreaction we might, also on Dr Fabing's suggestion, inject an extra stimulant drug such as coramine, so as to add further excitement and emotion to the remembering of an incident; later we used intravenous methedrine. We found, in some instances at least, that it was the severity of the emotional upheaval itself that mattered in treatment, regardless of what had brought it about. Non-specific abreaction could disrupt recently implanted attitudes and fears, and could be curative, especially in recently ill but previously normal patients. Again I must stress that we did not and could not use this method to make a new stable personality out of somebody lacking previous qualities of stamina, drive, stability, or powers of resistance to ordinary stress. We did, however, seem able to restore the *status quo*, though still modified by a persisting sensitization to the overwhelming experience which had caused the breakdown. You cannot, I must repeatedly emphasize, ever make a silk purse out of a sow's ear by so simple a technique. But because an increased state of suggestibility is a result of the treatment, it may be possible afterwards to *redirect* the basic drives and previous constitutional strengths of some patients to new ends, as this book will repeatedly show.

Pavlov's researches proved useful at this time because they seemed to bring some order and sense into what we had been seeing for so long but did not really understand. But Pavlov provided nothing like the whole explanation. His work seemed most applicable to what was happening to the human nervous system when subjected to the severest stresses of modern war, stresses so great that they are rarely seen in peacetime and can finally result in even the most normal nervous system breaking down abruptly and completely. Such stresses only occur in peacetime when specifically created in situations such as are described in this book, or in disasters like train accidents and aeroplane crashes; or sometimes, of course, in overwhelming disasters of a personal nature, or following very long periods of stress, which can be disruptive and terrible in their total effects on man. Past history shows how often man has created for himself imagined terrors such as burning in eternal hell-fire, which may come to dominate his imagination and damage him as severely as a more justifiable wartime fear of being burned alive in a tank.

Pavlov stressed that dogs—and the same has been shown to be the case in human beings—varied in their response to severe stress according to their respective innate and inherited constitutions. After over twenty years of research, he distinguished four main constitutional temperaments in his dogs, which he found to be the same as the four basic temperaments of man described centuries ago by the great Greek physician Hippocrates. There were the two extremes, a strong excitatory and a weak inhibitory temperament; and the two intermediate types, the controlled excitatory and the stable plethoric temperaments. The strong excitatory dog or man tends to respond with an excess of excitement to perhaps quite ordinary upsetting stimuli. The controlled excitatory type meets similar upsetting stimuli with controlled excitement or aggression, which does not go beyond the bounds of an accepted normality. The plethoric temperament can only be upset by anything in its environment with great difficulty; it remains remarkably stable under all sorts of different stresses. The weak inhibitory individual, on the other hand, after perhaps only a short period of excitement, responds by developing a progressive and finally paralysing inhibition of normal brain function. Pavlov found that what he called this 'transmarginal' (it has also been called 'ultra-boundary') inhibition eventually overcame all types of nervous system if stresses were too great. When it supervened, the brain had been reduced to the only means it had left of avoiding further damage due to continued nervous stress and fatigue, by developing a 'protective inhibition'.

One of Pavlov's most important findings describes what happens to conditioned implanted behaviour patterns when the brain of a dog—and again this has been shown to be true of man—is 'transmarginally' stimulated by aggression, fear or conflict, beyond its capacity for showing its habitual response, resulting in what he called a 'rupture in higher nervous activity'. Three distinct but progressive stages of 'transmarginal' inhibition succeed each other. The first is the *equivalent* phase of transmarginal brain activity. In this phase all stimuli of whatever contrasting strength produce the same sort of final result. For instance, normal people, during periods of great fatigue following stress, may find that there is little difference between their emotional reactions to important and trivial experiences. When well, the feelings of a normal healthy person will vary greatly according to the strength of the stimuli experienced, but when ill he may complain of being unable to feel joy or sorrow or any emotion as he would do normally.

When even stronger stresses are endured by the brain, the equivalent stage of brain inhibition may be succeeded by a *paradoxical* phase. Here weak and formerly ineffective stimuli can produce more marked responses than stronger stimuli. The stronger stimuli now only serve to increase the existing protective brain inhibition. But the weaker stimuli produce stronger positive responses, as there is less resulting brain inhibition. In this state a dog will refuse food accompanied by a strong stimulus, but accepts it if the stimulus is a weak one. This behaviour is often seen in human beings when behaviour and emotional attitudes change in a manner which seems quite irrational, not only to the detached observer but even to the patient himself—unless either of them happen to have studied Pavlov's experiments. As a simple example, the harder you try to remember something the less you succeed. When you stop trying to remember consciously, the forgotten name or incident soon comes to mind.

In the third stage of protective inhibition, the *ultraparadoxical* phase, positive conditioned behaviour and responses suddenly start to switch to negative ones, and negative ones to positive. The dog may then, for instance, be fond of the laboratory attendant he has previously hated, or attack the master he has previously loved. His behaviour, in fact, suddenly becomes exactly opposite to all his previous conditioning. In both men and dogs, after great stresses, one set of behaviour patterns can thus be temporarily replaced by other diametrically opposed ones. This is difficult to achieve by persuasive intellectual arguments alone, but can be done quite simply by imposing intolerable stresses and strains, either physical or psychological, on to a hitherto normally functioning brain.

One other important finding, which is relevant to all the material we shall be discussing, is that when transmarginal inhibition begins to supervene in dogs, a state of brain activity results which is similar to that seen in human hysteria. This can cause greatly increased suggestibility (or sometimes equally great counter-suggestibility). The individual suddenly starts to take notice of happenings and influences around him, to which he would normally have paid little or no attention. In this 'hypnoid' phase of brain activity, human beings become open to the uncritical adoption of thoughts and behaviour patterns, present in their environment, which would normally not have influenced them emotionally or intellectually. Hypnoid, paradoxical and ultraparadoxical states of brain activity can also cause a splitting of the stream of consciousness, so that certain thoughts, memories or patterns of behaviour implanted in the brain somehow become isolated and totally divorced from the main stream of consciousness, memory and behaviour. And we shall also frequently encounter the final inhibitory collapse phase, with its wiping clean of the brain-slate as regards recent happenings: this is often called the 'little death', preceding rebirth to a new life, in primitive tribal rituals.

To sum up, then, human beings respond to imposed stresses or complex situations according to their different types of inherited temperament. A person's reaction to normal stress also depends on the environmental influences to which he has been exposed, though they do not change his basic temperamental patterns. Human beings break down when stresses or conflicts become too severe for the nervous system to master, or as we might now say, to 'compute'. At this point of breakdown their behaviour begins to vary from that normally characteristic of their temperamental type and previous conditioning. The amount of stress that can be endured without breaking down varies also with the physical condition. Fatigue, fever, drugs, glandular changes in the body, and other physical factors can lower resistance to stress. If the nervous system is stimulated transmarginally—beyond its capacity to respond normally—for long periods, inhibition sets in, regardless of temperamental type. In the two less stable types, the weak inhibitory and the strong excitatory, breakdown is likely to occur sooner than in the two stronger types.

Transmarginal inhibition, once it sets in, can produce three distinguishable phases of abnormal behaviour—the equivalent, paradoxical and ultraparadoxical phases. And finally, stresses imposed on the nervous system may result in transmarginal protective inhibition, a state of brain activity which can produce a marked increase in hysterical suggestibility (or, more rarely, extreme counter-suggestibility) so that the individual becomes susceptible to influences in his environment to which he was formerly immune. All this has been set out in detail in *Battle for the Mind*, to which reference can be made for further factual and experimental data.

Some of the soldiers from the Normandy beach-head who arrived at our emergency hospital unit in England were still extremely frightened, weeping, speechless or paralysed. One such had served four years in the Army before his breakdown and had never reported sick with nerves, but he had suddenly been converted from a truck driver into an infantryman, and was then sent out to the front line where he broke down under mortar-fire and shelling. Not responding to immediate treatment in France, he was returned to England and on admission to our unit appeared to be mentally slow, tense and apprehensive. His condition did not change much during the first week; he walked slowly with bent back, his features were rigid and his fear and slowness of thinking made it difficult for us to get the story out of him. First, an intravenous barbiturate, sodium amytal, was injected, and he was then asked to say what had happened. He described being under mortar-fire for eight days in the same section of the front. He had then gone into a wood and become increasingly nervous, beginning to tremble and shake. Several men were killed by mortar-fire near him; he finally lost his voice, burst into tears and became partially paralysed. His recital of what happened, produced by the drug, released very little emotion and there was little change immediately after treatment, or on the following day. That afternoon he was given another abreaction, this time using ether instead of a barbiturate. Then we went over the same ground and he told the story with far greater release of emotion and at the end became confused and exhausted. He tried to tear off the ether mask and over-breathed in a panic-stricken way. When he came to, he got off the couch and an obvious change had occurred in him. He smiled for the first time and looked much less tense. A few minutes later he said that most of his troubles seemed to have gone with the ether, and a week later he was still feeling a different fellow. 'I feel fine,' he said, and the improvement was maintained for the next fortnight.

A further case illustrates the dispersal of what can be called an obsessive stereotype of behaviour, again by the use of ether abreaction, though the use of ether was not in itself sufficient to induce a complete release of emotion and, after a preliminary failure, the patient's excitement was deliberately stimulated again until he was brought to the necessary point of collapse. After this, the stereotype of his behaviour pattern broke up and he was very much better. In this soldier the neurosis had only come on gradually after he had been in action for several weeks. He, too, had been given front-line sedation treatment in France, but he had not responded and was sent back to our hospital in England. He was depressed and apathetic, complained of dizziness and inability to stand the noise of gun-fire or aircraft. He could not rid his mind of the thought of his friends who had been killed in France. In his imagination he constantly pictured a scene in which one of his comrades had died with a hole through his head, the chin of another had been blown off, and blood was spurting from the head of a third. When given the first ether abreaction and made to relive the scenes, he became excited and said he thought he was going to be the next to be killed, but the abreaction never went on to a phase of collapse. On coming back to full consciousness he wept. In the next abreaction he was made to relive another frightening experience which had taken place some time before his final breakdown. He had been subject to mortar-fire and dive-bombing in a churchyard, and when the therapist suggested to him, under ether, that he was back there again he began clawing at the couch, imagining that he was in a ditch. We deliberately played on his fears by giving him realistic comments on an ever-worsening situation until, reaching a crescendo of excitement, he suddenly collapsed and lay almost as if dead. Transmarginal inhibition had dramatically supervened. This time on regaining consciousness he smiled and said that 'everything had gone, everything was different', he felt more open. 'I feel better than I did when I came here.' What was interesting in this patient was that when asked if he remembered his friend's face being blown off, he grinned and said, 'I seem to have forgotten about it. France is not worrying me any more.' And when questioned about this incident, he said, 'Yes, the fellow with a hole in his head.' He could still remember it but the whole weight of the memory had been lifted from his mind. When asked why this had happened, he simply said he could not explain it. But he was now able to discuss the whole scene freely without his usual display of emotion, and later in the day he said he felt a lot better, it had gone out of his system. 'I know all about it and it does not affect me in the same way.' He then began to improve rapidly.

What is most important to emphasize about this case is that we used, as a means of stirring his excitement to the state of final collapse, a memory which was not the particular one which had been haunting him. But by creating a deliberate but artificial emotional explosion, harping on some other fear-provoking stimuli, we cleared away a whole chapter of recent emotional history and its associated behaviour patterns, which had been building up owing to the patient's growing inability to stand up to continued battle stress.

A woman in her fifties, on her admission to hospital could not get out of her mind some of the scenes which had occurred when the V-rockets were landing on London in 1944. Eventually her own A.R.P. helmet had been blown off by a severe rocket explosion, and she had been hit on the back of the head. She said, 'I saw terrible sights, plenty of people cut to pieces under the debris.' And fifty people had been killed or injured around her. As soon as she closed her eyes to try to sleep, she saw people cut and bleeding, and the same sort of picture plagued her dreams; this had been going on for six months before she finally entered hospital. She was depressed and worried, unable to concentrate; she had lost quite a lot of weight and complained of giddiness, unreal feelings, disturbed sleep and weakness in the legs. This last symptom practically immobilized her. A neighbour reported that she had been a very energetic and bright person, but since her illness had become listless, forgetful and 'flat'.

Ether was again used, and she relived the rocket explosion incident with great emotion and intensity, describing how she was buried under the debris with her husband until she was rescued by her brother. She interrupted her recital under ether, frantically shouting out for her husband, 'Where are you? Where are you?' She repeated this several times at the top of her voice, at the same time groping with her fingers as though searching for him among the debris. The climax came when she described the rescue, at which point she suddenly fell back and collapsed inert. On regaining consciousness, she found she had complete use of her limbs and a clear mind with no fears or visions. The improvement was maintained and she was very much better as a result of the treatment she had received.

It must be emphasized again that it was *not* always essential in these abreactive treatments to make a patient recall the precise incident which had precipitated the breakdown. It was often enough to create in them a state of excitement and keep it going until the patient finally collapsed; he might then start to improve very rapidly. Imaginary situations might have to be invented or actual events distorted, especially when the patient, remembering the real experience which had caused the neurosis or reliving it under drugs, had not reached the transmarginal phase of collapse necessary to disrupt his morbid behaviour patterns. One other important fact must be mentioned. If any patient is subjected to repeated abreaction on the couch, as in psychoanalysis and other more intensive forms of psychotherapy, and if this occurs over a period of months or years, he often becomes increasingly sensitive and suggestible to the therapist's suggestions and interpretations of symptoms. A hypnoid state of brain activity may result. Patients may come to feel that in some way they are in the hands of a person of almost divine wisdom; they avidly accept suggestions from the therapist about altering their behaviour, which would have been quite unacceptable to them in their more normal state of mind. Quite bizarre interpretations are accepted and false memories are believed as facts if they fit in with the analyst's own beliefs. It is necessary to emphasize as strongly as possible that in this stage of brain activity, brought about by continually stirring up the nervous system, and whether or not the transmarginal inhibitory collapse phase is finally reached, the patient can become sensitized, suggestible (or, rarely, pathologically unsuggestible), and often much too willing to adopt new attitudes and new behaviour patterns which he would never have dreamt of accepting before. Freudians refer to this sort of thing occurring in psychoanalysis as the 'transference situation' or as 'gaining insight'. I intend in this book to show how it happens in states of supposed religious possession.

NOTES

1 W. Sargant and H. J. Shorvon, 'Acute War Neuroses: Special References to Pavlov's Experimental Observations and Mechanism of Abreaction'. *Arch. Neurol. Psychiat.* 1945, **54**, 231.
2 W. Sargant, 'Some Observations on Abreaction with Drugs'. *Digest Neurol. Psychiat.* 1948, **16**, p. 193.
3 C. Kelly, *Journal of John Wesley*, Standard Edition. London, 1909–16.
4 R. Grinker and J. P. Spiegel, *War Neuroses in North Africa*. Josiah Macy Foundation, New York, 1943.
5 I. P. Pavlov, *Conditioned Reflexes and Psychiatry*. Lawrence & Wishart, London, 1941.

2

Mesmerism and Increased Suggestibility

The curious and alarming behaviour reported among audiences at Wesley's revival meetings was exhibited again by some of Mesmer's patients in Paris later in the eighteenth century. Mesmer was born in 1734 and studied medicine at Vienna. About 1766 he coined the term 'animal magnetism' for a supposed fluid or force which he thought existed everywhere in nature and was concentrated in the human nervous system and also in magnets. The idea that the human body has magnetic properties which respond to outside magnetic influences goes back far beyond Mesmer's day and attempts had long been made to use magnets in the cure of disease. Mesmer at first treated his patients with magnets but then discovered that they were unnecessary, because the 'magnetic' curative influence flowed more effectively from the doctor's own nervous system to the patient. What in fact he had discovered was 'mesmerism' or what we now call 'hypnosis'.

Mesmer fell foul of the orthodox medical profession in Vienna and in 1778 went to Paris, where his reputation had preceded him and patients flocked to him for treatment. As he could not treat so many individually, he used a large wooden tub or *baquet* round which thirty patients could sit and be magnetized at the same time. In the *baquet* was a layer of powdered glass and a number of bottles containing iron filings. The necks of some of these bottles slanted over towards the centre of the tub and others slanted towards the patients. The bottles usually stood in water but the *baquet* could, if necessary, be a dry one. Protruding from the *baquet* were jointed iron rods, held by the patients, who were arranged round the tub in several rows and were connected to each other by holding hands and by cords which were passed round their bodies.

Mesmer spared no pains to make the scene as impressive and emotionally tense as possible and to create the effect of powerfully mysterious and magical forces at work. Soft music filtered in from an adjoining room and the patients, in the dim religious light of the thickly curtained main hall, had to keep absolutely silent while Mesmer walked about in a coat of lilac silk, carrying a long iron wand with which he touched the afflicted parts of their bodies. He magnetized them by staring at them, by making mesmeric 'passes' with his hands or by stroking them, and this might be continued for some hours. Initially he might seat himself opposite the subject, foot against foot, knee against knee, gently rubbing the affected region, and moving his hands to and fro, perhaps lightly touching the ribs.

The effects of the treatment varied considerably. Some patients felt nothing at all, some felt as if insects were scampering over their bodies, some coughed, spat, felt slight pain or a local or general heat which made them sweat. Some patients, however, fell into convulsions. This was called 'the crisis' and was considered extremely salutary.

Bailly, who was one of the Commissioners appointed to investigate the phenomenon by the French Royal Society of Medicine, reported on the convulsions as follows:

'These convulsions are remarkable for their number, duration, and force, and have been known to persist for more than three hours. They are characterized by involuntary, jerking movements in all the limbs, and in the whole body, by contraction of the throat, by twitching in the hypochondriac and epigastric regions, by dimness and rolling of the eyes, by piercing cries, tears, hiccoughs, and immoderate laughter. *They are preceded or followed by a state of languor or dreaminess, by a species of depression, and even by stupor.* The slightest sudden noise causes the patient to start, and it has been observed that he is affected by a change of time or tune in the airs performed on the pianoforte; that his agitation is increased by a more lively movement, and that his convulsions then become more violent. Patients are seen to be absorbed in the search for one another, rushing together, smiling, talking affectionately, and endeavouring to modify their crises.'[1]

Bailly noted that the great majority of subjects who experienced the crisis were women, and that it took two or three hours to establish the crisis. 'When the agitation exceeds certain limits, the patients are transported into a padded room; the women's corsets are unlaced, and they may then strike their heads against the padded walls, without doing themselves any injury.[2]

Besides reporting on the greatly increased suggestibility of the patients, for example in their response to the piano music, Bailly also observed the formation of a strong positive 'transference' to the magnetizer: 'They are all so submissive to the magnetizer that even when they appear to be in a stupor, his voice, a glance, or sign will arouse them from it. It is impossible not to admit, from all these results, that some great force acts upon and masters the patients, and that this force appears to reside in the magnetizer.'[3]

Alfred Binet and Charles Féré, who published their extremely interesting book on mesmerism in 1887, remarked: 'It must have been curious to witness such scenes. So far as we are now able to judge, Mesmer excited in his patients nervous crises in which we may trace the principal signs of the severe hysterical attacks which may be observed daily. Silence, darkness, and the emotional expectation of some extraordinary phenomenon, when several persons are collected in one place, are conditions known to encourage convulsive crises in predisposed subjects. It must be remembered that women were in the majority, that the first crisis which occurred was contagious, and we shall fully understand the hysterical character of these manifestations. We must again draw attention to some of the characteristics of these convulsive crises. The movements of all the limbs and of the whole body, the contraction of the throat, the twitchings of the hypochondriac and of the epigastric regions, are manifest signs of hysteria . . .'[4]

The mesmeric crisis appears to have been essentially the same phenomenon which we observed in the drug abreaction of battle neuroses during the Second World War, following the identical pattern of mounting nervous excitement and tension, leading on to states of collapse, temporary sleep and highly increased suggestibility. The same pattern of behaviour among Wesley's audiences had been put down to 'possession' and it is significant that animal magnetism and mesmerism had an important influence on the development of Spiritualism, which in Europe and America today is the principal organized stronghold of the age-old belief in spirit possession. Communications delivered through a medium in trance come, in the first instance at least, from her 'control' or 'guide', who is believed to be the discarnate intelligence of someone who formerly lived on earth and who temporarily takes possession of the medium to communicate through her. An approved Spiritualist author defines the term *possession* to mean 'the invasion of the living by a discarnate spirit or spirits, tending to complete possession for the purpose of selfish gratification. Trance mediumship operates on the same principle but is the result of co-operation between an intelligent spirit and the medium.'[5] Non-Spiritualist observers generally tend to regard the 'control' as a subordinate personality of the medium herself, temporarily split off from her normal consciousness, but the number of people in the West who believe in the possibility of obsession or possession by the spirits of the dead is by no means negligible.

Mesmer and his disciples regarded the convulsions of the crisis as essential to the cure, and Deslon, one of Mesmer's principal assistants, believed that it was only by means of the crisis that the magnetizer could effect a cure. Binet and Fréré say: 'We are now aware that these crises are real phenomena, of which the cause is generally admitted to be hysterical neurosis. Moreover, a considerable number of facts demonstrate that, under the influence of such crises, certain forms of paralysis, which have persisted for months, and even for years, may suddenly disappear. There was, therefore, a certain truth in the curative virtue of these convulsive phenomena.'[6]

The members of the official Commission of Investigation were particularly struck by the fact that these curative crises did not occur unless the subjects were aware that they were being magnetized. If a patient's eyes were bandaged but she knew that she was being magnetized, she might have a crisis, but if the magnet or other magnetic agents were brought near her without her knowledge, nothing happened. Suggestibility obviously played a very important part.

So many people wanted treatment that the mesmerists were driven to magnetize trees and attach dozens of ropes to them. This enabled large groups of poor people to stand round the tree, holding the ropes and each other's hands, and so receive the magnetic treatment; and the same abreactive crises followed.

The members of the Commission gave it as their opinion

that they had demonstrated: 'that imagination apart from magnetism, produces convulsions, and that magnetism without imagination produces nothing.

They have come to the unanimous conclusion with respect to the existence and utility of magnetism, that there is nothing to prove the existence of the animal magnetic fluid; that this fluid, since it is non-existent, has no beneficial effect; that the violent effects observed in patients under public treatment are due to *contact, to the excitement of the imagination, and to the mechanical imitation which involuntarily impels us to repeat that which strikes our senses.*[7]

The Commission also prepared a special private report for the King in addition to the one publicly published. This dealt with the possible moral dangers of 'magnetic' treatment. They said:

'Women are always magnetized by men; the established relations are doubtless those of a patient to the physician, but this physician is a man, and whatever the illness may be, it does not deprive us of our sex . . . The long-continued proximity, the necessary contact, the communication of individual heat, the interchange of looks, are ways and means by which it is well known that nature ever effects the communication of the sensations and the affections . . . It is not surprising that the senses are inflamed . . . When this kind of crisis is approaching, the countenance becomes gradually inflamed, the eye brightens, and this is the sign of natural desire . . . The crisis continues, however, and the eye is obscured, an unequivocal sign of the complete disorder of the senses . . . the eyelids become moist, the respiration is short and interrupted, the chest heaves rapidly, convulsions set in, and either the limbs or the whole body is agitated by sudden movements. In lively and sensitive women *this last stage, which terminates the sweetest emotion, is often a convulsion: to this condition there succeed languor, prostration, and a sort of slumber of the senses,* which is a repose necessary after strong agitation.[8]

Obviously the Commission was hinting that attacks of mesmeric excitement leading to trance and collapse were akin to what happens in female orgasm, as is indeed also the case, as we shall see, in some other applications of the same basic method. Deslon was asked point blank by Lieutenant-General Lenoir of the police, 'whether, when a woman is magnetized and passing through the crisis, it would not be easy to outrage her.'[9] Deslon agreed that it would be, though there was no evidence at all that such abuses were occurring.

The private report ended with the warning that there was nothing to prevent the convulsions from becoming habitual in certain patients, or from producing an epidemic of the type earlier reported in convents. The Commission even suggested that the damage caused to patients by mesmeric treatment might be 'transmitted to future generations', and they felt that there might be an injurious effect on public morals.

It is particularly interesting that the Commission noticed the parallel between the behaviour of Mesmer's patients and the outbreaks of 'demonic possession', in nunneries in the sixteenth and seventeenth centuries (which we shall consider in more detail in a later chapter). In both cases most of those affected were women, hysterical excitement was contagious and spread rapidly from one person in a group to others, the behaviour of women patients was orgasmic, and the patients became highly suggestible.

The first signatory of the report to Louis XVI was Benjamin Franklin. Lavoisier, the great chemist, was one of the eight others who signed it. Issued in 1784, it finally resulted in Mesmer having to leave France. He first settled at Spa in Belgium, where he established a free mesmerism clinic, and then went to Constance in Germany. The King of Prussia invited him to practise in Berlin, but he refused. However, a Chair of Mesmerism was established at the Berlin Academy and a hospital devoted solely to mesmerism was founded there.

In the same year, 1784, that the Commission's report was issued, the Marquis de Puységur, a physician living in retirement on his estate, started to magnetize patients after the manner of Mesmer, and he reported another important phenomenon, which we shall see repeated time and again. 'A young peasant named Victor, 23 years of age, who had been suffering for four days from inflammation of the lungs, was thrown by magnetism into a peaceful sleep, unaccompanied by convulsions or suffering. He spoke aloud, and was busied about his private affairs. It was easy to change the direction of his thoughts, to inspire him with cheerful sentiments, and he then became happy, and imagined that he was firing at a mark or dancing at a village fête. In his waking state he was simple and foolish, but during the crisis his intelligence was remarkable; there was no need of speaking to him, since he could understand and reply to the thoughts of those present. He himself indicated the treatment necessary in his illness, and he was soon cured.'[10]

This early report on the occurrence of the mesmeric *trance state* was virtually ignored by Mesmer himself, who was too preoccupied with producing therapeutic states of excitement and collapse, but it is also most important to our theme. Puységur had also magnetized a tree, which grew on the village green near his house. The patients were seated on stone benches around this tree, with cords connecting its branches to the affected parts of their bodies, and they formed a link by joining their hands together. An eye-witness, Cloquet, has given us a very valuable account of the states of trance produced. He says that the patients' eyes became closed, and there might be no sense of hearing unless they were awakened by the voice of the master. One had to be careful not to touch the patient during a crisis, or even the chain on which he was seated, as this might produce a convulsion which only Puységur himself could subdue. To arouse the patients from trance, however, Puységur had only to touch their eyes, or tell them to go and embrace the tree. They would get up while still in trance, go straight to the tree and soon afterwards open their eyes. What is more, *the patients had no recollection of what had occurred during the three or four hours of what was then termed a 'mesmeric crisis.'*[11]

Puységur was mainly interested in curing diseases, but he observed the same phenomena so constantly reported by the mesmerists and later by the hypnotists. One of the reasons why mesmerism influenced the development of Spiritualism was that a mesmerized patient often appeared to possess what seemed to be supernatural healing power, which Spiritualists later put down to the activities of spirit doctors. It was sometimes enough for a mesmerized patient merely to touch another sick person brought to him. The mesmerized person was also supposed to be able in his trance to suggest remedies for other people's illnesses. Puységur, who did not use a *baquet* like Mesmer, explained his successes more in terms of the transmission of a supposed mesmeric fluid between persons, than through the production of violent crises accompanied by cries, sobs, contortions, or hysterical attacks, stressed by Mesmer, and which ended in the patient often drifting off into mesmeric sleep. We now know that both these mechanisms are very important.

Puységur also observed that the obedience of the magnetized person to the magnetizer's orders enabled the latter to direct the patient's thoughts and acts at his whim, and he stressed the phenomenon, which was rediscovered by Freud a hundred years later, of an increasing sensitivity, of 'transference' arising between the therapist and the patient. For instance, Puységur said that the magnetizer alone should touch the sleeping patient, for fear of producing suffering and convulsions if anybody else interfered. Other observers reported that a subject in mesmeric trance was often able to read the thoughts of the person magnetizing him. Many instances were cited of people being able to read papers held behind their backs, and of many other examples of what is now called 'extrasensory perception'. Such thought-reading feats under hypnosis have never been fully confirmed under the very strictest of experimental conditions, but it is clear that a person in hypnotic or mesmeric trance can become extremely sensitive to the lightest remarks and tiniest movements, and probably even to minute alterations in the breathing of those near him. In other words, we do see the person in trance becoming extremely sensitized and suggestible or, rarely, pathologically contra-suggestible, to the person who has put him into trance, and also to others who are near by.

Despite official medical disapproval, investigations continued and in 1813 Deleuze announced that faith was important to the success of mesmeric treatment. In the same year, Faria, an Italian mesmerist, gave demonstrations in Paris in which he seated a sensitized subject in an arm-chair, with closed eyes, and then simply cried out in a loud voice, 'Go to sleep!' After a certain amount of movement the subject would often fall into a condition of trance, which Faria in 1813 called 'a lucid slumber'. And he found that this 'lucid slumber' could be induced most easily if the subject wished for it, but sometimes even when he did not, and even when the patient had put up a great resistance to being mesmerized.[12]

Later in the nineteenth century the term animal magnetism itself fell out of use, but people went on experimenting with the basic techniques, and continued to produce the same startling effects of nervous function and to obtain the same impressive treatment successes in some patients. In 1843, Dr James Braid, in England, changed the name of mesmerism to 'hypnotism', but insisted that it was exactly the same phenomenon. He stressed the need for further inquiries into the phenomena of hypnotism, which have been going on right up to the present time. Numerous disputes have occurred about the causes of what happens under hypnosis, but we hope to convince the reader that the same phenomena have been seen and reported over and over again, and not merely since Mesmer's time but all through history.

What are these phenomena, so constantly reported and given so many different names and explanations? The first two can be termed 'hypnotic lethargy' and 'trance'. The patient may appear to be in deep sleep, the eyes closed or semi-closed, the eyelids quivering perhaps; the face is expressionless; the head may be thrown back; the limbs hang loosely down and, if raised, they fall back into the same position in a lifeless manner. Movements of the muscles show that they have a heightened tone, and if you try to move the limb in certain directions you may get pronounced opposition. Sometimes the whole limb may stiffen and resist all movement, and there may be a state of 'cataplexy' in which the subject will maintain certain attitudes into which his limbs and body have been placed for quite long periods of time. The arms can be gently raised or bent, since this generally produces no resistance. In deeper trance the eyes may remain wide open, the gaze is fixed, and the face and eyes are expressionless.

In these conditions, despite the general body lethargy, there may be strong contractions of individual limbs. The hands may be tightly closed, and one arm may become quite stiff and rigid; the more you try to move the arm the more rigid it becomes; or the muscles contract and do just the opposite to what you are trying to do with the limb. The skin can also become very sensitive to the lightest touch. In hypnotized subjects special zones of the body seem to produce certain actions; pressure on one zone, for instance, may bring about an attack of acute hysteria, which stops as soon as the pressure is removed. Patients may be breathing rapidly and shallowly, or sometimes very deeply and quietly.

During hypnotic lethargy the senses may be mostly in abeyance, with the exception perhaps of the sense of hearing. Sometimes they become highly sensitive to small stimuli, just as in the paradoxical phase of brain activity; subjects may even feel the moving air produced by someone else's breathing at a distance of several yards away; they may be very sensitive to even the whispered words of the hypnotist. The hypnotized subject, on waking, *seldom remembers what has occurred during the hypnotic sleep*, unless he has been specially ordered to do so by the hypnotist during trance. On the other hand, when the subject is in a hypnotic trance state *he may remember all sorts of facts about his past life which he cannot remember when he is awake*.

We observed exactly the same phenomena when we put people into what might well be called a mesmeric or hypnotic trance state, using drug abreaction instead of hypnosis, in the Second World War. Then the subject would be able to remember again, and to relive in the greatest detail, things forgotten in waking life—repressed battle experiences or memories of being bombed during the Blitz. In lighter mood, people have been reported singing songs when in trance which they cannot remember in their normal waking state, and one of the familiar techniques of the stage-hypnotist is to put subjects back into childhood to recall events and behave in ways which their normal adult selves have long forgotten and abandoned. It certainly seems clear that the brain's memory bank, as we might now call it, is far more extensive than is generally realized.

Writing in 1887, Binet and Fréré described what they regarded as two opposite types of 'somnambulism', the old term for hypnotic trance. These were the active and passive types:

'The latter remains motionless with closed eyes, without speech or expression, and, if asked a question, she replies in a low voice . . . the subject retains her consciousness of places and of persons, and hears all that is said in her presence. The other subject is a singular contrast to the one we have just described, since she is in a state of perpetual movement. As soon as she is thrown into a somnambulist condition, she rises from her chair, looks to the right and left, and will even go so far as to address the persons present with familiarity, whether she is acquainted with them or not . . . In the majority of subjects there is no marked difference between their normal life and that of somnambulism. None of the intellectual faculties are absent during sleep. It only appears that the *tone* of the psychical life is exaggerated; excessive psychical excitement is nearly always present during somnambulism. This is clearly shown in the emotions. It is, in general, perfectly easy to make a subject shout with laughter, or shed tears. He is deeply moved by a dramatic tale, and even by words in which there is no sense, if they are uttered in a serious tone. It is curious to note the influence of music; the subject expresses in all his attitudes and gestures an emotion in accordance with the character of the piece . . . Instances have been given of subjects who could, during somnambulism, perform intellectual feats of which they were incapable in the waking state. We ourselves have ascertained nothing decisive on this point, except that we have sometimes observed hypnotized subjects, who could read printing in an inverted position more rapidly than when they were awake, and who could even supply the omitted letters of a double acrostic. There is, indeed, nothing improbable in this quickening of the intellect. There are several instances of a thinker having, when dreaming at night, resolved problems to which he had devoted the fruitless study of many days.'[13]

So suggestible are subjects under hypnosis that they can be made to experience hallucinations—to hear non-existent voices, for instance—or to do things which they would refuse to do in their normal conscious state. Although there is much greater reluctance to perform acts which are morally repugnant to the hypnotized subject, yet there is evidence that under hypnosis some people can even be induced to attempt murder. However, if a suggested act is too offensive to his moral principles, the subject very often wakes up abruptly.

Deep anaesthesia can also be produced under hypnosis, so much so that in the days before the use of ether and chloroform mesmerists reported that major operations could be carried out with the patient in trance. These included the surgical removal of women's breasts. Major operations were performed in India by Esdaile, using hypnosis as his only anaesthetic.

There is also the interesting phenomenon of 'post-hypnotic' suggestion. While the patient is in trance he is instructed to go and put a certain clock forward an hour at some stated moment after he has come round, or to take off his clothes, or to do something startlingly foolish. He duly does so, and when he is asked why, he usually rationalizes, by saying for instance that he took his clothes off because it was too hot. He generally has no memory of the suggestion having been given to him while he was in hypnotic trance.

In the 1880s the famous French neurologist Charcot classified the symptoms shown by people under hypnosis into three categories. The first of these is the cataleptic state in which the subject is motionless and apparently awake but 'fascinated', as if spellbound, with complete insensibility to pain though some of the senses, including hearing and sight, are still active. The second is the lethargic state, resembling sleep, which Charcot thought occurs primarily under the influence of fixing the gaze on some distant object, or alternatively is brought on in darkness. Charcot's last category, of 'artificial somnambulism', was a state apparently between sleep and waking in which it was easy to induce the subject to perform very complex actions.

But it later became clear that in classifying hypnotic behaviour in this orderly way, all that Charcot was really demonstrating is that if you want a patient to exhibit this, that or the other symptom, then he will do so, simply because of *his greatly heightened suggestibility to your wishes and beliefs.* Other quite different states were produced for other investigators, and all the phenomena we have been discussing were lumped together in the end; quite rightly, because symptoms will always vary from patient to patient, depending on the particular doctor's influence and the patient's particular surroundings.

The ways in which these early experimenters produced trance states are of great interest and importance. Binet and Fréré suggest that 'sensorial excitement' produces hypnotic trance in two ways; either when it is strong and abrupt, or when it is fainter but is continued for a prolonged period. Charcot did not need Mesmer's *baquet.* In the end he could produce strong and sudden states of acute excitement in susceptible persons by the sudden introduction of light into a darkened room, by making the patient try to fix his gaze on the sun, or by the sudden incandescence of a strip of magnesium or the sudden turning on of an electric light. In an increasingly sensitized hysterical subject, any sudden excitement might suddenly bring on an equally sudden state of trance.

'If the patient is seated at work, is standing, or walking, she is transfixed in the attitude in which she was surprised, and fear is expressed in her countenance and in her gestures. The same effect may be produced by an intense noise, like that of a Chinese gong, by a whistle, or by the vibration of a tuning-fork. When the subject is predisposed, comparatively slight, but unexpected noises, such for instance as the crackling of a piece of paper, or the clinking of a glass, are enough to produce catalepsy.'[14]

If the excitement is moderate rather than violent, it may have to be prolonged in order to cause the onset of hypnotic or abreactive trance. One method is to fix the gaze on an object, which may be slightly luminous or altogether dark, such as a black stick, which should be held near the eyes and a little above them to produce a convergence of the eyes. What one is trying to do is to tire the subject out, because maintaining the inward convergent focusing of the eyes is very hard work, and will sometimes result in the patient suddenly falling into hypnotic sleep after a minute or two's concentrated effort. Monotonous sounds can also produce hypnotic sleep. Some workers have produced hypnosis by causing the subject to listen to the ticking of a watch, and a faint but continuous musical sound may have the same effect. All sorts of prolonged excitements and stresses can also exhaust the nervous system. Music, singing, dancing, monotonous repetitive talk, prolonged questioning and answering can all be used. Trance can even be caused in sensitized persons by hearing a nurse's lullaby, or by the noise of the wind, or by the reciting of prayers. By a process analogous to Pavlov's conditioning, all such stimuli may eventually come to have marked effects on brain function, in producing hypnotic sleep and states of increased suggestibility.

Though many workers have insisted that the patient's co-operation is essential, the fact is that subjects can be hypnotized against their will. There are some people, mostly highly obsessive or obsessional personalities, who cannot be hypnotized, and when normal people refuse to co-operate or actively resist, they may be very difficult to 'put under'. But equally, when a normal person actively resists, he so exhausts his nervous system that if pressure is maintained it may in the end become quite easy to put him into trance. Though the first attempt to hypnotize a subject frequently fails, repeated attempts are likely to succeed, and, once a subject has been hypnotized, the length of time needed to send him into trance will rapidly decrease with subsequent repetitions of the experience. When a subject has become accustomed to be hypnotized, he may be put into trance without realizing what is happening to him, as Binet and Fréré noted:

'Many persons are agitated by the idea that a stranger may influence and dispose of them as if they were mere automata. This is certainly dangerous to human liberty, and it is a danger which increases with the repetition of experiments. When a subject has been frequently hypnotized, he may be unconsciously hypnotized in several ways: first, during his natural sleep, by a slight pressure on the eyes; next, in the case of an hysterical patient, by surprising her when awake by some strong excitement, such as the sound of a gong, an electric spark, or even a sudden gesture. Some curious anecdotes are told on this subject. An hysterical patient became cataleptic on hearing the brass instruments of a military band; another was hypnotized by the barking of a dog; another, who had hypnogenic zones in her legs, fell asleep in the act of putting on her stockings.'[15]

These were obviously subjects who had become extremely sensitive to a particular hypnotic mechanism, but the really crucial point which the whole history of hypnotism demonstrates is that the people most susceptible to hypnotic states are *normal* people. Hypnotism has never been very successful in treating the severely mentally ill, who have in fact been remarkably unresponsive to all the efforts of Mesmer, Charcot and succeeding generations of hypnotists. When patients develop schizophrenia, severe depression, severe anxiety states, obsessional neuroses and the like, they become far less amenable to hypnotic techniques. *They have generally become much less open to suggestion than normal people.* Many normal people, on the other hand, become hysterical under stress, and, when they do, they become amenable to hypnotism and to techniques which depend on the same brain mechanisms.

It is not the mentally ill but ordinary normal people who are most susceptible to 'brainwashing', 'conversion', 'possession', 'the crisis', or whatever you wish to call it, and who in their hundreds or thousands or millions fall readily under the spell of the demagogue or the revivalist, the witch-doctor or the pop group, the priest or the psychiatrist, or even in less extreme ways the propagandist or the advertiser. At the root of this all too common human experience is a state of heightened suggestibility, of openness to ideas and exhortations, which is characteristic of subjects under hypnosis and which is discussed in a broader context in the next chapter.

NOTES

1 A. Binet and C. Féré, *Animal Magnetism*. Kegan Paul, London, 1887, p. 9. In this and all the other quotations the italics are mine, unless otherwise stated.
2 Binet and Féré, p. 10.
3 Binet and Féré, p. 10.
4 Binet and Féré, pp. 11, 12.
5 Norman Blunsdon, *A Popular Dictionary of Spiritualism*. Arco Publications, London, 1962, p. 148.
6 Binet and Féré, pp. 14–15.
7 Binet and Féré, p. 17.
8 Binet and Féré, pp. 19–20.
9 Binet and Féré, p. 22.
10 Binet and Féré, p. 27.
11 Binet and Féré, p. 28.
12 Binet and Féré, p. 32.
13 Binet and Féré, pp. 144–7.
14 Binet and Féré, pp. 88–9.
15 Binet and Féré, pp. 101–2.

3

Hypnosis and Possession

A state of heightened suggestibility, intense sensitivity to one's surroundings and a readiness to obey commands even when they go against the grain, is one of the most striking characteristics of hypnotized behaviour, and hypnosis has given its name to the 'hypnoid' phase of brain activity. As described in the first chapter, this phase can be caused by stress and creates a state of greatly increased suggestibility in which a human being uncritically adopts ideas to which he would not normally be open. Breuer was interested in this phenomenon at the end of the last century and his findings, reported in a masterly chapter which he contributed to a joint book with Freud, were repeatedly confirmed in our own experience with drug abreactions during the war. Breuer begins by quoting Moebius as saying, in 1890: 'The necessary condition for the (pathogenic) operation of ideas is, on the one hand, an innate—that is, hysterical—disposition and, on the other, a special frame of mind . . . It must resemble a state of hypnosis: it must correspond to some kind of consciousness in which an *emerging idea meets with no resistance from any other—in which, so to speak, the field is clear for the first comer.* We know that a state of this kind can be brought about not only by hypnotism but by emotional shock (fright, anger, etc.) and by exhausting factors (sleeplessness, hunger, and so on).'[1]

This account of a state of mind in which the ideational field is clear for the first comer, created not only by hypnotism but by emotional shock and by exhaustion, is of great importance. Excitement and stresses of various kinds, leading to the onset of protective brain inhibition and the hypnoid phase, may suddenly open the mind in a most uncritical manner to the implantation of new ideas. This 'imprinting' phase of brain activity, as it has been called, is normally present in very young children and can be induced artificially in adults.

In the hypnoid phase of brain activity, the mind may also become split. Pavlov showed with his dogs how one small special area of cortical brain activity could be so specially excited that it resulted in reflex inhibition of much of the rest of the ordinary cortical activity. Pavlov thought that the alterations were sited in the cortex, but we now know that the process could easily be initiated by alterations in the other part of the brain, for example, the reticular area of the mid-brain.

When it occurs in man, the subject may have no memory of long periods of time while in this hypnoid state of brain activity; but if later he is put back into it, he will remember exactly what happened during the time he was last in it. It is common knowledge that when a person is in a somnambulistic, hysterical or hypnoid trance, he can talk and behave apparently quite rationally. This happened to many soldiers in the war. During a hysterical loss of memory, which could last for days, weeks or in some instances years, soldiers still behaved quite rationally to all outward appearances, but later had no memory of what had happened in the amnesic state. They were living, in effect, two separate mental lives, and Breuer has this to say of the delusions which can flourish in 'auto-hypnotic states': 'The amnesia withdraws the psychical products of these states, the associations that have been formed in them, from any correction during waking thought; and since in auto-hypnosis criticism and supervision by reference to other ideas is diminished, and, as a rule, disappears almost completely, the wildest delusions may arise from it and remain untouched for long periods.'[2]

He goes on to point out, as we amply confirmed with our own patients, that all sorts of hysterical symptoms, which may have lasted for years, 'immediately and permanently disappeared when we had succeeded in bringing clearly to light the memory of the event by which they were provoked and in arousing their accompanying affect (emotion), and when the patient has described that event in the greatest possible detail and has put the affect into words'.[3]

Breuer and Freud unfortunately went their separate ways after this, largely because Freud came to believe that all traumas causing hysterical dissociation symptoms were sexual in origin. Whereas Breuer knew very well, and experience in two world wars confirmed, that hysterical breakdown and dissociation can be the result of traumas which have nothing to do with sex. Our drug abreaction treatments during the war centred about the uncovering of repressed traumatic memories which had been implanted when the brain was in a hypnoid suggestible state and under great stresses, other than sexual ones. These memories had been repressed and shut off from the normal stream of consciousness, but they still remained operative on total brain function. We had to bring them back again into the normal flow of thoughts and memories. To do this, as Breuer suggested, it is sometimes, though not always, necessary to make the patient verbalize the events in great detail, and put all the accompanying emotions into words. Freud, too, emphasized that an abreaction or catharsis obtained without any release of emotion expressed in words was generally ineffective. But we found that the amount of excitement produced in abreaction might be much more important than the content of the repressed memories, and that reintegration and redirection of the mind could follow an emotional explosion engineered around events which were not those that had caused the trouble, or even around events which were entirely fictitious. This is extremely significant for an explanation of what really happens when a person is converted under emotional stress to faith in an idea or a person which he would not accept in his normal state of mind.

The mind sometimes splits in such a way that an apparently well-balanced person begins to live in two different mental worlds, one of which is dominated by hypnoid and highly suggestible brain activity. His previous intellectual training and habits of rational thought have no influence in preventing the acceptance of ideas which he would normally find repellent or even patently nonsensical. The new constellation of beliefs then coexists with his more usual habit of critically examining new ideas, and accepting or rejecting them in the light of his prevailing outlook, his experience and his educational and intellectual background. His newly acquired set of ideas is shut off from and unrelated, or even diametrically opposed, to his other ideas, which have developed in a state of clear and critical consciousness. For reasons which he cannot explain but which have to do with the equivalent, paradoxical and ultraparadoxical phases of brain activity discussed in Chapter 1, white is suddenly black, friends are enemies and enemies friends, small matters are more important than larger issues, or perhaps nothing seems to matter any more at all. Irrational attitudes and beliefs now live cheek by jowl with rational and critical thinking about other topics. When this hysterical split-mindedness is partial, hysterical behaviour, hypnoid states, uncritical belief and sudden conversion can occur in people whose thinking processes are still normal in other respects, though their behaviour may seem bizarre and incomprehensible to detached observers.

We have seen how under hypnosis people become both hypersensitive to their surroundings and able to call on memories and abilities to which they do not have access in ordinary waking consciousness. In hypnoidal states people can remember languages which they have consciously long forgotten, or they can construct new languages. They can act or give impersonations or produce art or music with a degree of skill which is not normally available to them. They may also feel convinced that they are in touch with divine powers or with the spirits of the dead and that they are vouchsafed special experiences which are unavailable to others.

Examples can be found in mesmeric, hypnotic, Spiritualist and religious literature, and in the annals of psychical research, and are legion. A recent case which attracted much excited attention was that of Mrs Rosemary Brown, of Balham, London, who appeared to be, and no doubt sincerely believed herself to be, in touch with famous composers of the distant past who dictated to her music which they had composed after death. They included Liszt, Beethoven, Brahms, Chopin and Schubert. As a girl Mrs Brown had been passionately interested in music and had received some musical training, but after her marriage circumstances had forced her to give up music entirely and concentrate her energies on years of difficult struggle to make ends meet. It seems likely that her production of music in the characteristic manner of celebrated composers of the past was the result of the mental mechanisms we have been considering and that, as Rosalind Heywood has suggested, she belongs to 'the type of sensitive whom frustration, often artistic, drives to the automatic production of material beyond their conscious capacity'.[4]

The true explanation of some remarkable cases of 'automatic writing', the production of written material by someone who is not fully in conscious control of the pen or the typewriter, is very much in dispute, but they do suggest, as we know from other evidence, that the brain absorbs and records far more information than is normally remembered, but which can come to the surface in abnormal states of mind. The same thing underlies leave in *the* phenomenon of 'speaking in tongues', which the early Christians experienced and which has revived dramatically in recent years. It has never been satisfactorily proved that anyone has spoken a foreign language with which they had no previous acquaintance, and while proving a negative is notoriously difficult, we do know that people in hypnoid states can sometimes remember foreign words and phrases which they learned in the past but have forgotten. In their suggestible state they may well come to believe that they are 'speaking in tongues', and they may easily convey this conviction to others around them who are equally uncritical because the whole group is in a state of heightened suggestibility. A good example of such a greatly increased state of group suggestibility is given in the following description of events:

'About 1892 Mr Tout took part with some neighbours in a series of spiritualistic *seances*. Subjective lights were occasionally seen by himself and one other member of the circle. The ladies present were affected with spasmodic twitchings and other movements, sometimes of a violent character, chiefly in the fingers and arms. Mr Tout felt a strong impulse to imitate these motions, and occasionally gave way to the impulse, though never to such an extent as to lose complete control of his limbs. At later *seances* he on several occasions yielded to similar impulses to assume a foreign personality. In this way he acted the part of a deceased woman, the mother of a friend then present. He put his arm round his friend and caressed him, as his mother might have done, and the personation was recognized by the spectators as a genuine case of "spirit control". On another occasion Mr Tout, having under the influence of music given various impersonations, was finally oppressed by a feeling of coldness and loneliness, as of a recently disembodied spirit. His wretchedness and misery were terrible, and he was only kept from falling to the floor by some of the other sitters. At this point one of the sitters made the remark, which I remember to have overheard, "It is father controlling him", and then seemed to realize who I was and whom I was seeking. I began to be distressed in my lungs, and should have fallen if they had not held me by the hands and let me back gently upon the floor. As my head sank back upon the carpet I experienced dreadful distress in my lungs and could not breathe. I made signs to them to put something under my head. They immediately put the sofa cushions under me, but this was not sufficient —I was not raised enough yet to breathe easily—and they then added a pillow. I have the most distinct recollection of a sigh of relief I now gave as I sank back like a sick, weak person upon the cool pillow. I was in a measure still conscious of my actions, though not of my surroundings, and I have a clear memory of seeing myself in the character of my dying father lying in the bed and in the room in which he died. It was a most curious sensation. I saw his shrunken hands and face, and lived again through his dying moments; only now I was both myself—in some indistinct sort of way—and my father, with his feelings and appearance.'[5]

Another fascinating account was communicated to the Society for Psychical Research many years ago by William James, who knew the author. Here the trance state takes on more extreme characteristics.

'Mr Le Baron (pseudonym) is a journalist, and has published some work on metaphysics. In 1894 he stayed for some time at an American Spiritualist camp meeting, and joined a circle which held seances at midnight in the pine woods for converse with the invisible brethren. At one of these meetings Mr Le Baron became conscious of new and strange sensations. He felt his head held back until he was forced flat on the ground. Then, "the force produced a motor disturbance of my head and jaws. My mouth made automatic movements, till in a few seconds I was distinctly conscious of *another's voice*—unearthly, awful, loud, weird—bursting through the woodland from my own lips, with the despairing words, 'Oh, my people!' Mutterings of semi-purposive prophecy followed."

'A few days later he spoke again in the same involuntary manner to the friend with whom he was staying, in the character of her recently deceased mother. Again, after sleeping in the bed for some years occupied by his friend's father, who had been lame, he awoke lame, and limped painfully for some hours. He soon began both to write and speak sentences of semi-prophetic and mystical character, such as, "He shall be a leader of the host of the Lord"; "I shall be in thy heart, and thou shalt answer to My voice." He learnt to converse by means of a pencil and paper with this invisible monitor, which, or whom, he not very happily christens "the psychophysical spontaneity". Various journeys were enjoined on him . . . Later he learnt that he was the reincarnation of Rameses, and received many messages concerning his high mission. Finally, it was given to him to speak in an unknown tongue, and to furnish himself translations of the same. Some of these fragments were written down at the time by himself; others were spoken into a phonograph in the presence of Professor James and Dr Hodgson. Here is a specimen, together with its translation:

' "*The Unknown Tongue*. Te rumete tau. Ilee lete leele luto scele. Impe re scele lee luto. Onko keere scete tere luto. Ombo te scele to bere to kure. Sinte lute sinte Kuru. Orumbo imbo impe rute scelete. Singe, singe, singe, eru. Imba, Imba, Imba.

' "*Translation*. The old word! I love the old word of the heavens! The love of the heavens is emperor! The love of the darkness is slavery! The heavens are wide, the heavens are true, the heavens are sure. The love of the earth is past! The King now rules in the heavens!" '

'It is said that Mr Le Baron hoped that the unknown tongue he had been talking would prove to be a real language, and be some form of primitive human speech, and he spent a considerable period of time endeavouring to find the origin of the language in Coptic or Romany or some Dravidian tongue.

'It has recently been found experimentally that the "gift of tongues" generally comes to a person for the first time only when he takes part in a group happening. It rarely comes first when the person is *quite alone*, and without there being somebody present whom he knows has already been affected. But afterwards he may continue to speak with 'tongues' on his own, and may also infect others.'[6]

Podmore, in *Mediums of the 19th Century*, from which the two above interesting and important quotations were taken, also points out that: 'The two cases last quoted aptly illustrate two stages of automatic action. Mr Tout yields himself to the impulse to personation, and is yet half conscious that he is acting a part. He is apparently in the same psychological condition as subjects in a light stage of hypnosis, who wil' faithfully fulfil the hallucinations imposed upon them by the hypnotist, but will be partly aware all the time that they are making themselves ridiculous, and that the comedy or tragedy which they are set to enact is but an affair of pasteboard and tinsel after all. There seems to be here a real division of consciousness, the one part acting as spectator and critic of the performance directed by the other. Traces of the same conflict of separate systems of ideas occur in dreams, and it is said to form a marked feature in the delirium caused by hashish.'[7]

Many similar examples are provided by a vast literature, but another quotation from Podmore's book, referring to Janet's famous patient in France at the end of the last century, is particularly appropriate. For it firmly links up the phenomena which have been discussed so far *with the phenomena and feelings of 'possession'*.

'Achille is a French peasant of bad family history, his mother, in particular, and her family having been given to drunkenness. Achille himself in his youth was feeble, delicate, and timid, but not markedly abnormal. He married at twenty-two, and all went well until one day in his thirty-third year, after returning home from a short absence, he became afflicted with extreme taciturnity, and in the end completely dumb. He was examined by various physicians, who successively diagnosed his ailment, one as diabetes, another as angina pectoris. Achille's voice now returned, he manifested symptoms appropriate in turn to either malady, and incessantly bewailed his sufferings. In the final stage, he fell into a complete lethargy, and remained motionless for two days. At the end of that period he awoke and burst into a fit of Satanic laughter, which presently changed into frightful shrieks and *complaints that he was tortured by demons*. This state lasted for many weeks. He would pour forth blasphemies and obscenities; and immediately afterwards lament and shudder at the terrible words which the demon had uttered through his mouth. He drank laudanum and other poisons, but did not die; he even tied his feet together, and threw himself into the water, ultimately coming safe to land. In each case he ascribed his deliverance to the fact that his body was doomed to be for ever the abode of the damned. He would describe the evil spirits which tormented him, their diabolic grimaces, and the horns which adorned their heads.

'Ultimately he came under Professor Janet's charge, and the latter satisfied himself that the unhappy man had all the signs of genuine possession as described by mediaeval chroniclers; that his blasphemies were involuntary, and many of his actions unconsciously performed. Janet even made the devil write at his bidding—in French not too correctly spelt—poor Achille the while not knowing anything of the matter; and further established the fact that during the convulsive movements of the upper part of the body, Achille's arms were insensible to pricking and pinching—an old-time proof of demoniacal possession.

'In the end this most guileful of modern exorcists (Janet) persuaded the devil, as a proof of his power over the unhappy man, to send poor Achille to sleep; and in that suggested sleep Mr Janet interrogated the demoniac, and learnt the secret of his malady. He had been acting out for all these months the course of a most unhappy dream. During the short absence which preceded his attack he had been unfaithful to his wife. Possessed with a morbid terror of betraying his fault, he had become dumb. The physicians who had been called in had unwittingly suggested, by their questions, the symptoms of one or two fatal maladies, and his morbid dream-self had promptly seized upon the hints, and realized them with a surprising fidelity.

'In the slow development of his uneasy dream the time came for the man to die; and after death there remained for such a sinner as he nothing but damnation. The lesser devils struck nails into his flesh, and Satan himself, squeezing through the holes so made, entered on an ambiguous co-tenancy of the tortured body. It is pleasant to record that the skilful exorcist was able to dispel the evil dream, and restore the sufferer to his right mind.'[8]

Quite early on, subjects in hypnotic trance not only experienced the phenomenon of possession by demons, or by God or the Devil, but, as today, also travelled through space on tremendous imaginary journeys. 'Mesmeric space exploration' was all the rage even in the early 1800s. In November, 1813, we read of a girl of fifteen, daughter of a Mr Römer, seized with convulsive attacks, followed by catalepsy:

'Ultimately she became somnambulic, prescribed for her own ailments and those of her father and other persons, rejecting all other medical treatment than her own. Römer frequently asserts that she displayed in the trance knowledge which she could not possibly have acquired from normal sources . . . further, she was conducted, sometimes by a deceased relative, but more frequently by the spirit of a still-living companion, one Louise, to the moon. But, alas! her description of her first voyage reveals a conception of the solar system scarcely more adequate than that of the Blessed Damosel, watching "from the gold bar of Heaven". . . . It was night when she left the earth—5.30 on a January afternoon—and continued night, apparently, as she voyaged to the moon, for she describes how that luminary, at one point, showed forty times larger, but there is no mention of the sun. However, she enjoyed a unique astronomical experience. She watched the sun rise over the lunar mountains, basked in his rays for a whole lunar day, witnessed his setting, and returned to the earth in time for supper. Miss Römer was probably not aware that in the ordinary course of nature about a fortnight would elapse between the rising and the setting of the sun on our satellite.'[9]

Profound spiritual convictions resulted from these states of abnormal brain activity in some people, who adopted them with overwhelming, uncritical and unshakeable faith:

'The central point of these teachings is that man consists of body, soul, and spirit, the two latter surviving death and forming the spiritual man. But the soul itself is clothed, for the time at least, after leaving the body by an ethereal body (Nervengeist) which partakes rather of the nature of body than of soul, and ultimately with progressive spirits, according to some somnambules, decays and leaves the soul free . . . There is, he says, but one absolutely immaterial Being—that is God. Below God there is an infinite chain from seraph to grain of sand, from highest self-consciousness to most absolute unconsciousness, each link in the chain having more of earth intermixed with its spiritual nature than that which went before. The soul of man occupies some intermediate position in this universal procession.'[10]

Despite this wealth of extraordinary spiritual phenomena being experienced by so many persons, sometimes gathered together in groups, Braid in England as early as 1842 insisted that all such strange experiences and effects, all the apparent thought-reading by mesmerized subjects and their supposed ability to diagnose their own and other people's complaints, were *explicable in terms of states of increased suggestibility*. Like the French Commissioners before him, he maintained that all the phenomena were caused by the subject's imagination, acting on hints unconsciously furnished by the experimenters, who had failed to allow for the enhanced sensitivity and acuteness of patients in mesmeric trance. He also repeated the Commissioners' demonstration that the presence or absence of magnets and other paraphernalia made no difference to the behaviour of patients, who responded according to the suggestions made to them.

Believers in mesmerism, magnetism, Spiritualism and all the other 'isms' dependent on trance states and heightened suggestibility, were entirely unaffected by Braid's comments. One of the earlier workers in the field, Deleuze, who was an agnostic, found himself towards the end of his life being presented with a series of phenomena which almost converted him to a belief in heavenly spirits. A Dr G. P. Billot, treating hysterical patients, found that by means of leading questions (a technique which had been employed earlier by exorcists in demonic possession cases) he could induce patients in trance to announce that they were possessed by spirits. The spirits claimed to be the guardian angels of the patients, through whom they communicated, 'confessed the Catholic verities', and on occasion made the sign of the cross. Billot reported all this at great length to Deleuze between 1829 and 1833. In one of his last replies to Billot, Deleuze wrote: 'I have unlimited confidence in you, and cannot doubt the truth of your observations. You seem to me to be destined to effect a change in the ideas generally held on Animal Magnetism. I should like to live long enough to see the happy revolution, and to thank Heaven for having been introduced into the world of angels.'[11]

NOTES

1 Freud and Breuer, *Studies on Hysteria*. Avon Library, 1966, pp. 258–9.
2 Freud and Breuer, p. 260.
3 Freud and Breuer, pp. 264–5.
4 Rosalind Heywood, 'Notes on Rosemary Brown', *Journal of the Society for Psychical Research*, vol. 46, no. 750, December 1971.
5 F. Podmore, *Mediums of the 19th Century*. University Books, New York, 1963, Vol. 2, pp. 303–4.
6 Podmore, Vol. 2, p. 304.
7 Podmore, Vol. 2, p. 305.
8 Podmore, Vol. 2, pp. 309–10.
9 Podmore, Vol. 1, pp. 98–9.
10 Podmore, Vol. 1, p. 107.
11 Podmore, Vol. 1, pp. 79–80.

4

States of Possession

States of supposed 'possession' have probably been with man always, and certainly remain with him still. What is believed to happen is that God or the Holy Spirit or the Devil, angels or evil spirits, satans or zars or pepos, or whatever the entities are called, enter a man's body and take control of him. For thousands of years all over the globe certain forms of madness and other major abnormalities of behaviour have been accounted for in this way. But possession has also very often been deliberately induced, to give a human being the most direct and immediate possible experience of a deity, by becoming its living vessel, and to enable him to act as a channel of communication between gods and spirits and their worshippers on earth. The effects of this experience in creating and maintaining faithful adherence to systems of belief have been profound and far-reaching.

My argument in this book is that states of possession are products of the same mental mechanisms discussed in earlier chapters. We have already seen examples of the similarity between possessed states and somnambulistic or hypnotic states, and T. K. Oesterreich, in his classic book on *Possession*, first published in German in 1921, pointed out their fundamental identity: 'A state . . . in which the normal individuality is temporarily replaced by another and which leaves no memory on return to the normal, must be called, according to present terminology, one of somnambulism. Typical possession is nevertheless distinguished from ordinary somnambulistic states by its intense motor and emotional excitement, so much so that we might hesitate to take it for a form of somnambulism but for the fact that possession is so nearly related to the ordinary form of these states that it is impossible to avoid classing them together . . . the most important thing is to see that we are dealing with a state in which the subject possesses a single personality and a defined character, even if this is not the erstwhile one. The subject . . . considers himself as the new person, the "demon", and envisages his former being as quite strange, as if it were another's: in this respect there is complete analogy with the ordinary somnambulistic variations in personality . . . the statement that possession is a state in which side by side with the first personality a second has made its way into the consciousness is also very inaccurate. Much more simply, it is the first personality which has been replaced by a second.'[1]

The age-old method of curing the possessed and getting rid of undesirable entities which have invaded them follows the same sort of pattern as our drug abreaction treatments of battle neuroses. The 'possessed' patient is worked up into a condition of frenzied emotional excitement, in which he expresses intense anger and fear, and this leads very often to a collapse, which may be followed by a feeling of calm and release from the 'demon' which has been tormenting him, just as our patients felt released from traumatic memories.

In a case familiar to us from the Bible, the main elements are the frenzied excitement and convulsion, the commanding voice of the exorcist, ordering the demon to leave its victim, the collapse, and the subsequent recovery. 'And they brought the boy to him: and when the spirit saw him, immediately it convulsed the boy, and he fell on the ground and rolled about, foaming at the mouth . . . (And Jesus) rebuked the unclean spirit, saying to it, "You dumb and deaf spirit, I command you, come out of him, and never enter him again." And after crying out and convulsing him terribly, it came out, and the boy was like a corpse; so that most of them said, "He is dead." But Jesus took him by the hand and lifted him up and he arose.'[2]

Lucian's *Philopseudes*, sardonically describing the same method of treatment in the second century A.D., emphasizes the importance of identifying the possessing spirit, which is a common feature of accounts of exorcism and corresponds to the way in which our wartime patients relived, and so identified, the experiences which had been preying on their minds. 'What about those people who exorcize ghosts and cure victims of demonic possession? There's no need to quote individual instances, for everyone knows about that Syrian in Palestine who specializes in such cases. His patients are the sort who throw fits at the new moon, rolling their eyes and foaming at the mouth. Yet he always manages to cure them, and sends them home perfectly sane, charging a large fee for his services. When he finds them lying on the ground, the first question he asks is, "What are you doing in there?" The patient makes no reply, but the devil explains, either in Greek or in some foreign language, who it is, where it comes from, and how it got into the man. Then the Syrian starts swearing at the devil and, if necessary, threatening it until it goes away.'[3]

In Ethiopia in 1966 I watched a Coptic priest expelling possessing spirits, using the same technique which was employed by Jesus and so many others two thousand years ago, and with the same beneficial results as we obtained with drug abreactions during the war. Different explanations of the symptoms and the treatment have been given down the ages but the phenomenon itself has remained the same.

For instance, in the fourth century A.D., a Christian author, Cyril of Jerusalem, gives this very interesting description of a typical possession state: 'The unclean devil, when he comes upon the soul of a man . . . comes like a wolf upon a sheep, ravening for blood and ready to devour. His presence is most cruel; the sense of it most oppressive; the mind is darkened; his attack is an injustice also, and the usurpation of another's possession. For he tyrannically uses another's body, another's instruments, as his own property; he throws down him who stands upright . . . he perverts the tongue and distorts the lips. Foam comes instead of words; the man is filled with darkness; his eye is open yet his soul sees not through it . . .'[4]

Another author of the same period, Zeno of Verona, describes the methods of relieving states of possession. They are again very reminiscent of what we saw in the treatment of battle neuroses, though Zeno believed that the condition was caused by the souls of the dead. 'But as soon as we enter into the field of the divine combat (exorcism) and begin to drive them forth with the arrow of the holy name of Jesus, then thou mayest take pity on the other—when thou shalt have learnt to know him—for that he is delivered over to such a fight. His face is suddenly deprived of colour, his body rises up of itself, the eyes in madness roll in their sockets and squint horribly, the teeth, covered with a horrible foam, grind between blue-white lips; and limbs twisted in all directions are given over to trembling; he sighs, he weeps; he fears the appointed day of Judgment and complains that he is driven out; he confesses his sex, the time and place he entered into the man . . .'[5]

As this description suggests, successful exorcism generally depends on working the patient's emotional excitement up to the highest possible pitch. There is frequently a violent verbal battle between the exorcist and the possessing demon, in which the demon expresses mounting anger and fear, the two emotions which we found to play so crucial a role in treating our wartime patients. A typical case is reported from Germany in the eighteenth century, when a pastor attempted to expel Satan from a possessed woman. He had the woman brought into church, and read from the Bible, while Satan jeered at him through her mouth. Presently: 'Satan broke into complaints against me: "How dost thou oppress, how dost thou torment me! If only I had been wise enough not to enter the church!" . . . When at last I addressed to him the most violent exhortations in the name of Jesus, he cried out: "Oh, I burn, I burn! Oh, what torture! What torture!" or loaded me with furious invectives . . . During all these prayers, clamourings and disputes, Satan tortured the poor creature horribly, howled through her mouth in a frightful manner and threw her to the ground so rigid, so insensible that she became as cold as ice and lay as dead, at which time we could not perceive the slightest breath until at last with God's help she came to herself . . .'[6]

Justinus Kerner, a German physician, recorded the following case in the nineteenth century:

'Without any definite cause which could be discovered, she was seized, in August, 1830, by terrible fits of convulsions, during which a strange voice uttered by her mouth diabolic discourses. As soon as this voice began to speak (it professed to be that of an unhappy dead man) her individuality vanished, to give place to another. So long as this lasted she knew nothing of her individuality, which only reappeared (in all its integrity and reason) when she had retired to rest . . . During five months all the resources of medicine were tried in vain . . . On the contrary, two demons now spoke in her; who often, as it were, played the raging multitude within her, barked like dogs, mewed like cats, etc. . . .'[7]

During the famous epidemic of demonic possession at Loudun in the seventeenth century, one of the nuns was possessed by the demon Asmodeus:

'Asmodeus was not long in manifesting his supreme rage, shaking the girl backwards and forwards a number of times and making her strike like a hammer with such rapidity that her teeth rattled and sounds were forced out of her throat. That between these movements her face became completely unrecognizable, her glance furious, her tongue prodigiously large, long, and hanging down out of her mouth, livid and dry . . . Monsieur (brother of Louis XIV who went to Loudun to see the possessed women) having desired to see all the devils which possessed this girl appear, the Exorcist made them come into her face one after another, all making it very hideous but each one causing a different distortion.'[8]

This is a fascinating example of how one person can influence the mind of another who is in a state of such extreme suggestibility that she can be made to behave as if possessed by various different demons. Three hundred years later, the celebrated medium Hélène Smith took on the supposed character of Marie Antoinette, Cagliostro and other figures of the past. She also believed herself to have travelled in spirit to the planet Mars and gave a detailed account of conditions there, including a complete Martian language. Describing the Cagliostro possession, Flournoy reported: 'Soon, after a series of hiccups, sighs, and various sounds showing the difficulty which Leopold experiences in taking possession of the vocal organs, comes speech, grave, slow and powerful, a man's strong bass voice, slightly thick, with a foreign pronunciation and a marked accent which is certainly rather Italian than anything else . . . When she (Hélène) incarnates her guide, she really takes on a certain facial resemblance to him, and her whole bearing has something theatrical, sometimes really majestic, which is entirely consistent with what may be imagined of the real Cagliostro.'[9]

Trance and possession can occur in quite young children, and at a very noisy and excited service in Nigeria in 1966 I saw a girl of 11 'possessed' by the Holy Ghost. An anonymous German work published in 1892 reported the case of a boy of 10 who could not say a prayer or bear the presence near him of any object which had been blessed without falling into fits of violent rage. If he had to walk past a church or a wayside shrine or crucifix, he became uncontrollably agitated and fell down unconscious. He was exorcized by Father Remigius and Father Aurelian. The latter gave an account of what happened:

' . . . the possessed uttered a terrible cry. We seemed no longer to hear a human voice, but that of a savage animal, and so powerful that the howlings—the word is not too strong— were heard at a distance of several hundred metres from the convent chapel, and those who heard them were overcome with fear . . . we had him bound hand and foot with straps . . . we exposed the fragment of the Holy Cross. When the Sign of the Cross was made with it, the young man uttered an appalling scream. All the time he did not cease to spit forth vile insults against the fragment of the Cross and the two officiants . . . The clamour and the spitting lasted without interruption until the recitation of the litanies of the saints. Then took place the exorcism, which we pronounced in Latin. To all our questions the possessed made no reply, but he showed great contempt for us and spat upon us each time.'[10]

We must also recognize a different type of possession, which has been termed 'lucid', when the possessed person knows what is happening to him and does not afterwards lose his memory of what took place while he was possessed. In Oesterreich's words: 'In the midst of the terrible spectacle which he presents in the fit, he remains fully conscious of what is happening; he is the passive spectator of what takes place within him.' This form of possession was described by one of the victims of an outbreak of demonic possession at a convent in Madrid in the seventeenth century:

'When I began to find myself in this state I felt within me movements so extraordinary that I judged the cause could not be natural. I recited several orisons asking God to deliver me from such terrible pain. Seeing that my state did not change, I several times begged the prior to exorcize me; as he was not willing to do so and sought to turn me from it, telling me that all I related was only the outcome of my imagination, I did all that in me lay to believe it, but the pain drove me to feel the contrary . . . I then felt the presence of the demon who was in my body; I began without thinking to run, muttering, "Lord Peregrino calls me," so I came where the demon was, and before arriving there was already speaking of whatever thing they had under discussion and of which I had no previous knowledge.'[11]

Similarly, Kerner reported the case of an old man who remained fully conscious during convulsions which threw him to the ground or hurled him out of bed at night. While in these fits he insulted and abused his dearly-loved wife and children for, without being able to give any reason, he felt he could not endure them. Though normally a gentle and responsible person, he would quite suddenly, perhaps in the middle of a conversation, be seized with raging anger and his expression, tone of voice and gestures would change dramatically.

The same phenomenon was frequently described in a setting of mesmerism and animal magnetism. One of Kerner's women patients said: 'When the magnetism (the hypnosis) had been applied during three weeks I was obliged immediately after the magnetization to pronounce, in part mentally and in part by soundless movements of the lips, beautiful religious sentences from which I drew great hope of a cure, and the fits became less frequent. But after three weeks had elapsed the Evil One who was hidden within me began to rage again. I was obliged almost without ceasing to utter cries, weep, sing, dance, and roll upon the ground where I went into horrible contortions; I was forced to jerk my head and feet in all directions, howl like a bear and also utter the cries of other animals . . . I am never absent, I always know what I am doing and saying, but I cannot always express what I wish; there is something within me which prevents it . . .'12

These reports contain clear examples of the equivalent, paradoxical and ultraparadoxical phases of brain activity. Pierre Janet, for example, described the ultraparadoxical phase in one of his patients in a state of lucid possession in which in a deep and solemn voice he spoke curses and blasphemies against God, the Trinity and the Virgin Mary. Then in a higher voice and with his eyes full of tears, he said: 'It is not my fault if my mouth says these horrible things, it is not I . . . it is not I . . . I press my lips together so that the words may not come through, may not break forth, but it is useless; the devil then says these words inside me, I feel plainly that he says them and forces my tongue to speak in spite of me.' In a case reported by Sollier in 1903 a woman said that she felt 'that another person is drawn out of me, as if my limbs were stretched to form new ones . . . The person is absolutely similar to myself . . . She speaks just as I do, but is always of a contrary opinion . . . I feel her especially in my head, preventing me from speaking so that she may say the opposite of what I think. This lasts for whole days and exasperates me when I am obliged to hold a conversation. It leaves me with a head like a block of wood for a long time.'[13]

Sister Jeanne des Anges, one of the possessed nuns of Loudon, wrote her memoirs in the 1640s. Her account of what happened to her includes striking examples of the paradoxical and ultraparadoxical states of brain activity, which resulted in her doing and feeling just the opposite of what she normally wanted to do:

'My mind was often filled with blasphemies and sometimes I uttered them without being able to take any thought to stop myself. I felt for God a continual aversion and nothing inspired me with greater hatred than the spectacle of his goodness and the readiness with which he pardons repentant sinners. My thoughts were often bent on devising ways to displease him and to make others trespass against him. It is true that by the mercy of God I was not free in these sentiments, although at that time I did not know it, for the demon beclouded me in such a way that I hardly distinguished his desires from mine; he gave me, moreover, a strong aversion for my religious calling, so that sometimes when he was in my head I tore all my veils and such of my sisters' as I could lay hands on; I trampled them underfoot, I chewed them, cursing the hour when I took the vows. All this was done with great violence, I think that I was not free . . . As I went up for Communion the devil took possession of my hand, and when I had received the Sacred Host and had half moistened it, the devil flung it into the priest's face. I know full well that I did not do this action freely, but I am fully assured to my deep confusion that I gave the devil occasion to do it.'[14]

Father Surin, one of the Jesuit exorcists of the nuns of Loudun, finally became possessed himself by the spirits he was exorcizing. On 3 May 1635 he wrote to a friend, and the following further excellent examples of paradoxical and ultraparadoxical brain activity following stress may be quoted:

'I have engaged in combat with four of the most potent and malicious devils in hell . . . At all events, for the last three and a half months I have never been without a devil at work upon me . . . I cannot explain to you what happens within me during that time and how this spirit unites with mine without depriving me either of consciousness or liberty of soul, nevertheless making himself like another me and as if I had two souls, one of which is dispossessed of its body and the use of its organs and stands aside watching the actions of the other which has entered into me. The two spirits fight in one and the same field which is the body, and the soul is as if divided. According to one of its parts it is subject to diabolic impressions and according to the other to those motions which are proper to it or granted by God.'[15]

Father Surin then goes on to complain that in the ultraparadoxical phase his feelings were as follows:

'When I wish to speak my speech is cut off; at Mass I am brought up short; at table I cannot carry the morsel to my mouth; at confession I suddenly forget my sins; and I feel the devil come and go within me as if he were at home. As soon as I wake he is there; at orisons he distracts my thoughts when he pleases; when my heart begins to swell with the presence of God he fills it with rage; he makes me sleep when I would wake; and publicly, by the mouth of the possessed woman, he boasts of being my master, the which I can in no way contradict.'[16]

Father Surin finally developed a state of severe persistent melancholia, and his mental illness lasted for no less than twenty years. But eventually he recovered and was able to write his reminiscences of what had happened to the possessed nuns of Loudun and to himself. And no better description, in terms of the various phases of brain inhibitory activity under stress, and the suggestibility induced by the possession state, can be given than this fascinating document, penned by a sincere believing Catholic and Jesuit priest of the seventeenth century.

It is important to distinguish between the type of person who can become possessed while retaining his state of normal consciousness, and the type of person who becomes possessed, goes into trance, and subsequently has no recollection of what happened while he was possessed. The first type will almost certainly have many more obsessive or obsessional components in his personality. Strong obsessive and obsessional traits are generally a bar to states of complete hysterical mental dissociation, but they do not prevent states of equivalent, paradoxical and ultraparadoxical brain activity from being experienced in clear consciousness. Thus it is found that 'normal' people, who are not markedly obsessive, may experience complete dissociation under many varied stresses; while those with marked obsessional tendencies are much more likely to experience 'possession', if at all, in comparatively clear consciousness. Today many compulsive obsessional symptoms, the result of paradoxical and ultraparadoxical brain activity, are still reported by such people. They include a compulsion to curse God, an unnatural and persistent preoccupation with the sexual life of Jesus Christ, an urge to utter terrible blasphemies against Jesus, and the like. The only difference today is that these compulsions are not generally attributed to demons.

This is, of course, an important difference. In his study of the Loudun case, Aldous Huxley remarked that what began as hysteria was turned into an epidemic of demonic possession by the exorcists, playing on the heightened suggestibility of the nuns, and that this explanation was put forward at the time, by an author who preferred, not surprisingly perhaps, to remain anonymous. ' "Granted that there is no cheat in the matter," wrote the author of the anonymous pamphlet, "does it follow that the nuns are possessed? May it not be that, in their folly and mistaken imagination, they believe themselves to be possessed, when in fact they are not?" This, continues our author, can happen to nuns in three ways. "First, as a result of fasts, watchings and meditations on hell and Satan. Second, in consequence of some remark made by their confessor—something which makes them think they are being tempted by devils. And thirdly, the confessor, seeing them act strangely, may imagine in his ignorance that they are possessed or bewitched, and may afterwards persuade them of the fact by the influence he exercises over their minds." ' Huxley concluded that the epidemic at Loudun 'was due to the third of these causes' and that it was 'produced and fostered by the very physicians who were supposed to be restoring the patients to health'.[17]

It is clear that states of possession reflect and serve to confirm the beliefs of bystanders and observers, and that they also tend to confirm or inculcate these same beliefs in the possessed persons themselves. The unfortunate Jeanne des Anges at Loudun did not initially believe herself to be possessed, but was convinced of it by the exorcists, as she recorded in her memoirs. When a subject goes into trance or shows an increased state of suggestibility, it becomes much easier for him to accept beliefs which he would have regarded critically in his normal state of mind. Disbelievers and scoffers can be brought to accept that they really have been invaded by a god or spirit, good or evil, and they may now accept religious beliefs which they previously doubted but which are held by those around them.

This is, in fact, the essence of the sudden conversion or faith state. A person suddenly accepts quite uncritically ideas and beliefs which he would formerly have subjected to critical examination. Now he no longer does so, and his new set of beliefs remains fixed and immune from criticism. One of the particular features of Moebius and Breuer's 'hypnoid' state is the lack of criticism of any idea imprinted on the brain in this phase. Given the right circumstances and surrounding beliefs, a person in this state of brain activity can even become possessed by the spirit of a fox, as in a case reported in 1907 from Japan. A seventeen-year-old girl was lying in bed, suffering from exhaustion and nervous irritability after a bad attack of typhoid. Her female relatives were sitting round her bed, discussing a ghostly presence, resembling a fox, which had been seen near the house. Hearing this, the sick girl trembled and the fox-spirit possessed her. It spoke through her mouth several times a day in a domineering fashion, abusing and tyrannizing over her.[18]

The important part played by a heightened state of suggestibility to one's surroundings in determining the content of states of possession is shown by the case of a patient admitted to a French hospital, where she was told that it was the Devil who was making her ill. 'Presently under the influence of this idea her malady redoubled in intensity and in the delirious period of the convulsive fits she saw the devil . . . "He was tall, with scales and legs ending in claws; he stretched out his arms as if to seize me; he had red eyes and his body ended in a great tail like a lion's, with hair at the end; he grimaced, laughed, and seemed to say: 'I shall have her!' " The nuns and the almoner had persuaded her that she was possessed by the devil because she did not pray enough, and that she would not recover. She had masses said, for which she paid a franc or one franc fifty; she confessed and took Communion; the almoner sprinkled her with holy water and made signs over her.' When she was later removed from this atmosphere and taken to a psychiatric hospital in Paris, she was still seeing visions of the Devil, but while there she went to church less and no one talked to her about the Devil, with the result that the visions ceased and she discarded the idea that she belonged to the Devil.[19]

Among our Normandy beach-head casualties we found that

highly obsessive patients could only be made to abreact with great difficulty and that we were unable to exorcize their 'demons', the thoughts and fears which obsessed them. Similarly, as we have seen, in the history of demonic possession, people like Father Surin, who thought they were possessed, but were so in clear consciousness, and who did not experience trance and dissociation, because of a strong obsessive temperament, could not be helped simply by the abreactive method of casting out devils. They differed from persons in whom it was easier to bring about dissociation, trance, collapse and a temporarily heightened state of brain suggestibility. If a person cannot be put into such a dissociated state, and his abreactive excitement increased to the point of sudden collapse, strong suggestions associated with the casting out of their devils are less successful.

The similarity of some states of possession to induced states of clinical hysteria in normal persons has been recognized for many years. Charcot and his pupils in Paris were able to produce states of hysteria through strongly-given suggestions to otherwise normal people. States have been repeatedly produced which are, in fact, identical with those thought in the Middle Ages to be due to possession by evil spirits, with or without loss of consciousness. For example:

'Suddenly terrible cries and howlings were heard; the body, hitherto agitated by contortions or rigid as if in the grip of tetanus, executed strange movements; the lower extremities crossed and uncrossed, the arms were turned backwards and as if twisted, the wrists bent, some of the fingers extended and some flexed, the body was bent backwards and forwards like a bow or crumpled up and twisted, the head jerked from side to side or thrown far back above a swollen and bulging throat; the face depicted now fright, now anger, and sometimes madness; it was turgescent and purple; the eyes widely open, remained fixed or rolled in their sockets, generally showing only the white of the sclerotics; the lips parted and were drawn in opposite directions showing a protruding and tumefied tongue . . . The patient had completely lost consciousness.'[20]

Oesterreich pointed out that the only real difference between these hysterical states and states of possession, reported all over the world and in every age and culture, is purely 'psychic'. In states of possession the person possessed generally believes that he is possessed *from the outside.* In modern civilized cultures most individuals know that hysteria is an illness of the nervous system, and so they tend to blame themselves and their weak nervous systems for the symptoms which they would previously have taken to be caused by some higher power outside. However, Oesterreich took this to indicate a cardinal difference between states of hysteria and possession: '. . . difference so radical that, at least from the psychological point of view, it is impossible to speak of the states as in any way identical.'

I think this is a totally wrong opinion. A person only speaks spontaneously in his mesmeric or hypnotic dissociated state if he really believes that he is possessed by the Devil, or by some other spiritual agency able to speak through him. If on the contrary he believes that the condition he suffers from is due to hysteria and is basically his own fault, and if he does not believe in spirit possession, and is not living among others who do, he will only talk about himself and his past and present fears and weaknesses. Even if he goes into trance he never discusses the part being played by supposed metaphysical agencies.

It is instructive in this connection to examine the material obtained from hysterical and suggestible patients, suffering from exactly the same symptoms, when they are interviewed or abreacted by psychiatrists of different schools of thought. Given a psychiatrist who is interested in birth trauma, or in faulty parental attitudes, most hysterical and suggestible patients will finally produce many examples of disturbing parental attitudes, and may even remember in startling detail some supposed highly traumatic birth experience. But given another psychiatrist who is interested in quite different matters, such as whether or not the patient is mother-fixated, or has been sexually assaulted by the father, the hysterical patient, because of his state of greatly increased suggestibility, will produce a quite different set of memories which fit that psychiatrist's explanation of the symptoms. Freud once made twelve consecutive patients remember and abreact what proved to be imaginary sexual assaults by the father, implanted by Freud's belief, at the time, that sexual assault by the father was the major cause of hysteria. Later he realized how wrong he had been and proceeded to develop a concept of the sexual unconscious, which is now believed in by thousands who have been analysed and have come to explain their life-experiences in terms of later Freudian metaphysics. Where some people in the past heard the still small voice of God, and some heard those of the Devil and his minions, few in our modern Western cultural climate hear either. But the fact that many disturbed people nowadays accept explanation of their troubles which differ from those customary in the past should not obscure the fundamental identity of the mental processes at work.

NOTES

1 T. K. Oesterreich, *Possession.* Kegan Paul, London, 1930, p. 39.
2 Mark 11: 20–7.
3 Lucian, *Satirical Sketches*, translated by Paul Turner. Penguin Books, Harmondsworth, 1961, p. 205.
4 Oesterreich, p. 7.
5 Oesterreich, p. 7.
6 Oesterreich, p. 10.
7 Oesterreich, pp. 10–11.
8 Oesterreich, p. 18.
9 Oesterreich, p. 19.
10 Oesterreich, p. 24.
11 Oesterreich, p. 41.
12 Oesterreich, p. 42.
13 Oesterreich, pp. 42–5.
14 Oesterreich, pp. 49–50.
15 Oesterreich, p. 51.
16 Oesterreich, p. 52.
17 Aldous Huxley, *The Devils of Loudun.* Harper, N.Y., 1953, pp. 188–9.
18 Oesterreich, p. 95.
19 Oesterreich, p. 99.
20 Oesterreich, pp. 126–7.

5

More About Possession

A study of states of possession suggests that the brain function of man has altered very little, if at all, over thousands of years. The same phenomenon is reported in higher civilizations and in more primitive societies, in the distant past and still to this day. The art of prehistoric hunting peoples in Europe includes representations of human dancers dressed in animal costumes. For example, 'one of the most perfect engraved drawings on deer antler, found at Teyjat, is of three small masked dancers disguised as chamois bucks. They are jumping in upright position, and their mighty leaps cause the skins to puff out and swirl. The legs of youthful dancers protrude from under the chamois skins.[1] Rhythmic dancing and leaping are among the principal methods of inducing states of ecstasy in which a man feels taken over by a force or being greater than himself. The dancer dressed as an animal, imitating the animal's characteristic movements and sounds, bringing all his mental and emotional resources to bear with intense concentration on pretending to be the animal, can come to feel that he actually *is* it. He may also feel that he is a supernatural being, a god or spirit, since he is after all in a 'supernormal' state of mind, markedly different from his ordinary, everyday condition. The most famous of the animal dancers of prehistoric art, the 'great sorcerer' of the Trois Frères cave, wears the hide and antlers of a stag, the mask of an owl, bear-like paws and the tail of a horse. It seems likely that he was both a god and the priest who represented the god, not merely in the sense of impersonating him but in the sense of feeling himself to be the living god walking on the earth.

The Australian aborigines who, when first investigated by anthropologists in the nineteenth century, lived in a Stone Age culture, perform long and complex traditional rituals in which they identify themselves with their ancestors and penetrate the dimension of time in which the ancestors live, called the Dreamtime or Dreaming. They do this by acting out the story of the ancestors' adventures, by dressing up as the ancestors, by dancing and chanting. Through intense concentration and elaborate mimicry carried on over many hours they feel that they have become their ancestors: 'the chanting goes on and on; the decorated actors appear; but they are no longer the men of a few hours previously. They are now the heroes of the Dreaming.'[2]

In the ancient world kings and priests acted the parts of deities in dramatic rituals and no doubt at solemn moments felt that they literally embodied the gods whom they represented. At the Sed-festival in Egypt, for example, the pharaoh, who even in his ordinary everyday frame of mind, was regarded as a god, was given a fresh access of divine energy by being assimilated to the god Osiris, who had been killed and revived again. After long and exhausting ceremonies, attended by statues of the gods brought from all over the country, the pharaoh was dressed as Osiris, was formally identified with him, and was told: 'Thou beginnest thy renewal, beginnest to flourish again like the infant god of the Moon, thou art young again year by year, like Nun at the beginning of the ages, thou art reborn by renewing thy festival of *Sed*.'[3]

It was not only through acting or dancing that people might be possessed. In ancient Mesopotamia all forms of sickness, including psychological illnesses, were put down to possessing spirits and so numerous were the demons and evil ghosts that might fasten on a man that fear of them has been described as 'one of the most important factors in the daily life of a Babylonian'.[4] Specialist priests exorcized the sufferers. Their principal technique was to transfer the disease-demon to an animal or object by means of impressive and repeated incantations which, with a disturbed patient in a state of heightened suggestibility, may well have had the desired effect.

In Israel, where diseases and psychological disorders were again put down to invading demons, there was also a long tradition of inspired prophecy, in which the prophet in an ecstatic state believed himself to be the mouthpiece of God, the temporary vessel of the divine, which spoke through him.[5] In the Greek world at certain celebrated oracles the gods possessed priestesses whom we should now call 'mediums' or 'sensitives'

and spoke through their utterances in trance. The pronouncements of Apollo at Delphi, delivered through a priestess in
trance and interpreted by priests, were regarded with the utmost
respect and affected all sorts of important political and personal
decisions, even though they were famous for being double-edged
and deceptive. In the *Aeneid* Virgil gives a graphic description
of the sibyl of Cumae, possessed by Apollo. Cumae was the
oldest Greek colony in Italy and behind the temple of Apollo on
the hill there, among the caves still to be seen in the rock, the
sibyl had her lair. 'There is a cleft in the flank of the Euboean
Rock forming a vast cavern. A hundred mouthways and a
hundred broad tunnels lead into it, and through them the Sibyl's
answer comes forth in a hundred rushing streams of sound.'
While Aeneas prayed to the god, 'the prophetess who had not
yet submitted to Apollo ran furious riot in the cave, as if in hope
of casting the God's power from her brain. Yet all the more did
he torment her frantic countenance, overmastering her wild
thoughts, and crushed her and shaped her to his will.' She spoke
his answer and 'the cavern made her voice a roar as she uttered
truth wrapped in obscurity. Such was Apollo's control as he
shook his rein till she raved and twisted the goad which he held
to her brain.'[6]

    In Tibet, until the Communist conquest, the Dalai Lama and
his advisers consulted the state oracle on all important matters,
the oracle being a young monk through whose mouth the god
spoke. This oracle decided whether the last Dalai Lama was to
leave the country when Chinese troops invaded. 'In order to
function as an oracle,' Heinrich Harrer explained, 'the monk
has to be able to dislodge his spirit from his body, to enable the
god of the temple to take possession of it and to speak through
his mouth. At that moment the god is manifested in him.' Harrer
described the actual possession as follows: 'He began to concentrate . . . He looked as if the life were fading out of him.
Now he was perfectly motionless, his face a staring mask. Then
suddenly, as if he had been struck by lightning, his body curved
upward like a bow. The onlookers gasped. The god was in possession. The medium began to tremble; his whole body shook
and beads of sweat stood out on his forehead . . . The trembling
became more violent. The medium's heavily laden head wavered
from side to side, and his eyes started from their sockets. His
face was swollen and covered with patches of hectic red. Hissing

sounds pierced through his closed teeth. Suddenly he sprang up. Servants rushed to help him, but he slipped by them and to the moaning of the oboes began to rotate in a strange exotic dance . . . The medium became calmer. Servants held him fast and a Cabinet Minister stepped before him and threw a scarf over his head. Then he began to ask questions carefully prepared by the Cabinet about the appointment of a governor, the discovery of a new Incarnation, matters involving war and peace. The Oracle was asked to decide on all these things.'[7]

One of the major techniques of theurgy, developed as part of the pagan resistance to the rising tide of Christianity in the early centuries after Christ, was to induce the presence of a god in a human being, and the philosopher Proclus defined theurgy as 'in a word all the operations of divine possession'. The god's words, spoken through the human medium, were recorded: 'Seraphis, being summoned and housed in a human body, spoke as follows.' A distinction was made where consciousness was completely in abeyance and superseded by the god, and cases where the medium's normal consciousness persisted. E. R. Dodds has pointed to the similarities between theurgy and modern Spiritualism, though the theurgists were concerned with communications from gods, not from the human dead.[8]

The pagans lost the battle against Christianity and theurgy was banned in the sixth century, but the Christians themselves in fact had specialized in another phenomenon associated with spirit possession, 'speaking in tongues'. On the day of Pentecost, not long after the Ascension, Jesus's followers were gathered together. 'And suddenly a sound came from heaven like the rush of a mighty wind, and it filled all the house where they were sitting. And there appeared to them tongues as of fire, distributed and resting on each one of them. And they were all filled with the Holy Spirit and began to speak in other tongues as the Spirit gave them utterance.'[9]

This phenomenon of possession by the Holy Spirit continued and evidently played an important role in impressing pagans, making converts, and cementing the faith of the converted. 'From Paul's first letter to the Church in Corinth we have as nearly a detailed picture of the assemblies of a church of the first generation of Christians as has come down to us . . . Paul implies that the assemblies were open to non-Christians as well as Christians, and that they were often noisy and confusing.

Several might simultaneously "speak with tongues". At the same time two or more might be "prophesying", that is, voicing a message which they believed had been given them by the Spirit, perhaps in the form of a "revelation". There were some who were gifted with the ability to "interpret tongues", or to put into the common speech the meaning of what had been spoken in an unknown tongue. There were those who broke out in spontaneous prayer in a "tongue" or in the vernacular. Apparently it was the custom for the hearers to say "Amen"—"so be it"—a sign of emphatic agreement, at the end of a prayer, especially if it were one of thanksgiving. There was singing, perhaps at times in a "tongue", at other times with a psalm.'[10]

The picture could scarcely be closer to that of the revivalist and fundamentalist type of worship, of which I give some examples in later chapters, in which possession by the Spirit of God creates and reinforces convinced faith among people in a highly emotional and highly suggestible state of mind. When Christ was baptized in the Jordan, the Spirit of God descended upon him, or 'into him', according to one early manuscript of St Mark's gospel, and it was held in the early Church that it was through this possession that Christ became imbued with the divine. St Paul, in his turn, experienced the possession by the divine which enabled him to say, 'It is no longer I who live, but Christ who lives in me.'[11] The religion of the early Church and its appeal to the spiritually unsatisfied was rooted in this direct experience of the presence of the divine. 'The distinctive quality of the mysticism which is the essence of Pauline and Johannine Christianity is indicated in the term "Christ-mysticism". The experience in which it centres is union with Christ . . . Since Christ is Spirit, he can live in men—can possess them, and speak through them, and become the inner principle of their being . . . and they can live in him.'[12]

Early on, however, St Paul found that possession by the Spirit and the gift of tongues caused serious difficulties, precisely because they created a state of fervent belief which, though edifying, was uncritical and confused. On the day of Pentecost itself, St Peter found it necessary to tell the astonished onlookers that the possessed Christians were not drunk, and St Paul, who was worried by the irrationality of the phenomenon, lectured the Corinthian Christians on the need for greater order and good sense, and the importance of interpreting the 'tongues'. For one who speaks in a tongue speaks not to men but to God; for no one understands him, but he utters mysteries in the Spirit . . . Therefore, he who speaks in a tongue should pray for the power to interpret. For if I pray in a tongue my spirit prays *but my mind is unfruitful* . . . If, therefore, the whole church assembles and all speak in tongues, and outsiders or unbelievers enter, will they not say that you are mad? . . . do not forbid speaking in tongues, but all things should be done decently and in order.'[13]

St Paul himself, however, had experienced a severe attack of dissociative mental collapse on the road to Damascus, in which he had been converted to Christianity and had suddenly and uncritically embraced beliefs which he had previously been busy attacking. And he made it clear to the Corinthians that he himself had the gift of tongues and spoke in them more often than anybody; in other words, he still had recurrent bouts of ecstatic hysterical trance.

The gift of tongues is still present and observable in various religious movements. All cases, when carefully examined, seem to be typical hysterical and dissociative phenomena, and there is really nothing to suggest that the early Christian speaking in tongues was anything different.

It is now time to return to some of the earlier observations which aroused my own interest in this whole topic. These are Wesley's recorded experiences of the power of the Holy Spirit and the Devil's nefarious activities. There is no doubt about the effectiveness of Wesley's preaching methods. He made converts in droves and the church he founded is still one of the largest in the Christian world. People coming to hear him, especially in the early days of his preaching, were presented with a dire alternative; either they must accept God's forgiveness, obtain 'saving faith' and adopt a new way of life, or they would suffer an eternity of torment in hell. The results were experiences of the type with which we are now familiar.

In Volume II of his Journal[14] we read:

'1739, Monday, Jan. 1st. Mr. Hall, Kinchin, Ingham, White-field, Hutchins, and my brother Charles were present at our lovefeast in Fetter Lane, with about sixty of our brethren. About three in the morning, as we were continuing instant in prayer, the power of God came mightily upon us, insomuch that many cried out for exceeding joy, and many fell to the ground. As soon as we were recovered a little from that awe and amazement at the presence of His Majesty we broke out with one voice, "We praise Thee, O God; we acknowledge Thee to be the Lord." '

And again:

'While I was speaking one before me dropped down as dead, and presently a second and a third. Five others sank down in half an hour, most of whom were in violent agonies. The "pains" as "of hell came about them, the snares of death overtook them." In their trouble we called upon the Lord, and He gave us an answer of peace. One indeed continued an hour in strong pain, and one or two more for three days; but the rest were greatly comforted in that hour, and went away rejoicing and praising God.'

And again:

'About ten in the morning, J. C., as she was sitting at work, was suddenly seized with grievous terrors of mind, attended with strong trembling. Thus she continued all the afternoon; but at the society in the evening God turned her heaviness into joy. Five or six others were also cut to the heart this day, and soon after found Him whose hand make whole; as did one likewise who had been mourning many months, without any to comfort her.'

Wesley was, however, much more critical of the same sort of phenomena when they resulted from rival preaching.

'Jan. 28, 1739. I went . . . to a house where was one of those commonly called French prophets. After a time she came in. She seemed about four or five and twenty, of an agreeable speech and behaviour. She asked why we came. I said, "To try the spirits, whether they be of God." Presently after she leaned back in her chair, and seemed to have strong workings in her breast, with deep sighings intermixed. Her head and hands, and, by turns, every part of her body, seemed also to be in a kind of convulsive motion. This continued about ten minutes, till, at six, she began to speak (though the workings, sighings, and contortions of her body were so intermixed with her words, that she seldom spoke half a sentence together) with a clear, strong voice, "Father, Thy will, Thy will be done" . . . She spoke much (all as in the person of God, and mostly in Scripture words) of the fulfilling of the prophecies, the coming of Christ now at hand, and the spreading gospel all over the earth . . . Two or three of our company were much affected, and believed she spoke by the Spirit of God. But this was in no wise clear to me. *The motion might be either hysterical or artificial* . . . But I left the matter alone; knowing this, that "if it be not of God, it will come to nought." '

Wesley's own preaching continued to produce similar effects, especially in those who had become very excited or angry with him.

'March 2nd, 1739. One of the most surprising instances of His power which I ever remember to have seen was on the Tuesday following, when I visited one who was above measure enraged at this *new way*, and zealous in opposing it . . . I broke off the dispute, and desired we might join in prayer, which she so far consented to as to kneel down. In a few minutes she fell in an extreme agony, both of body and soul, and soon after cried out with the utmost earnestness, "Now I know I am forgiven for Christ's sake" . . . And from that hour God hath set her face as a flint to declare the faith which before she persecuted.'

'March 8th, 1739. In the midst of the dispute one who sat at a small distance felt, as it were, the piercing of a sword, and before she could be brought to another house, whither I was going, could not avoid crying out aloud, even in the street. But no sooner had we made our request known to God than He sent help from His holy place.'

Southey, in his biography of Wesley, was impressed by the fact that the most striking psychological manifestations were caused, not by the 'emotional and overwhelmingly eloquent preaching of Whitefield', but by the 'logical, expository, and eminently theological discourses of John Wesley'. He could not explain it; he also reported the interesting 'conditioning' effect that not only the spoken but even the printed word of Wesley was liable to produce the same results. But Wesley's quiet but eloquent insistence on the crucial choice confronting his listeners could be terrifying.

When preaching on the alternatives of hell or salvation by faith to condemned felons in Newgate Prison, who were due to be hanged very soon anyway, his message was peculiarly effective.

'April 26th and 27th, 1739. While I was preaching at New-gate on these words, "He that believeth hath everlasting life!" . . . Immediately one, and another, and another sunk to the earth; they dropped on every side as thunderstruck. One of them cried aloud. We besought God in her behalf, and He turned her heaviness into joy. A second being in the same agony, we called upon God for her also; and He spoke peace unto her soul . . . One was so wounded by the sword of the Spirit that you would have imagined she could not live a moment . . . All Newgate rang with the cries of those whom the word of God cut to the heart.'

Later on, Wesley was forced to wonder whether some of these manifestations were the work of the Devil rather than the Holy Ghost, as in a case like the following:

'23rd October, 1739. Returning in the evening, I was extremely pressed to go back to a young woman (Sally Jones) in Kingswood. The fact I nakedly relate, and leave every man to his own judgement on it. I went. She was nineteen or twenty years old; but, it seems, could not write or read. I found her on the bed, two or three persons holding her. It was a terrible sight. Anguish, horror and despair, above all description, appeared in her pale face. The thousand distortions of her whole body showed how the dogs of hell were gnawing her heart. The shrieks intermixed were scarce to be endured. But her stony eyes could not weep. She screamed out, as soon as words could find their way, "I am damned, damned; lost for ever. Six days ago you might have helped me . . . I have (now) given myself to him. His I am. Him I must serve. With him I must go to hell. I will be his. I will serve him. I will go with him to hell. I cannot be saved. I will not be saved. I must, I will, I will be damned." She then began praying to the devil . . . We continued in prayer till past eleven; when God in a moment spoke peace into her soul, first of the first tormented, and then of the other. And they both joined in singing praise to Him who had "stilled the enemy and the avenger".'

Wesley's converts were often thought of as mad because of their behaviour. Wesley's mother wrote to him on 13 December 1740:

'I am somewhat troubled at the case of poor Mr McCune, I think his wife was ill-advised to send for that wretched fellow Monroe, for by what I hear, the man is not lunatic, but rather under strong conviction of sin, and hath much more need of a spiritual than a bodily physician.'

Wesley and Dr Monro, head physician of Bethlem Hospital, then sited at Moorfields, were on bad terms. But Wesley highly praised the treatment given to the mentally ill at the new St Luke's Hospital in Old Street, also near to Wesley's Chapel in City Road. Religious possession was often being mistaken for madness, and *vice versa*. And madness at that time was generally treated by combating the body's supposed 'abnormal' humours and vapours, which had now taken the place of evil spirits as a supposed medical causative factor. But unfortunately, patients still received the same sort of treatments which had been regarded for many centuries as essential to drive 'spirits' of all sorts out of madmen.

Wesley's abreactive shock techniques could have interesting effects in some states of depression accompanied by religious preoccupations, as seen in the following:

'January 21st, 1739. We were surprised in the evening, while I was expounding in the Minories. A well-dressed, middle-aged woman suddenly cried out as in the agonies of death. She continued so to do for some time, with all the signs of sharpest anguish of the spirit. When she was a little recovered, I desired her to call upon me the next day. She then told me that about three years before she was under strong convictions of sin, and in such terror of mind that she had no comfort in anything, nor any rest day or night . . . A physician was sent for accordingly, who ordered her to be blooded, blistered and so on. But this did not heal her wounded spirit. So that she continued much as she was before; till the last night.'

He had even developed some interesting physiological theories as to what might be happening: 'How easy it is to suppose that strong, lively and sudden apprehension of the hideousness of sin and the wrath of God, and the bitter pains of eternal death, should affect the body as well as the soul, suspending the present laws of vital union and interrupting or disturbing the ordinary circulation and putting nature out of its course.'

William James in his *Varieties of Religious Experience*[15] concluded that: 'In the end we fall back on the hackneyed symbolism of a mechanical equilibrium. A mind is a system of ideas, each with the excitement it arouses, and with tendencies impulsive and inhibitive, which mutually check or reinforce one another . . . a new perception, a sudden emotional shock, or an occasion which lays bare the organic alteration, will make the whole fabric fall together; and then the centre of gravity sinks into an attitude more stable, for the new ideas that reach the centre in the rearrangement seem now to be locked there, and the new structure remains permanent.' He went on to quote Professor Leuba's conclusion that: 'The ground of the specific assurance in religious dogmas is then an affective (emotional) experience. The objects of faith may even be preposterous; the affective stream will float them along, and invest them with unshakeable certitude. The more startling the affective experience, the less explicable it seems, the easier it is to make it the carrier of unsubstantiated notions.'[16]

This is what Breuer also noted in dealing with the occurrence of a 'hypnoid' state of brain activity in situations of stress, leading to uncritical acceptance of certain ideas. It is worth remembering that Wesley wanted to convert his hearers to a set of beliefs which may well seem to be, on the face of it, unlikely: that God had a son who was born of a virgin and lived on the earth for a time long ago in Palestine, and died and rose from the dead and was taken up into heaven: that they had achieved faith in the presence and power of God's Spirit; that their past sins were now forgiven them, and that they were sure to go to heaven rather than burn for eternity in hell-fire. Wesley found to his surprise that conversion to these beliefs was, on his methods, always something which happened suddenly. The explanation is surely that they could only be accepted in a hypnoid and suggestible state of brain activity. It seems very unlikely, in fact, that so strange a set of beliefs could ever be accepted as a result of purely intellectual processes.

Many other religious sects have relied on states of possession and trance to inculcate faith. In the early days of the Quakers, so called because they shook and trembled before the Lord, men and women and small children foamed at the mouth and roared aloud. Their leader, George Fox, described what happened to one of their critics, Captain Drury:

'This Captain Drury, though he sometimes carried fairly, was an enemy to me and to Truth, and opposed it; and when professors came to me (while I was under his custody) and he was by, he would scoff at trembling, and call us Quakers, as the Independents and Presbyterians had nicknamed us before. But afterwards he once came to me and told me that, as he was lying on his bed to rest, in the day time, he fell atrembling, that his joints knocked together, and his body shook so that he could not get off the bed; he was so shaken that he had not strength left, and cried to the Lord. And he felt His power was upon him . . . and said he never would speak against the Quakers more, and such as trembled at the word of God.'[17]

George Salmon, who was Provost of Trinity College, Dublin, published in 1859 a factual account of supposed possession by the Holy Ghost, in the great Belfast revival of that year; the after-effects of which have profoundly influenced the religious life of the town right up to the present day.[18]

'Strong men burst into tears; women fainted, and went off in hysterics. The piercing shrieks of those who called aloud for mercy, and the mental agony from which they suffered, were, perhaps, the most affecting that you could imagine. The penitents flung themselves on the floor, tore their hair, entreated all around to pray for them, and seemed to have the most intense conviction of their lost state in the sight of God.'

He went on to say that: 'The physical affections are of two kinds. (1) The patient either becomes deeply affected by the appeals which he or she may have heard, and bursts into the loudest and wildest exclamations of sorrow, and continues praying and pleading with God for mercy, sometimes for hours; or (2) *falls down completely insensible,* and continues in this state for different periods varying from about one hour to two days . . . During continuance of the state (2), the person affected remains perfectly tranquil, apparently unconscious of everything going on around; the hands occasionally clasped as in prayer, the lips moving, and sometimes the eyes streaming with tears; the pulse generally regular, and without any indications of fever . . . and the persons who have recovered from it represent it as the time of their "conversion". There is a most remarkable expression in their countenances, a perfect radiance of joy, which I have never seen on any other occasion. I would be able to single out the persons who have gone through this state by the expression of their features.'

In Russia, well into this century, the Holy Ghost has manifested itself in a variety of strange ways, as among the sect of Khlysty: 'They claimed to be inspired with the Word and to incarnate Christ. They attained this heavenly communion by the most bestial practices, a monstrous combination of the Christian religion with pagan rites and primitive superstitions. The faithful used to assemble by night in a hut or in a forest clearing, lit by hundreds of tapers. The purpose of these *radenyi,* or ceremonies, was to create a religious ecstasy, an erotic frenzy. After invocations and hymns, the faithful formed a ring and began to sway in rhythm, and then to whirl round and round, spinning faster and faster. As a state of dizziness was essential for the "divine flux", the master of ceremonies flogged any dancer whose vigour abated. The *radenyi* ended in a horrible orgy, everyone rolling on the ground in ecstasy, or in convulsions. They preached that he who is possessed by the "Spirit" belongs not to himself but to the "Spirit" who controls him and is responsible for all his actions and for any sins he may commit.'[19]

Finally, the extraordinary effectiveness of methods of this sort in altering a person's beliefs, interrupting the normal 'flow of consciousness' and allowing uncritical acceptance of new and strange beliefs, which are afterwards held with absolute conviction, is reported once again by Thomas Butts, who examined the effects of the supposed work of the Holy Ghost or the Devil among Wesley's followers: 'As to persons crying out or being in fits, I shall not pretend to account exactly for that, but only make this observation: it is well known that most of them who have been so exercised were before of no religion at all, but they have since received a sense of pardon, have peace and joy in believing, and are now more holy and happy than ever they were before. And if this be so, no matter what remarks are made on their fits.'[20]

NOTES

1 Johannes Maringer, *The Gods of Prehistoric Man*. Weidenfeld & Nicolson, London, 1960, pp. 102–3.

2 A. P. Elkin, 'Australia', in *Man, Myth & Magic*. Purnell, London, 1970–72, vol. 1, p. 180.

3 E. O. James, *The Beginnings of Religion*. Hutchinson, London, p. 65.

4 S. H. Hooke, *Babylonian and Assyrian Religion*. Hutchinson, London, 1953, p. 77.

5 See J. Lindblom, *Prophecy in Ancient Israel*. Basil Blackwell, Oxford, 1962.

6 Virgil, *Aeneid*, translated by W. F. Jackson Knight. Penguin Books, Harmondsworth, 1956, pp. 148–50.

7 Heinrich Harrer, *Seven Years in Tibet*, translated by Richard Graves. Reprint Society, London, 1955, pp. 206–208.

8 See E. R. Dodds, *The Greeks and the Irrational*. University of California Press, 1951, appendix 1; 'Theurgy', in *Man, Myth & Magic*, op. cit., vol. 7, pp. 2821–4.

9 Acts 2: 2–4.

10 Kenneth Scott Latourette, *A History of Christianity*. Harper, N.Y., 1953, p. 196.

11 Galatians 11: 20.

12 Sidney Spencer, *Mysticism in World Religion*. Penguin Books, Harmondsworth, 1963, pp. 216–17.

13 I Corinthians 14.

14 C. Kelly, *Journal of John Wesley*, Standard Edition. London, 1909–16.

15 W. James, *The Varieties of Religious Experience*. Longmans Green, London, 1914.

16 H. Leuba, *American. Journ. Psychology*, 1895, **7**, p. 345.

17 *The Journal of George Fox*, Everyman Edition. Dent, London.

18 G. Salmon, *The Evidence of the Work of the Holy Spirit*. Hodges, Smith; Dublin, 1859.

19 F. Youssoupoff, *Lost Splendour*. Cape, London, 1953.

20 W. L. Doughty, *John Wesley*. Epworth Press, London, 1955.

6

Mystical Possession

When the great British physiologist, Sherrington, was taken round Pavlov's laboratory at Leningrad, he was shown an experiment in which one small focal area of a dog's brain had been so strongly excited that it had produced a reciprocal state of inhibition in many other functions of the higher nervous system. Sherrington, after watching the experiment, said he still did not accept all of Pavlov's theories. But this particular experiment did show how it was possible physiologically for the Christian martyrs to die happily, even when being eaten by the lions in the Roman Colosseum or being burnt at the stake, and sometimes without any apparent suffering. With their minds so strongly focally excited, and fixed firmly on the glory of God and the rewards to come in Heaven, normal pain sensations and fear of death might be inhibited reflexly, just as had happened in this experiment with Pavlov's dogs.

Strong focal excitation of one part of the brain, with reflex generalized inhibition of other parts, is seen constantly in hypnosis and hysteria. For instance, an actor, who had what he himself described as a 'histrionic' temperament, told me after the last war how, as a prisoner of the Japanese, he had to go each day to receive orders from the local Japanese camp commandant. He never knew whether he was going to be beaten up or praised or just ignored. When he was beaten up, which happened frequently, he found that if he could succeed in fixing his thoughts on a certain mountain in Wales, and keep his mind completely concentrated on it, he could often inhibit much of the physical pain of the beating. Pain and other strong sensory impressions can sometimes be completely inhibited in a moment of great crisis, with its heightened state of nervous excitement, and also in states of hypnosis. With the mind entirely focused on some present danger, it is possible to remain unaware that you have been seriously hurt at the time; you only realize it afterwards. Not everybody reacts to stress with severe reciprocal inhibition. Some do so more easily than others. Under very great stresses, however, severe inhibitory effects can occur quite involuntarily, even in those of previously stable temperament. This was seen very commonly during the war, when many cases of acute hysteria occurred in people of normally stable personality. A soldier might be admitted to hospital complaining mainly of, say, a bad pain in the ear, and apparently entirely unaware of other major nervous dysfunctions he was showing at the same time, such as a patchy amnesia or loss of memory or even an injured, shaking or paralysed limb. His brain had developed a state of focal excitation about the pain in the ear, which had resulted in generalized reflex inhibition and a lack of appreciation of many other disabilities present. People of obsessional temperament were the least affected in this way. Their brains showed generalized inhibition reflexly only under very extreme stresses. Like elephants, their fault generally lies in their never inhibiting enough to forget past traumas, rather than quickly repressing them as is so often seen in hysteria.

So far, we have seen how the brain and nervous system of man can be furiously excited, by music, dancing, hell-fire preaching and the stirring up of great fear or anger. And it has been emphasized that this can induce various abnormal states of brain activity. There is another quite different method of achieving the same results, by using an exactly opposite technique. Here most of the nervous system is progressively relaxed, instead of being continuously excited. And as the mind becomes more and more quiescent, a state of generalized inhibition also finally results. Only a small focal part of the higher nervous system remains active and excited.

Pavlov showed that the small remaining focal areas of brain excitation, surrounded by generalized inhibition, such as are also seen in hypnosis, could exhibit the same types of 'equivalent', 'paradoxical' and 'ultraparadoxical' inhibitory behaviour as the larger areas. This occurs in the *focally isolated and excited area only*, and causes a drastic disorganization of higher nervous activity in the individual concerned, especially in regard to his personal judgements of the strange sensory impressions he starts to receive while in this state. A woman dominated by fear of being sexually assaulted, and dwelling constantly on this fear to the exclusion of all else, may suddenly switch to a state of *paradoxical* activity of the already focally excited area of the brain. She suddenly 'internalizes' the fear and feels that she is actually being sexually assaulted, and feels the penis inside her. It is almost certainly the paradoxical and ultraparadoxical phases of brain activity that make her feel that the assault is now happening *within herself* and not, as before, remaining only as an outside threat. A person who fears that other people are talking about him may suddenly start to hear the actual conversations about him going on in his head. The connection with states of 'possession' is clear. The person who fears that the Devil is near him, suddenly starts to feel with absolute certainty that the Devil is actually in him, and possessing him. Exactly the same mechanism is behind sudden feelings of possession by God, of God dwelling within one or of becoming part of God.

Every great religion has its 'mystical' and 'solitary' as well as its 'revivalistic' and 'orgiastic' means whereby the individual can be 'saved'. In solitary prayers and meditations, the mystic can bring himself into direct touch with the particular god or spirit of his particular religion. He can, by using certain techniques, come to feel the actual presence of a god, spirit or devil *within* him, to feel that he is part of the good or bad possessing spirit, or that the spirit has suddenly become part of himself. When such paradoxical or ultraparadoxical phases of brain activity occur, the individual finds it extremely difficult, and sometimes quite impossible, to explain in ordinary language what he has been experiencing. His description may become just as 'paradoxical' as his brain activity. He uses paradoxical phrases, such as 'a brilliant darkness' or a 'white darkness', or talks about feelings of 'painless pain' and 'fearless states of fear'. Descriptions of mystical experience of this sort suggest that the brain is, in fact, functioning highly abnormally, and that the person concerned is trying to describe abnormal states of paradoxical brain activity. These sensations are very difficult to describe simply because they do not approximate to the normal reality generally experienced at other times.

It must also be emphasized that when one small focal area of the brain is strongly excited, and this small area switches over into paradoxical or ultra paradoxical inhibitory behaviour, the individual can also become more suggestible. For the sensory impressions received at the time may easily be isolated and shut off from all the rest of the ordinary brain activity, so that they are not subjected to the usual criticism of sensory impressions which are judged in the light of past experiences. In fact, critical judgement about this particular set of abnormal impressions may be entirely absent.

The literature of mysticism contains many sets of instructions and detailed recorded experiences which confirm what we have said about the mechanisms involved. Here is a classical example of how a monk was advised to proceed, if he wished to be filled with certainty of the presence of God within him:

'Seated in a quiet cell, off in a corner . . . lift your intelligence beyond every vain and temporal object. Then, resting your beard upon your chest and turning your bodily eyes with all attentiveness upon the center of your stomach (which is to say, upon your navel), limit the air that passes through your nose so that you are breathing with difficulty and search with your mind the interior of your belly and there find the habitation of your heart . . . In the beginning you will find darkness and a stubborn density. But if you persevere and engage in this occupation day and night you will find—O wonder!—felicity unlimited . . .'[1]

This could as well have been a Yogi talking as a Christian priest; another method, which has also been used in Christianity and Eastern religions alike, is to repeat a phrase over and over again, not usually aloud but silently in the mind, concentrating on it and emptying one's consciousness of everything else. The auto-hypnotic effect of this procedure has frequently been observed. An example of such a phrase is 'Jesus Christ, Son of God, have mercy on me, a sinner.' Other religions use other words and phrases, such as the *mantras* of Hinduism. In different religions the same methods are used to attain quite different truths, and mystics employing the same techniques feel themselves possessed by different deities.

Among the Sufis the term *dhikr* refers to the glorification of God in certain set phrases, which are repeated over and over again. They may be recited aloud by a group or by a solitary worshipper but are perhaps most effective when repeated silently in the mind and accompanied by special breathing techniques and physical movements. The Sufi al-Hallaj regarded the mystical union with God as the actual inhabitation of the human soul by the divine, and spoke of the 'incarnation' of the divine in the human body and the 'identity' of the mystic and God. He was crucified at Baghdad in 922, partly because he had announced that he was God. Other Sufis hesitated to go so far but it is clear from what the mystic and poet al-Ghazali says that while in the state which he calls being 'drunk with a drunkenness in which their reason collapsed' they felt utterly possessed by God:

'One of them said, "I am God (the Truth)." Another said, "Glory be to me! How great is my glory", while another said, "Within my robe is naught but God." But the words of lovers when in a state of drunkenness must be hidden away and not broadcast. However, when their drunkenness abates and the sovereignty of their reason is restored—and reason is God's scale of earth—they know that this was not actual identity, but that it resembled identity as when lovers say at the height of their passion:

"I am he whom I desire and he whom I desire is I;
We are two souls inhabiting one body." '2

The reference to the union of lovers is significant, and we shall return to it later on, but for the moment the point is the stress which al-Ghazali places on a 'collapse' of reason as a condition of attaining the sense of mystical union, just as St Paul observed the uncritical irrationality of ecstatic forms of worship in the early Church. This suggests that it is *the brain of man and not his soul* which is affected by mystical techniques, though the possessing deity or spirit will be identified differently against varying religious backgrounds. The Christian mystic does not become obsessed by the bloodthirsty Hindu goddess Kali, and *vice versa*.

St Edmund Rich, who died in 1240, said the following about the technique of attaining possession by the Christian God. Relaxation and emptying of the mind is specially emphasized, as in most mystical techniques:

'The first step in contemplation is for the soul to retreat within itself and there completely to recollect itself. The second step in contemplation is for the soul to see what it is when it is so collected. The third step is for the soul to raise itself beyond itself and to strive to see two things; its Creator, and His own nature. But the soul can never attain to this until it has learned to subdue every image, corporeal, earthly and celestial, to reject whatever may come to it through sight or hearing or touch or taste or any other bodily sensation, and to tread it down, so that the soul may see what in itself is outside of its body . . . After this, when you have in this way looked at your Creator and His creatures, put every corporeal image outside your heart, and let your naked intention fly up above all human reasoning and there you shall find such great sweetness and such great secrets that without special grace there is no one who can think of it except only him who has experienced it.'[3]

Another good example of the need to empty the mind before the paradoxical and ultraparadoxical phase of brain activity supervenes and allows feelings of possession to occur is contained in an account of a group of people who were called 'The Friends of God':

'When it comes into Nothing all natural marks disappear and the soul becomes unoccupied and rests in pure peace. It is then that the spirit arrives at the source from which it flowed. In this way natural knowledge is negated, and in this way it is necessary that one should become empty of his natural knowledge if he desires true spiritual poverty.'[4]

Tauler also says in the fourteenth century: 'That is wherein you should penetrate, using your entire strength to leave far behind every thought of your worldliness, which is as remote and alien to the inner self as only an animal can be, living, as it does, without knowledge, perception or awareness or anything except its senses.'[5] He goes on to give a very good example of the paradoxical and ultraparadoxical phases of brain activity which can then result, and he has to describe them in highly *paradoxical* phraseology: 'Then you will contemplate the *divine darkness, which by its blinding clearness appears dark to human and even to the angels' understanding,* just as the resplendent orb of the sun appears dark to the weak eye; for it is in the nature of all created understanding that, compared with the divine clarity, it is as small as a swallow's eye when compared with the size of the sun and as far as this understanding is merely of the natural order it must be beaten back into consciousness so that it can do no more harm.'[6]

Another very good account of the method of obtaining Christian mystical union is given by Jan Van Ruysbroeck:

'The first is that he must be well ordered in all virtues from without, and that within he be unhindered, and that he be empty of all outward works, just as though he performed nothing. For if within he is preoccupied with any work of virtue, so he is distracted by images. As long as this lasts in him, he is unable to contemplate. Secondly, he must within depend upon God with compelling intention and love, just as a kindled and glowing fire that never again can be put out. And when he feels himself to be thus, then he is able to contemplate. Thirdly, he must have lost himself in a lack of manner, and in a darkness in which all contemplative men fare in delectation, and can never again find themselves in any way natural to the creature. In the depths of this darkness, in which the loving spirit has died to itself, begins the revelation of God and the eternal life. For in this darkness there shines and there is born an incomprehensible light, which is the Son of God, in Whom we contemplate eternal life. And in this light we see.'[7]

Finally, Walter Hilton, also in the fourteenth century, sums up the points already made, as follows:

'The third degree of contemplation is the highest that is attainable in this life. Both knowing and loving go to make it up. It consists in knowing God perfectly and in loving God perfectly, and that is when a man's soul is first cleansed of all sins and is formed anew, through the fulness of virtue, into the image of Jesus and then, at the visitation of grace, is withdrawn from all earthly and fleshly affections and from vain thoughts and musings on bodily matters and is, as it were, rapt out of his bodily senses; and then, by the grace of the Holy Spirit, he is enlightened so that he can see by his understanding the truth which is God and see spiritual things with a soft sweet burning love in him, which is so perfect that by the ravishing of this love he is united for a time to God and is conformed to the likeness of the Trinity.'[8]

This ecstatic state, in which there is absolute certainty of possession by God, is regarded as the supreme gift of God in several different religions. The same basic technique to attain it is reported, and with similar results. It is generally explained that in this final stage God actually enters and becomes conjoined with man, and that this is the act of God himself. It is not considered to have anything to do with the brain acting abnormally, along the lines suggested here. But one of the main purposes of this book is to consider the part played by the brain itself in the phenomenon. Sometimes the 'mystical union' can occur suddenly, with the individual being quite unprepared for it. St Teresa of Avila says:

'For often when a person is quite unprepared for such a thing, and is not even thinking of God, he is awakened by His Majesty, as though by a rushing comet or a thunderclap. Although no sound is heard, the soul is very well aware that it has been called by God, so much so that sometimes, especially at first, it begins to tremble and complain, though it feels nothing that causes it affliction. It is conscious of having been most delectably wounded, but cannot say how or by whom.'[9]

We can also see, in St Teresa's account, how an increased state of suggestibility present when one has attained to a mystical state causes ready acceptance of the doctrines and beliefs of the particular religious viewpoint with which one is in contact. Here is a good example of the way in which 'proof' of the Holy Trinity is acquired:

'First of all the spirit becomes enkindled and is illumined, as it were, by a cloud of the greatest brightness. It sees these three persons, individually, and yet, by a wonderful kind of knowledge which is given to it, the soul realizes that most certainly and truly all these three Persons are one Substance and one Power and one Knowledge and one God alone; so that what we hold by faith the soul may be said here to grasp by sight, although nothing is seen by the eyes, either of the body or of the soul, for it is no imaginary vision. Here all three Persons communicate Themselves to the soul and speak to the soul.'[10]

Marie of the Incarnation described the attainment of these states of possession, which create such total faith, very well indeed: 'The state which I now experience, compared with what I have previously described, is a completely extraordinary clearness about the ways of the adorable Spirit of the Word Incarnate. I know, experientially in great pureness and certainty, that here is Love Himself intimately joined to me and joining my spirit to His and that "all that He has said has spirit and life" in me. Particularly does my soul experience being in this intimate union with Him.' She also insists: 'It is a reality so lofty, so ravishing, so simple, and so beyond the scope of what falls within the meaning of human discourse that I am unable to express it otherwise than to say that I am in God, possessed by God, and that God would soon overwhelm me by His loving gentleness and strength were I not sustained by another impression which follows it and does not pass but tempers His greatness as something not to be sustained in this life.'[11]

In Quietism there is again the emptying of the mind, which Madame Guyon described in answering the question, what must the soul do to be faithful to God?

'Nothing and less than nothing. It must simply suffer itself to be possessed, acted upon, and moved without resistance . . . letting itself be led at all times and to any place, regardless of sight or reason, and without thinking of either; letting itself go naturally into all things, without considering what would be best or most plausible.'[12]

Ronald Knox, who used this quotation in his book *Enthusiasm*, said that it shows the resemblance of Quietism to the later Quaker methods of achieving what is called the 'Inner Light'. Fénelon described Madame Guyon's 'perfect souls' as those who 'are without action, without desire, without inclination, without choice, without impatience, in a state of complete death, seeing things only as God sees them, and judging them only with God's judgment'.[13]

Mystical contemplation has very real dangers. Sometimes quite unexpectedly, when the nervous system is being progressively relaxed, almost total inhibition of much of the higher nervous system may occur, and this does not lift again at will. Some people experience severe mental depression. Knox points out the complications:

'There is, however, an extreme case in which the counsel of abandonment seems to reach further. It is the general testimony of souls which have attained a high degree of mystical experience that they did so only by means of, and at the cost of, acute spiritual trials. The chief of these takes the form of an overpowering conviction that the soul has been deserted by God's love and is marked down for reprobation. During these periods of dereliction, ought such a soul to meet the temptation face to face, in an effort to fight it down by returning to deliberate acts.'[14]

It is in fact a commonplace that the road to union with the divine often leads through a 'valley of the shadow', a stage of hopeless despair and deep sense of unworthiness which has all the symptoms that we now recognize in psychiatry as indicative of depressive illness. It is only after this depressive inhibitory phase of brain activity that the person achieves the ecstatic experience of divine possession, a certainty of salvation and forgiveness of sins, or a conviction of having found the truth. This final stage brings with it a sense of certainty which may not be at all related to the previous beliefs and experiences of the person concerned, and which need not harmonize with his other existing beliefs. An isolated focus of experience creating convinced belief can now remain quite uninfluenced by the rest of the person's outlook.

William James summarizes the position of the emptying of the mind and the relaxing of worry as a means of preparing for the mystical entry of the desired God, or the sudden attainment of faith:

'From Catholicism to Lutheranism, and then to Calvinism; from that to Wesleyanism; and from this, outside of technical Christianity altogether, to pure "liberalism" or transcendental idealism, whether or not of the mind-cure type, taking in the mediaeval mystics, the quietists, the pietists, and quakers by the way, we can trace the stages of progress towards the idea of an immediate spiritual help, experienced by the individual in his forlornness . . . There are only two ways in which it is possible to get rid of anger, worry, fear, despair, or other undesirable affections. One is that an opposite affection should overpoweringly break over us, and the other is by getting so exhausted with the struggle that we have to stop—so we drop down, give up, and don't care any longer. *Our emotional brain-centres strike work, and we lapse into a temporary apathy. Now there is documentary proof that this state of temporary exhaustion not infrequently forms part of the conversion crisis.* So long as the egoistic worry of the sick soul guards the door, the expansive confidence of the soul of faith gains no presence.'[15]

James even described, long before Pavlov had demonstrated the physiology in his dogs, the existence of the paradoxical phases of brain activity.

'You know how it is when you try to recollect a forgotten name. Usually you help the recall by working for it, by mentally running over the places, persons, and things with which the word was connected. But sometimes this effort fails; you feel then as if the harder you tried the less hope there would be, as though the name were jammed, and pressure in its direction only kept it all the more from rising. And then the opposite expedient often succeeds. Give up the effort entirely; think of something altogether different, and in half an hour the lost name comes sauntering into your mind, as Emerson says, as carelessly as if it had never been invited.'[16]

John Nelson, one of Wesley's converts, in despair just before his conversion, cried out, 'Lord, Thy will be done; damn or save!' And at that moment his soul was filled with peace.

Dr Starbuck, in discussing conversion, quotes other examples such as the person who said:

' "Lord, I have done all I can: I leave the whole matter with Thee," and immediately there came to me a great peace.'

Or another:

'All at once it occurred to me that I might be saved, too, if I would stop trying to do it all myself, and follow Jesus: somehow I lost my load.'

Yet another:

'I finally ceased to resist, and gave myself up, though it was a hard struggle. Gradually the feeling came over me that I had done my part, and God was willing to do his.'[17]

In this phase of relaxation or depression an increased state of suggestibility may develop, evidence of the hypnoid state of brain activity. And with the paradoxical and ultraparadoxical phases also supervening, outside events seem to sear themselves into the brain, uninfluenced by any criticism from past experience. Take for instance, Henry Alline's account of his own conversion, also quoted by William James. This occurred in 1775, and it seems that throughout the ages the same fundamental alterations in brain behaviour have occurred in similar circumstances. Alline writes:

'You have been seeking, praying, reforming, laboring, reading, hearing, and meditating, and what have you done by it towards your salvation? Are you any nearer to conversion now than when you first began?. . . These discoveries continued until I went into the house and sat down. After I sat down, being all in confusion, like a drowning man that was just giving up to sink, and almost in an agony, I turned very suddenly round in my chair, and seeing part of an old Bible lying in one of the chairs, I caught hold of it in great haste; and opening it without any premeditation, cast my eyes on the 38th Psalm, which was the first time I ever saw the word of God: it took hold of me with such power that it seemed to go through my whole soul, so that it seemed as if God was praying in, with, and for me . . . the burden of guilt and condemnation was gone, darkness was expelled, my heart humbled and filled with gratitude, and my whole soul, that was a few minutes ago groaning under mountains of death, and crying to an unknown God for help, was now filled with immortal love, soaring on the wings of faith, freed from the chains of death and darkness.'[18]

Jonathan Edwards, the great American revivalist, whose work preceded Wesley's by a few years, used to insist that despair—total religious despair, equivalent to the 'dark night of the soul' of medieval mystics—was an important precursor of effective and convincing feelings of salvation and possession by God. Wesley also thought that as a preliminary to conversion it was necessary to realize one's own sinfulness and the certainty of punishment in hell unless God intervened. He found that the change to a conviction of being 'saved' was generally instantaneous, a point repeatedly confirmed in accounts of mystical experiences:

'In London alone I found 652 members of our Society who were exceeding clear in their experience, and whose testimony I would see no reason to doubt. And every one of these (without a single exception) has declared that his deliverance from sin was instantaneous; that the change was wrought in a moment. Had half of these, or one third, or one in twenty, declared it was *gradually* wrought *in them*, I should have believed this with regard *to them*, and thought that *some* were gradually sanctified and some instantaneously. But as I have not found, in so long a space of time, a single person speaking thus, I cannot but believe that sanctification is commonly, if not always, an instantaneous work.'[19]

William James distinguished mystical conversions from other, more intellectual conversions. I should say that what in fact happens is that a variety of methods reach the same common endpoint, in which hypnoid, paradoxical and ultraparadoxical states of brain activity make conversion possible, whether the conversion is to religious belief, a political philosophy or any other system of ideas. James suggested that one important distinguishing mark of a mystical state of mind is that it defies expression and cannot adequately be described in words. It is impossibly difficult to impart or transfer the experience to others, even though it may occur in clear consciousness without accompanying trance or loss of memory. The experience carries with it a sense of insight into depths of fundamental truth which cannot be plumbed by what James called 'the discursive intellect'.

In other words, the mystic is carried 'beyond' reason precisely because he is in an abnormal and non-rational state of mind. But this characteristic of mystical experience is also characteristic of conversion in general. It is a matter of common observation that faith—in religious or other doctrines—is essentially non-rational. Prodigies of intellectual effort may be devoted to supporting a belief rationally once it has been accepted, but this comes after the event. And once the edifice of rational argument has been constructed, it does not by itself succeed in making fresh converts. A potential convert may study theology and find it more or less persuasive intellectually but it is not the theology which converts him to *faith*. There is a great gulf fixed between intellectual adherence to a theological or other position and a state of faith in that position: and if the gulf is crossed at all, it is generally crossed suddenly and dramatically. Faith is a profound and non-rational conviction of the truth of propositions to which the unaided intellect can at best accord only a temperate allegiance. The recognition of this fact explains the Christian emphasis on divine grace, the contribution which God makes to the conversion process, the gift of faith which seems to come from a source outside the believer because it does not come from his normal, conscious, reasoning and critical self. And the converted find that the difficulty of explaining their acquisition of faith in plain language is insuperable.

This is not to say that reasoned argument or theological study play no part in the process which leads to conversion. They can play a part, because if long continued they may put a strain on the nervous system which contributes to the supervening of hypnoid, paradoxical and ultraparadoxical phases of brain activity, in the same way that the person who struggles on and on against attempts to hypnotize him will eventually suddenly succumb. One of the most famous and deeply appealing statements of faith ever made, after all, was Tertullian's Certum estquia imposibile est, 'it is certain because it is impossible'.

NOTES

1 E. O'Brien, *Varieties of Mystic Experience*. Holt, Rinehart; New York, 1964, pp. 98–9.

2 Quoted in R. C. Zaehner, *Mysticism Sacred and Profane*. Oxford University Press, 1961, paperback, pp. 157–8.

3 *V.M.E.*, pp. 137–9.

4 *V.M.E.,* p. 166.

5 *V.M.E.,* p. 172.

6 *V.M.E.*, pp. 172–3.

7 *V.M.E.*, p. 189.

8 *V.M.E.,* p. 217.

9 *V.M.E.*, p. 271.

10 *V.M.E.*, p. 273.

11 *V.M.E.*, pp. 297–9.

12 R. A. Knox, *Enthusiasm*. Clarendon Press, Oxford, p. 263.

13 Knox, p. 272.

14 Knox, pp. 255–6.

15 James, pp. 211–12.

16 James, p. 205.

17 James, 206–10.

18 James, p. 227.

19 James, pp. 217–18. Italics in original.

Sex and Possession

If man is thought to rise to the level of the divine in mystical experience, it has been believed by millions of people that he can attain the same level in the ecstasy of sex. The experience of being swept away in an overwhelming tide of desire, which carries the lovers irresistibly along with it, which smashes down all barriers of convention, which the lovers themselves may realize will hurt others close to them, but which they feel powerless to control, long ago suggested to humanity that to be passionately in love is to be seized by a force from outside oneself, a force which is superhuman and in some religions divine. A lover traditionally behaves like a madman, another sufferer frequently regarded as possessed by a god or a demon, and lovers in orgasm behave as if they were possessed, trembling, writhing, groaning, crying out, as blind and deaf to everything around them as if they were no longer on any earthly plane. Complete orgasm also often ends in a collapse phase, as in abreaction, ecstatic dancing and convulsion therapy.

It is significant that 'having', 'knowing' and 'possessing' are among our commonest expressions for sexual intercourse, for they suggest that the real goal and summit of sexual activity is not the procreation of children, or even erotic pleasure, but the sense of mingled identity which lovers briefly achieve, the acquisition of another human being who, if only momentarily, seems to become part of oneself. This ideal of mingled identity in sex has caused mystics to speak of the soul's union with and possession by God in sexual terms. In the previous chapter I quoted al-Ghazali's analogy between union with the divine and the union of lovers. Numerous Christian mystics have described the human soul as the female, surrendering to and possessed by God as the male. St John of the Cross, in one of his poems, a song of the soul in rapture at having arrived at the height of perfection, wrote:

Oh night that was my guide!
Oh darkness dearer than the morning's pride,
Oh night that joined the lover
To the beloved bride
Transfiguring them each into the other.[1]

The soul is in darkness, says the *Cloud of Unknowing*, but God pierces the darkness with a ray of love, the soul is 'inflamed with the fire of love', and so is 'one with God in spirit and in love' and 'made a God in grace'. According to Walter Hilton, 'God and the soul are no longer two but one . . . In this union a true marriage is made between God and the soul, which shall never be broken.' Heinrich Suso, a German mystic of the fourteenth century who refers to himself throughout his autobiography as 'she', again stresses the total mingling of identities. 'Earthly lovers, however greatly they may love, must needs bear to be distinct and separate from one another; but Thou, O unfathomable fullness of all love . . . pourest Thyself so utterly into the soul's essence that no part of Thee remains outside.'[2]

Earthly lovers, however, similarly sense a divine element in sexual union. Lovers in poetry and popular songs, and very often in everyday speech, 'worship' or 'adore' or 'idiolize' each other. In the marriage service, the bridegroom may say to the bride, 'with my body I thee worship'.

Previous chapters have thrown light on the probable physiological mechanism responsible for this connection between sex and concepts of the divine and possession. During the sexual act, especially if it ends in mutual orgasm, both partners achieve an intense, often uncontrolled and uncontrollable, state of temporary brain excitement, which leads on to a state of sudden temporary nervous collapse and transient brain inhibition. We have already seen what effects this physiological process can have in creating greatly increased suggestibility and in producing paradoxical and ultraparadoxical phases of brain activity. Feelings of possession from outside, or of mutual possession of each partner by the other, can become extremely strong, and powerful and quite uncritical transference can build up. Relief from the accumulated tensions of everyday living also occurs frequently in the phase of final sexual collapse, when the brain-slate is wiped clean and left blank for new impressions and influences to write on. New loves can readily spring up, or old hates be dissolved, in states of aroused sexual tension and the final orgasm.

It is this physiological process which lies behind the use of normal and deviant sexual practices to induce possession by gods and spirits, which has an important role in certain oriental cults though Christianity, with its powerful strain of distrust of sex, woman, and the body, has generally been fiercely hostile to it and has played down and allegorized away the role of sex in mysticism. Even so, sexual means of inducing the presence of God in the worshipper were employed, usually in disguised and unrecognized forms, in medieval nunneries and monasteries, and there are accounts of sincerely pious nuns feeling themselves physically seduced, loved and possessed by Christ during mystical meditation, to the point of orgasm.

Several religious sects have practised the use of prolonged sexual intercourse without orgasm, called carezza, to increase states of suggestibility and fortify religious faith. Dr Alice Stockham in the 1880s describes its effects as follows: 'Manifestations of tenderness are indulged in without physical or mental fatigue . . . once the necessary control has been acquired, the two beings are fused and reach sublime spiritual joy . . . After an hour the bodies relax, spiritual delight is increased and new horizons are revealed with the renewal of strength.'[3] Later on, Dr Marie Stopes was also to recommend its use.

In crude American revivalism, making worshippers 'come through' sexually to Jesus was often deliberately encouraged, and the occurrence of such orgasm might be taken as the sign of the Holy Ghost entering a person's life and the sign that things would be 'new and different' for him from then on. Erskine Caldwell's novel *The Journeyman* describes this revivalist technique in the American South very well.

The act of sex and orgasm not only greatly increases suggestibility and so facilitates the implantation of belief, but the increased suggestibility then fires off further sexual excitement. Repeatedly induced orgasmic collapse has therefore been used to produce states of deep hysterical trance. Further, the implantation of confirmation of religious faith by techniques of this sort is often more effectively achieved in groups than by people in pairs or alone, hence the sexual orgy as a religious rite. Wesley's early followers were accused of doing this at their 'love feasts', as the early Christians had been long before.

Until comparatively recently, little was known in the West of the tantric cults of India, which are viewed with severe disapproval by many Hindus and Buddhists. Tantrism is of considerable antiquity, so much so that some authorities believe it to be the oldest of all Indian cults, the religion of the pre-Aryan inhabitants of India and the prototype of yoga.[4]

It uses sexual intercourse to strengthen religious group feelings and to bring about states of possession by divine and demonic powers. To bank up energy, sexual indulgence is reduced to a minimum for some days before a ceremony. If actual sexual intercourse is employed in the ceremony, it is in the 'left-hand tradition'; while the 'right-hand tradition' substitutes symbols for actual sex practices. Left-hand tantrism involves actual sexual intercourse with a woman, and it is accepted that the tantric's wife and any other woman, from any caste, are equally eligible.

Agehananda Bharati's book on *The Tantric Tradition*[5] explains that the person who is to be initiated should be beaten up by the guru, and if he trembles and is frightened this is a sign of his readiness for initiation into left-hand practices. In other words, the candidate is first reduced by strong physical and nervous pressures to a suitably pliable and suggestible state (and this is a feature of initiation into many other cults and groups in other parts of the world). Benjamin Walker also stresses the importance of fear in tantrism:

'An important feature in tantrism is the element of the direful and the awe-inspiring, to which the term *bhairav*, "terror", is applied. Its source is Siva in his aspect of Bhairava and his consort Sákti in her aspect of Bhairavi (Kali, Durga, Chandi, etc.) who body forth the elements of universal dread. In the eight "terror" shapes of Siva he is described as black-limbed, destructive, wrathful, red-crested and so on . . . His companions are ghouls, demons and ogresses, and his *vahana* or vehicle is a misshapen dog with evil fangs and slavering jaws, who is as terrible to behold as the god himself. The bhairav or terror aspects of the deity are invoked in ceremonial maledictions, and form the subject of meditation of tantric devotees at graveyards during necrophilic rites.'[6]

We saw earlier what effects the arousal of intense fear can have on the brain, and the tantrics also make much use of *mantras*, magic words and phrases which are repeated over and over again and which have a hypnotic effect. All sorts of other long and complicated rituals have also to be gone through prior to the actual intercourse. Hemp (hashish) is very often taken, if possible an hour and a half before, so that the person is under its full effects at the time of ritual intercourse. In some rituals there is a circle of men and women sitting in pairs, with the leader and his own girl in the centre. Ritualistic intercourse is finally performed by the group and special mantras are repeated while this is going on. Hindu tantric worshippers are allowed to eject sperm but the Buddhist must not do so, he must conserve it. Bharati reports that these ritual sex practices 'engender the intensive, euphoric, oftentime hallucinatory and perhaps psycho-pathological feelings which go with religious experience —or which are religious experience . . . the method of tantrism is more radical than that of any other system, and the immediate aim of the tantric is to achieve enstacy (ecstasy).'

We are told that:

'Breath control is relatively easy to achieve . . . using the mantra as a time unit . . . This brings about a certain euphoric effect accompanied by mild hallucinations . . . Next he learns to practise breath control . . . with his consecrated female partner. With her he enters into sexual union, the procedure . . . taught orally by the guru (varies) according to the different somatic and psychological constitutions of the individual disciple and the (girl). Most frequently the female adept sits astride on the male yogi's lap, who himself takes one of the traditional yogic postures which are slightly modified to adapt him to the situation.'[7]

The purpose of these rituals, which one Hindu critic described as 'the most revolting and horrible that human depravity could think of', is to enable the worshipper to unite himself with demons and deities. Similarly, Indian temple prostitutes have been trained for centuries to help worshippers achieve trance and states of possession. And Indian temple sculpture demonstrates the Hindu view of the power of sex as a means of achieving religious ecstasy and mingling with the divine.

Allan Ross has described many examples of temple prostitution and the varied sex rites in and around Bombay used for the attainment of religious ecstasy. He attended, among other ceremonies, the Zatra festival in the Matheran hills near by. 'I saw some of the tortured penitents: every inch of one man's body was pierced with small hooks . . . A few naked women had arrows penetrating their breasts, stomach and buttocks, so they could neither sit nor lie down.' Near by on a peculiar wooden structure 'A woman was hanging from hooks attached to her breasts and vagina, the two centres of desire.'

For three days these penitents cannot eat, drink or bathe. Then ensued the religious ritual of firewalking. Going over the fire pits unharmed were among others 'the self torturing penitents with their Kavadis, their hooks, nails, arrows and pins skewering their bodies . . . Outside all around the temple, men were rolling on the ground in exaltation . . . women rolled along with the men in equal transports of sexual compulsion.'

Meanwhile a girl came up to the priest and Allan Ross, and started sexually provoking them. ' "What should I do?" I asked the priest as the girl tugged at me insistently. She was quite young with satiny gold skin. Her sari had become undone . . . "There is room for such things inside," said the priest coolly. "In such cases it is better to release one's emotions as God meant it, for a union with flesh is also a union with fire." He took the girl and me to a special room inside the temple . . . later, released, she looked at me as though I was a total stranger . . . completely oblivious to all that had taken place . . . I (too) left the temple still possessed.'[8]

In Western cultures, however, sexual methods have been driven underground by Christian ethics and automatically associated with heresy. The whole witch mania, if based on any reality at all, may have arisen from group sex practices in which the devotees believed themselves to be possessed by the Devil and his minions. It is possible that group religious sex practices may have survived underground when the Christian Church took control of religious life in Europe. But so many false confessions to witchcraft were forced from innocent people by torture and so much abnormal sexual psychopathology was based on the judges' own sexual imaginings that it is impossible to know what was the truth behind it all. However, every generation has bred its own sex adepts, using intercourse, as in India, to obtain feelings of possession by gods and devils, and so there may have been a small fire behind the clouds of enforced confession smoke.

In this century tantric theory and practice have spread to some groups of occultists in the West. I was fortunately able to examine the then unpublished diaries of Aleister Crowley, through the good offices of Gerald Yorke.[9] These throw a flood of detailed technical light on sexual means of attaining states of possession. They deserve discussion in a book of this nature since magic, witchcraft and demonology have absorbed the minds of many men for centuries, with too little understanding of the physiological and psychological effects of magical and sexual practices, and their faith-creating powers.

Aleister Crowley, a highly intelligent and persistent seeker after the means by which man could make contact with the inhabitants of the spirit world, and command gods and devils to do his bidding, made a detailed study of Indian mysticism and tantric practices. He was a member of a number of secret societies, including the Golden Dawn, among whose distinguished members was W. B. Yeats. Later, like others before him and since, he started to experiment with drugs to enable him to contact spirits more easily. From various psychedelic drugs he went on to 'hard' drugs like cocaine, and finally his writings became verbose and almost meaningless, as he mentally drifted further and further from reality. His day-to-day diaries are a mine of information on a subject which it is difficult to obtain correct information about because the use of abnormal and normal sexual practices for religious and spiritual ends conflicts with conventional attitudes. These methods are therefore still invariably practised in secret.

In the early 1900s Crowley was already showing interest in mysticism and esoteric Eastern practices, and he travelled and studied in the Orient from 1902 to 1906. He also claimed to have worked with Dr Henry Maudsley for some months and says in his diary for 1903:

'Dr. Maudsley, the greatest of living authorities on the brain, explained to me the physiological aspects of Dhyana (unity of subject and object in meditation) as extreme activity of one part of the brain, extreme lassitude of the rest. He refused to localize the part. Indulgence in this practice (mystical trance) he regarded as dangerous, but declined to call the single experience pathological.'

Crowley proceeded to join the Order of the Golden Dawn and later the Ordo Templi Orientis, a German occult society primarily concerned with sexual magic. He writes:

'The art was communicated to me in June 1912 by the O.H.O. (the Outer Head of the Order, Theodor Reuss). It was practised in a desultory manner until Jan. 1st, 1914, when I made the experiment described elsewhere (a homosexual working in Paris with Victor Neuburg). The knowledge thus gained enabled me to make further research and produce certain results . . . my bronchitis was cured in a day. I obtained money when needed. I obtained sex force and sex attraction . . . much of the great work done by me all this summer may be considered due entirely to this Act.'

Earlier, in 1911, Crowley had started to use a sexual trance technique which he later called 'Eroto-comatose Lucidity'. It helped him, he thought, to get into more direct contact with the spirit and demon world. Later, on the evening of 11 October 1911, for instance, he met a Mrs Mary d'Este Sturges at the Savoy Hotel in London, and their attraction was mutual. He met her again in London on 13 and 14 October and joined her in Paris a month later; then they went on to Zurich. On 21 November in Zurich, he records:

'At about midnight she was in a state of excitement, exhaustion and hysteria . . . one little removed from an amorously infuriated lioness . . . suddenly and without warning (this) gave place to a profound calm hardly distinguishable from prophetic trance, and she began to describe what she was seeing . . . The lady . . . had seen in a dream the head of 5 White Brothers . . . The person now appeared again to her. He was an old man with a long white beard . . . His first counsel to the seer was "to make himself perfectly passive" in order that he might communicate freely.'

Crowley then went on to ask Mrs Sturges, now in deep trance, questions as to the identity of the possessing spirit. The woman was put into trance by repeated sexual orgasm, and questioned about the spirits possessing her, to test their knowledge. His diary records the following questions and answers.

'Q. Do you claim to be a Brother of A.A.? (Crowley's own occult order).
A. He has A.A. in black letters on his breast.
Q. What does A.A. mean?
A. It means *ALL*.
Q. I want an intelligible significant word.

A.   I.T.O. but that isn't what he said. He sticks to his H.T.E. or something.'

In trance Mrs Sturges was also asked whether the possessing spirit would say where certain books were hidden and give other information, again designed to test the spirit's knowledge about happenings past, present and future.

Crowley persisted with sexually induced mysticism and magic which, to his believing mind, often produced concrete results. He went so far as to believe that: 'By the right use of this secret man may impose his will on Nature Herself . . . though all recorded knowledge is destroyed, it would be possible for an adept of this secret to restore it.'

Crowley describes how, after preliminary meditation, a full meal is taken three hours before the start of the ceremony; an assistant, either male or female, is required.

'. . . formed by Nature signally for physical tasks, robust, vigorous, eager and sensible, fat and healthy; flesh, nerve and blood being tense, quick and lively, easily inflamed and nigh inextinguishable . . . The phallus is the physiological basis of the Oversoul . . .' After ritual intercourse—'The semen is then collected and must be perfectly dissolved in a full portion of gluten or menstrual blood if possible. This is taken as a sacrament. It is said by the O.H.O. that of this perfect medicine a single dewdrop sufficeth, and this may be true. Yet it is our opinion that every drop generated (so far as may be possible) may be consumed . . . If indeed it be the contained Prana that operateth the miracle, then the quantity is as important as the quality.'

The details of producing sexual trance states are fully detailed in Crowley's writings. Both men and women may be used:

'The candidate is made ready for the ordeal by general athletic training and by fasting. On the appointed day he is attended by one or more experienced attendants whose duty it is to exhaust him sexually by every known means. The candidate will sink into a sleep of utter exhaustion but he must be again sexually stimulated and then again allowed to fall asleep. This alternation is to continue indefinitely until the candidate is in a state which is neither sleep nor waking, and in which his spirit is set free by perfect exhaustion of the body . . . communes with the most Highest and the Most Holy Lord God of its Being, Maker of Heaven and Earth.'

The 'Ordeal' terminates by its failure to work any longer, or by the achievement of a trance state in which the god or devil talks through the subject and various manifestations may occur. Ultimate waking is followed by another and final performance of the sexual act if possible.

He also writes that:

'Ordinary acts of love attract or create discarnate human spirits. Other (abnormal) sexual acts involving emission of semen therefore attract or excite other spirits, incomplete and therefore evil . . . Nocturnal pollutions bring succubi . . . Voluntary sterile acts create demons, and (if done with concentration and magical intention) such demons may subserve that intention.'

In view of the physiological effects of operations of this sort, it is not unduly surprising that by means of them Crowley obtained apparent visions and communications from gods and spirits. In 1914, in Paris, he carried out a series of important experiments or 'working' with the poet Victor Neuburg, using homosexual acts, and putting Neuburg repeatedly into states of trance and possession. Thus of the *Seventh Working* he writes:

'The temple open at 10: the Rite being done anally. We beheld the Universe of the most brilliant purple and Jupiter seated on his throne surrounded by the Four Beasts . . . Subsequently there appeared a great Peacock . . . The peacock is now crowned, and regards himself in a mirror.' *The Sixteenth Working.* 'The temple opened at about 10.20 (p.m.). After the semen had been ejaculated the god demanded blood. (Neuburg cut a 4 on Crowley's breast) . . . Next week the god demands . . . a sparrow (or if not a pigeon) shall be slain. The directions were obtained with difficulty and his (Neuburg's) *whole consciousness was wrapped up in God,* the only expression being these (repeated) words Sanguis and Semen.'

When the First World War broke out Crowley was in America, where he stayed and continued his work, mostly now using women rather than men as his magical assistants. By this time he was also employing various drugs, including ether, anhalonium lewinii, hashish and cocaine, to improve the trance and mystical phenomena obtained.

We read in his Diary:

'*July 23rd, 1916,* midnight (circa) Boston, Mass. Marie Roussel, French Canadian prostitute; great similarity to Maud Allen in face, form and manner. Object Glory to Hermes. Operation very good considering long abstinence. Elixir (semen and gluten) good. *Nov. 12th* 2.35 a.m. IX Degree (ceremony of O.T.O.) with Doris. Operation and Elixir wonderful. Object Wealth. Result. Immediate receipt of largest sum I have ever handled in 12 months . . . *Dec. 10th* 8.50 p.m. Irene Stanfield, extremely voluptuous and of greatest possible skill and good-will. Operation perfect. Elixir good, Dedication of myself to Tahuti at the beginning of this Great Magical Retirement.'

Ether and other drugs were used in these ceremonies, by both participants where helpful. Hashish was also extensively tested, and Crowley wrote an interesting early account of its mystical use. By 1922 he had become severely addicted to heroin, and made repeated attempts to master it, but without success. His diary now deteriorated, and he started to write more and more meaningless nonsense. His sexual workings became more bizarre. He set up a 'monastery' in Cephalù in Sicily. He is now 'the Beast 666 and Alostrael (Leah Hirsig) the Scarlet Woman, Leah my concubine, in whim all power is given, sworn unto Aiwaz, prostituted in every part of her body to Pan and the Beast, Mother of bastards, aborter, whore to herself, to man, woman, child and brute, partaker of the Eucharist of the Excrements in the Mass of the Devil, Sorceress of the Rite of Esau and Jacob.'

He also has a young American:

'A master magician of O.T.O. and a passed postulant to the secret chamber of the knights of the Temple, High Priest to the Beast before the Altar of Purple and Gold.'

The formula of this magic included making the American a 'God by ether' and then his having relations with the Beast 666 (Crowley) 'who thus becomes God'. The Scarlet Woman was also expected to have perverse sex with the Beast, using the right mantras. 'Ether is to be taken at leisure . . . Consume the elements of semen and gluten and perform any scrying or letter any prophesies as may be given, and at leisure and pleasure resume vestments and insignia and close Temple.' One of the initiates, Raoul Loveday, suddenly died and there was a public scandal. The Abbey of Thelema was hurriedly closed.

Crowley himself died in 1947, almost forgotten, and a registered and confirmed addict to heroin.

One of the principal purposes of the IX degree ceremony of the Ordo Templi Orientis, a rite of sexual magic to which Crowley refers in his diaries and which is practised by some Crowley-orientated magicians, is to induce possession by and union with a god. Francis King explains in his book *Sexuality, Magic and Perversion* that:

'The initiates of the IX degree claimed that success in almost any magical operation, from the invocation of a god to "procuring a great treasure", could be achieved by the application of the appropriate sexual technique. Thus to invoke the powers of a god into themselves they mentally concentrated on the god throughout their sexual intercourse, building up the form of the deity in their imaginations and attempting to imbue it with life. At the moment of orgasm they identified themselves with the imagined form, mentally seeing their own bodies and that of the god blending into one.'[10]

These details have been given because so little is known generally of the operations of small secret groups whose aim is sexual 'possession'. The witches of old are said to have practised these rites in their covens, and recently covens of self-styled witches have been formed in England and the United States in which sexual intercourse sometimes occurs within the magic circle during certain ceremonies, the participants acting the parts of, and evidently feeling themselves temporarily to be, the god and goddess of the witch religion.

It should be realized that the physiological states of brain excitement induced by sexual practices can be as conducive to the production of trance, heightened suggestibility and feelings of possession as the other methods we have already discussed. It is foolish to ignore the existence of these practices and their sway over the minds of those who use them, even though they are discredited by our present ethical codes.

NOTES

1 'St John of the Cross', *Poems*, translated by Roy Campbell. Penguin Books, Harmondsworth, 1960.

2 See, Sidney Spencer, *Mysticism in World Religion*, op. cit., pp. 237, 249–50.

3 *Forum Magazine,* 1972. Vol. 5, no. 9, p. 12.

4 See, Benjamin Walker, *Hindu World.* George Allen & Unwin, London, 1968, vol. 2, pp. 482 ff.

5 A. Bharati, *The Tantric Tradition.* Rider, London, 1965.

6 Walker, op. cit.

7 Bharati, p. 295.

8 A. Ross, *Bombay after Dark* (Vice in Bombay). Macfadden Bortell, London, 1968, pp. 149–55.

9 Duckworth has recently published some of these edited by Symonds and Grant in the *Magical Record of the Beast 666*, 1972.

10 Francis King, *Sexuality, Magic and Perversion*, Neville Spearman, London, 1971, p. 98.

Drugs, Magic and Possession

Like sexual techniques, drugs have also been used from time immemorial to induce feelings of possession by gods and spirits, and one of Aleister Crowley's disciples is entirely in harmony with thousands of years of religious and magical tradition, and too much modern tragedy, when he says that 'the only really legitimate excuse for resorting to drugs is the scientific one, i.e. for the acquisition of praeterhuman knowledge and power, which includes poetic inspiration or any other form of creative dynamism'.[1] Poetic inspiration, prophetic power and other forms of 'creative dynamism', whether drug-induced or not, have been regarded in many societies as the result of temporary possession of a human being by a supernatural being or force.

It is a pity that modern proponents of the use of marijuana, L.S.D. and the rest have so seldom inquired into the vast literature of this subject, for the effects produced by various different drugs have been reported time and time again in the past. In the East, the early Vedic hymns sang the praises of soma, the 'King of Plants', omnipotent, all-healing, the giver of immortality, consumption of which elevated the worshipper to the level of the divine, and which was itself considered a god. What soma was is uncertain, but it may have been a mushroom, *Amanita muscaria* or fly agaric. Tantric and other Indian sects 'have continually resorted to drugs to shift the plane of perception and attain ecstatic states and mystical illumination. Drugs, drinks, chemicals (e.g. mercury) and special medicinal preparations were and still are used for this purpose.'[2]

Gordon Wasson in his book on the Divine Mushroom quotes Endereli as describing its use as an abreactive and trance producing drug: 'And now there began an indescribable dancing and singing, a deafening drumming and a wild running about the (yard), during which the men threw everything about recklessly until they were completely exhausted. Suddenly they collapsed like dead men and promptly fell into deep sleep.' Wasson also quotes Kapec describing a journey in Asia. When in Siberia he met an 'evangelist' who recommended that he take these mushrooms 'that are I can say miraculous . . . they are the most precious creation of nature.' Kapec goes on, 'Hearing so many strange things about the merits of that mushroom . . . I ate half . . . Dreams came one after the other. I found myself as though magnetized . . . I started to have confidence in its supernatural qualities . . . For several hours new visions carried me to another world, and it seemed to me that I was ordered to return to earth so that a priest could take my confession . . . I should add only that as if inspired by magnetism I came across some blunders of my (confessor) and I warned him to improve in these matters, and I noticed that he took these warnings almost as the voice of Revelation.'[3]

The sacred plants of Mexico included the peyote cactus, from which mescaline is derived, the *psilocybe* mushroom, which was significantly called 'god's flesh', and *Datura stramonium* or thorn-apple. Peyote cults began to flourish among North American Indians in the 1870s and the peyote religion is now their principal cult. Stramonium was also smoked in North America, and in both California and Siberia a hallucinogenic toadstool was used to bring about communication with the divine and to induce ecstatic visions. Francis Huxley has commented that the use of hallucinogenic mushrooms 'may have been much more widespread in the past than we realize, and its effects quite possibly helped to give form to a number of traditional descriptions of heaven'.[4]

Alcohol is one of the drugs which has frequently been used in this way. Wine was evidently an important aid to ecstasy in the worship of Dionysus, who among numerous other roles was the god of wine. The worshippers were predominantly women and their rites have been summarized by Professor Guthrie as follows:

'Clad in fawnskins and taking in their hands the thyrsos, which was a long rod tipped with a bunch of ivy or vine-leaves, the god's own potent emblem, and with ivy-wreaths upon their heads, they follow their leader (a priest of the god) to the wildest parts of the mountains, lost in the bliss of the dance. Many carry snakes, wreathed about them, twined in their hair or grasped in the hand as may be seen in the vase-paintings. Their dance is accompanied by the heavy beat of the tympanum . . . and the strains of the reed-flute, as well as their own excited shouts and cries. Nothing is lacking which can serve to increase the sense of exaltation and of shedding the self of everyday existence; to the darkness, the music and the rhythmic dance are added the smoky light of torches and no doubt the god's especial gift of wine. Erotic enjoyment probably also contributed to producing the final state of *ekstasis* (standing outside oneself) and *enthousiasmos* (possession by the god). (In this state the worshippers saw visions, and nothing was impossible to them . . . Endowed with superhuman strength, they hurl themselves upon animals, wild or tame, and tear them to pieces with their bare hands for the "joy of the raw feast".)'[5]

Professor Dodds remarks that the Maenads, the female votaries of Dionysus, 'became for a few hours what their name implies—wild women whose human personality has been temporarily replaced by another', and that the tearing to pieces of animals and devouring of their raw flesh is based on a simple piece of primitive logic. 'If you want to be lion-hearted, you must eat lion; if you want to be subtle, you must eat snake; those who eat chickens and hares will be cowards, those who eat pork will get little piggy eyes. By parity of reasoning, if you want to be like god, you must eat god . . . And you must eat him quick and raw, before the blood has oozed from him: only so can you add his life to yours, for "the blood is the life".' The slaughtered animals are embodiments of the god, and it is likely that 'there once existed a more potent, because more dreadful, form of this sacrament, viz., the rending, and perhaps the eating, of God in the shape of a man . . .'[6]

Modern magicians in quest of the same objective also whip themselves up into a state of mental and emotional intoxication in which reason is overwhelmed, with or without the use of drink, drugs or sex. One of them gives this account of possession by what he calls an 'astral force' or a 'god-form', through whose power the magician hopes to achieve his purposes. 'The climax of all magical ritual occurs when the adept draws into himself the astral force he has evoked so as to project it towards a chosen object. To do this he must surrender his complete being to the astral force which is waiting to possess it, and this he does by cultivating a state of mind or, rather, madness, akin to the divine frenzy of the Bacchantes . . .' He goes on to say that,

'Some magicians cultivate the sweet madness by reciting one word over and over again . . . While engaged in this, the adept imagines that the god-form . . . is materializing behind his back. He visualizes this in as much detail as possible.' Slowly he begins to sense that it is towering in the magic circle behind him, and 'by now his heart will no doubt be beating furiously', but he must not panic. 'At last—and he will certainly know when—the god-form will take control of him. To begin with, the adept will feel an exquisite giddiness somewhere at the base of his skull and quickly convulsing the whole of his body. As this happens, and while the power is surging into him, he forces himself to visualize the thing he wants his magic to accomplish, and will its success.' Sex is frequently used to reach this climax. 'The outburst of power is effected at the same time as orgasm is reached, with possession occurring a few seconds before.'[7]

In his book *The Black Arts*, discussing the elaborate and exhausting techniques of European ceremonial magic, designed to summon up supernatural beings and subject them to the magician's control, Richard Cavendish has summed up the physiological effects on brain function which help to create belief in magic and in the reality of spirits and demons:

'The magician prepares himself by abstinence and lack of sleep, or by drink, drugs and sex. He breathes in fumes which may effect his brain and senses. He performs mysterious rites which tug at the deepest, most emotional and unreasoning levels of his mind, and he is further intoxicated by the killing of an animal, the wounding of a human being and in some cases the approach to and achievement of orgasm. Through all this he concentrates on a mental picture of the being he hopes to see. It does not seem at all unlikely that at the high point of the ceremony he may actually see it.'[8]

Frenzy, induced by sex, drugs, *mantras*, concentration, rhythmic music, chanting, dancing, jumping, twirling, over-breathing, is undoubtedly immensely effective in creating an absolute conviction of the presence of a god. For reasons already explained, it produces intense faith, not only in those who experience it but also very often in onlookers, who become much more suggestible in response to the excitement of the 'possessed' and who will then accept as true claims and beliefs of which they would normally be critical.

William James has the following to say about alcohol:

'The sway of alcohol over mankind is unquestionably due to its power to stimulate the mystical faculties of human nature, usually crushed to earth by the cold facts and dry criticisms of the sober hour . . . It (can) bring its story from the chill periphery of things to the radiant core. It makes him for the moment one with truth. Not through mere perversity do men run after it.'[9]

James then goes on to point out that nitrous oxide and ether stimulate mystical consciousness to an extraordinary degree, especially when given in suitably modified strength. 'Depth beyond depth of truth seems revealed to the inhaler . . . metaphysical revelation.' James was writing at the beginning of this century, and we are now seeing the same claims being monotonously repeated for any new drug that for the moment catches popular attention. James seems to have been greatly influenced and even 'converted' by his own drug experiences. After experimenting with nitrous oxide and ether, he came to the following conclusion:

'One conclusion was forced upon my mind at that time, and my impression of its truth has ever since remained unshaken . . . all about it (normal waking consciousness), parted from it by the flimsiest of screens, there lie potential forms of consciousness entirely different. We may go through life without suspecting their existence; but apply the requisite stimulus, and at a touch they are there in all their completeness . . . No account of the universe in its totality can be final which leaves these other forms of consciousness quite disregarded . . . Looking back on my own experiences, they all converge towards a kind of insight to which one cannot help *ascribing some metaphysical significance*. The keynote is invariably a reconciliation. It is as if the *opposites of the world*, whose contradictoriness and conflict make all our difficulties and troubles, *were melted into unity*.'[10]

Unfortunately, the schizophrenic in his temporary or permanent madness also finds similar unities occurring. And when he tries to explain them, they may be as nonsensical as many of the unities experienced through inhaling anaesthetics. One of Christopher Mayhew's correspondents—Mayhew himself will be quoted later—wrote about what happened when he was put under an anaesthetic for a short operation.

'I had a complete revelation about the ultimate truth of everything. I understood the entire works. It was a tremendous illumination. I was filled with unspeakable joy . . . When I came round I told the Doctor I understood the meaning of everything. He said, "Well, what is it?" and I faltered out, "Well, it's a sort of green light." '[11]

A schizophrenic doctor patient of mine suddenly woke up one day feeling that he had found the basic cause of all neurological illness, cancer and infections; he felt certain that he had suddenly stumbled overnight on a great universal discovery. When asked what the basic cause was, he said 'sin'! But with his recovery from the severe attack of schizophrenia, he lost this conviction. Now well and practising medicine, he might, however, still feel that something of real importance had been vouchsafed to him in his illness, if asked to be quite honest about his feelings. Such revelations, whether they occur under drugs or during a schizophrenic illness, carry with them a certainty which may override the normal intellectual standards and attitudes of the person experiencing them.

Another of Mayhew's correspondents, after having teeth removed under nitrous oxide, gave the following report of his anaesthetic experience:

'. . . of everlasting hell. I lost all consciousness of my surroundings . . . there was no consciousness of myself as the subject of suffering, but only an experience of suffering itself, outside time. It was this experience of being "caught in eternity" which . . . I shall never forget as long as I live.'[12]

J. A. Symonds, however, had a quite different experience under chloroform:

'I thought I was near death; when suddenly my soul became aware of God, who was manifestly dealing with me, handling me, so to speak, in an intense personal present reality. I felt him streaming in like light upon me . . . I cannot describe the ecstasy I felt. Then, as I gradually awoke . . . my relation to God began to fade . . . To have felt for that long dateless ecstasy of vision the very God, in all purity and tenderness and truth and absolute love, and then to find that I had after all no revelation, but that I had been tricked by the abnormal excitement of my brain . . . Yet, this question remains. Is it possible that the inner sense of reality which succeeded, when my flesh was dead to impressions from without, to the ordinary sense of physical relations, was not a delusion, but an actual experience? Is it possible that I, in that moment, felt what some of the saints have said they always felt, the undemonstrable but irrefragable certainty of God?'[13]

Both Symonds and James were profoundly affected by their anaesthetic experiences, which may have decided or fortified James's own brand of religious faith. Leuba[14] states that:

'In our experience Wm James has erred not in considering "pure" experience as unassailable, but in unwittingly regarding as such more than the given. He has confused pure experience with the elaboration of it . . . for what in mystical experience does James claim invulnerability? The uncritical mystic believes that Christ, or the Virgin, or some saint, has manifested himself to him . . . James regards them as illusory . . . They form, however, he affirms, a kernel immediately given, intuitional, and therefore invulnerable. What is this kernel? He answers that it consists in a feeling or conviction of vastness of reconciliation, of repose, of safety, of union, of harmony. In these terms does our distinguished philosopher define the kernel of unassailable truth revealed in mystical (drug) ecstasy . . . The truth-kernel of religious ecstasy is, as we have shown, no other than the truth-kernel of narcotic intoxication . . .'

And so the argument proceeds between those who have 'experienced' and so 'know', and those on the sidelines, who observe the variety of 'knowing', the contradictory variety of 'certainties', to which drugs, trances, mystical states of possession and the rest give birth in human minds.

Leuba goes on to say that if by 'union' William James had merely meant to indicate that, as the trance progresses, the mystic notices the gradual disappearance of boundary lines between objects, the merging of ideas into one another, the fusion of feelings, and that he enjoys a delightful sense of peace, there could be no objection to this observation: 'but James seemed to imply much more than this, a union with someone or something else . . . The universality of the mystical conviction is frequently offered as proof of its truth. But the truth of a belief is not proved by the fact that it is shared by all known men, (in fact) most of the users of narcotics and many of the subjects of spontaneous trance regard its contents just as they do their dreams, i.e. as having no other than a subjective validity . . . Hocking holds, with James and the mystic philosophers in general, that the immediate in ecstasy does not remain meaningless . . . it conveys a direct and truthful assurance of God and of the mystic's own relation to him; it is a divine substance known intuitively to come "from heaven" . . . it suffices to lift man above fatal doubt and disbelief.'

Whatever the truth of the matter, people have frequently acquired unshakeable faith from drug revelations, and continue to do so. Christopher Mayhew was convinced by his own experiences of mescaline that God exists, and that he had been in God's presence. When argued with, he would point out that he had *experienced* God under the drug, which the critics who questioned the reality of his experience had not done. He showed, after the mescaline experience, the calm unshakeable assurance of belief which can equally come from the other methods we have described.

Aldous Huxley, in his writings and in talking to me personally, also insisted that mescaline had taken him into the presence of God. But as in Mayhew's case perhaps, this was what Huxley was really interested in when he took the drug. Robert Graves, who was more interested in the beliefs of the ancient world, took the 'sacred' mushrooms which, he thought, might have been used in the Eleusian mysteries. Graves told me he did not, in consequence, enter God's presence like Huxley; he had a different type of drug experience which helped him to understand what the initiates of the mysteries had been trying to describe. He seemed to have a similar experience to theirs which, at the time, he wanted to do. People seem to obtain under drugs, or equally through mystical or revivalist or sexual techniques, what they want to obtain, or what they expect to obtain, or what conforms to the general setting and background. Converts were not possessed by Buddha at Wesley's revival meetings.

Another experience under ether shows the variety of religious experiences obtainable:

'I did not see God's purpose, I only saw his intentness and his entire relentlessness towards his means. He thought no more of me than a man thinks of hurting a cork when he is opening wine, or hurting a cartridge when he is firing . . . I realized that in that half-hour under ether I had served God more distinctly and purely than I had ever done in my life before . . . I was the means of achieving and revealing something, I know not what or to whom . . .'[15]

Sir James Crichton-Browne also reported many years ago that nitrous oxide inhalation provoked varying effects:

'In persons of average mental calibre they are pleasant and stimulating but in no way remarkable; but in persons of superior mental power they become thrilling and apocalyptic. A working man describes it as if he had had a little too much beer, and a philosopher announces that the secret of the universe had been, for one rapt moment, made plain to him.'[15]

Sir Humphrey Davy very early on had also found that in nitrous oxide inhalation in persons of intellectual training and distinction, the thoughts are in nine cases out of ten connected with some great discovery, some supposed solution of a cosmic secret.

One can suppose that those of Davy's scientific friends who agreed to experiment at so early a period were interested in just such things. Marghanita Laski in her book on *Ecstasy*, from which some of the quotations have been drawn, says in discussing drug ecstasy that:

'But from mescaline people may derive genuine religious overbeliefs yet not have had the kind of experiences generally regarded as religious ones. Mr Huxley believed he had attained the Beatific Vision. The female figure seen by Rosalind Heywood is described by her as "celestial" and as a messenger of the "High Gods". Alice Marriot describes her vision as "Paradise" and Mr Mayhew accepts the possibility of deriving religious experience from mescaline. Only Mr Mortimer and Professor Zaehner altogether deny that mescaline experiences are related to or can be assimilated to religious ones.'[16]

Yet if we start using L.S.D. in a non-religious setting, we get all sorts of non-religious effects, and the same applies to mescaline. But the non-religious 'truths' which take hold of a person under drugs can impress themselves on him with a religious certainty and fervour.

R. E. Masters in an article on chemically induced or enhanced eroticism reports that under L.S.D. 'A sexual union that in fact lasts thirty minutes or an hour may seem "endless" or to have "the flavour of eternity" . . . it may even take on symbolic and archetypal overtones. The couple may feel they are mythic, legendary . . . one has transcended the ordinary boundaries of self, the limits of time and space, so that something more, some infusion of the divine or supernatural, *must* have occurred . . .

with surprising frequency the feelings are shared . . . Religiously devout or mystically inclined people may have the *sense of a unity* that is also a trinity with God present in the oneness.'[17]

Another writer has said, 'That is the cosmic beauty of L.S.D. You flow in essence of god-love exactly to where you should be flowing in the manner and the moment you should be flowing. One day when we are all more highly evolved, more aware, in incarnations to come, it will all be happening without acid.' Hashish can give similar mystical and less dangerous effects. 'This is the very acme of love. This first moving in together . . . It's the beginning of time, the primordial chaos when all is formless and one, and in racking agony of pleasure, *two forms give birth to one another*. White light crashes through our minds. We are gone'.[18]

A patient of mine, previously under treatment by a doctor who believed in birth trauma, told me how under L.S.D. he had relived his own birth. He was in no doubt at all about it. After taking the drug, he had felt tight and constricted in the chest and abdomen, and very fearful. His breathing became laboured and rapid. Only a nurse was with him, and on his asking her what his symptoms meant, he was told to think hard and the answer would come to him. It suddenly did. He became quite certain that he was reliving his own birth; and as he felt himself coming out of his mother's womb and vagina, he had a sudden feeling of relief. Although he obtained no permanent mental relief from his drug-induced experience, and only recovered later when he was given electroshock therapy, he still persisted in the conviction that he had actually relived his own birth. He pointed out that no doctor had been present at the time, to suggest it to him or to brainwash him. However, he was living in an atmosphere of hospital group therapy where many patients were receiving L.S.D. Most of them were just as intellectually indoctrinated with the probability that birth trauma was a cause of their illness as was their doctor himself. They talked about it at meals and in spare moments. It is not surprising, therefore, that when claustrophobic and panicky feelings came upon this patient, and he asked what it meant and was told to think out the answer for himself, that it came to him that he had re-experienced his own birth trauma.

Other psychotherapists, using similar abreactive drugs, obtained and will always obtain quite different supposedly remembered experiences from patients, depending on their own or the patient's special interests. When during the war ether, pentothal and methedrine were all used to 'abreact' the horrifying war experiences of patients, it soon became obvious that, if pressed to do so, some soldiers would abreact experiences they had never had, sometimes made up on the spur of the moment to please the doctor or to put a good appearance on a cowardly act. Every abreacted experience had to be carefully examined and checked on, otherwise it might become all too real to the patient and come to be fully believed by him.

Freud, when he was working with Breuer, induced more than ten consecutive Viennese women under hypnosis to remember vividly having been slept with or interfered with sexually by their fathers. He thought he had stumbled on the basic cause of hysteria in women, until he realized that 10 out of 10 meant 100 out of 100, and that every Viennese father must be sleeping or sexually interfering with his daughter. This was obviously nonsense, and Freud was so disappointed that he said later that he nearly gave up psychoanalysis, which had led him so sorely astray. To solve his dreadful dilemma he invented his concepts of the sexual 'subconscious mind' and explained that many of his patients had 'subconsciously' wanted to sleep with their fathers, instead of actually having done so. Under drugs, hypnosis, induced abreactive excitement, or any other conscious or subconscious method of implanting suggestion, the patient will generally play back to the doctor what the doctor wants to hear. For a time Freud really believed that he had discovered the basic cause of hysteria, and in his letters at the time he described his sadness when it proved that the information obtained from his patients was false, entirely because of his eagerness to believe his theory. Similarly, Freudian and Jungian analysis of the same patient can produce quite different dreams, repressed memories and remembered incidents, proving that the analyst can readily obtain the information he needs to confirm his confidence in his own theories. The patient thus helps to re-brainwash the therapist.

All this is reported in detail in Ernest Jones's *Life of Freud*.[16] It is mentioned here to draw attention to the essential moral of this book. However real and vivid personal and apparently remembered experiences may seem, this is no evidence of their reality, if they are brought to the surface under conditions of stress and in states of abnormal brain activity and heightened suggestibility. And the overwhelmingly vivid and convincing nature of so many experiences reported in the same states of brain activity induced by meditation, drugs, sex, hellfire preaching, mob oratory or other mind-bending agencies, provides no evidence of their truth. Wesley's own beliefs about sudden conversion were confirmed when he found that more than 600 of his followers had all experienced it, and so he preached that sudden conversion was the only sure road to salvation. Good works alone, or intellectual adherence were of no value to Wesley and so were of no value to his vast congregations. But his converts never realized that their sudden and totally convincing state of faith had been brought about by Wesley's own beliefs and preaching methods, which in turn, in a circular way, their dramatic conversions had reinforced.

NOTES

1 Kenneth Grant, *The Magical Revival*, Frederick Muller, London, 1972, p. 91.

2 G. Wasson, *Soma, Divine Mushroom*. Harcourt Brace, New York, pp. 244–5.

3 Benjamin Walker, *Hindu World*, op. cit., vol. 1, p. 312.

4 *Man, Myth and Magic*, op. cit., vol. 2, p. 711.

5 W. K. C. Guthrie, *The Greeks and Their Gods*. Methuen, London, 1950, pp. 148–9.

6 E. R. Dodds, *The Greeks and the Irrational*, op. cit., appendix 1.

7 David Conway, *Magic: An Occult Primer*. Jonathan Cape, London, 1972, pp. 78, 130–32.

8 Richard Cavendish, *The Black Arts*. Routledge & Kegan Paul, London, 1967, pp. 256–7.

9 James, p. 387.

10 James, p. 388.

11 M. Laski, *Ecstasy*. Cresset Press, London, 1961, p. 261.

12 Laski, p. 262.

13 James, pp. 391–2.

14 J. H. Leuba, *Amer J. Psychology*. vii; 345; 1895.

15 James, pp. 392–3.

16 Laski, p. 276.

17 R. E. Masters, *The Sexual Revolution*. Playboy Press, Chicago, 1970, p. 134.

18 *Experience*, vol. 2, no. 10, 1972, p. 41 and vol. 2, no. 7, 1972, p. 43.

19 E. Jones, *Sigmund Freud: Life and Work*. Hogarth Press, London, 1955, 2 vols.

PART TWO

9

African Experiences

The second part of this book is mainly concerned with my personal studies of possession, trance, the creating and stabilizing of various faiths, and primitive healing methods, as seen, studied, photographed and filmed in many parts of the world. Opportunities to do this were made possible by my being repeatedly invited to lecture abroad, mostly on psychiatric problems. It was fortunately often possible at such times to make suitable research breakaways from the route of my ordinary medical travels.

The first to be discussed is a visit to the Samburu and Molo tribes in northern Kenya, when I was on my way to lecture at the Centenary of the Melbourne Medical School in Australia in 1962. We stopped off in Kenya for several days, finally reaching Australia via India. Owing to the kindness of John Brooke, my wife and I were able to use the Brooke Bond Company aeroplane to get to the Samburu and Molo tribes.

The Samburu are a nomadic tribe. They live in compounds called *manyattas* in the open pastoral areas of the country. These manyattas have to be moved every four months or so, to provide fresh grazing for the animals. Their boundaries are composed of cut thorn and other brushwood, to keep wild animals out and their own cattle in at night. The huts are mostly made of mud with a hole at the top for the smoke to get out.

These people are very subservient to their tribal and group leaders. Each manyetta had its own leader, and there were other leaders and tribal chiefs controlling groups of manyettas. The chiefs and leaders seemed to combine the functions of the priest and political leader in more sophisticated communities. During their initiation ceremonies, the adolescents are made to believe that their God will kill them at the request of a tribal leader.

The first thing that struck me, as an untrained observer, was the presence of the same basic personality types that one sees almost anywhere else in the world. Among these primitive people one saw dignified and competent chiefs who could well have been company directors in a more modern cultural climate. The girls had varied personalities very similar to those seen in mixed groups of girls in any civilized country. This was my first glimpse of so-called 'primitive' nomadic people, yet they seemed in temperament, outlook and general behaviour basically no different from the men and women of England or other supposedly more civilized countries. I find it hard to believe that the brain of man has altered much in the last million years. We see the same basic patterns of behaviour, temperament and mental illness in primitive tribes, in Greek, Roman, medieval and modern times. If it were not so it would be quite impossible for us to understand the behaviour of people in Shakespeare's plays, or in classical literature and history. And in classical times Hippocrates and Galen both described the same symptoms of nervous illness that are still to be seen in our day.

Because of the constant need to seek new grazing land, the Samburu tribal system has certain interesting features. There are, as usual, initiation rites at puberty in which both male and female adolescents are broken down as individuals and then reindoctrinated with the special beliefs and social behaviour patterns required of them by the custom of the tribe. We saw some of these recent initiates, who had been circumcised and were going through a very strenuous course of initiation training. They were dressed differently from the rest while they were being systematically indoctrinated and disciplined, and they danced incessantly. When they had gone through all this, the girls became marriageable and the men became Morans or warriors, who would be allowed no wives until their main fighting days were over. They had to fight for the new grazing land and the building of new manyattas. When they had earned by their labours a certain number of cattle which could be exchanged for a wife, they were allowed to become husbands. But they were given little chance of obtaining the required number of cattle for a wife until their early years as the advance guard of fighters were over; and in the meantime the elders took unto themselves the pretty young girl-friends of the Moran.

As there is no actual fighting to be done at the present time, these Moran seem to lead a pretty idle life. Their existence is almost psychopathic and vain; they dress up in elaborate costumes and do very little work. But they generally remain subservient to the tribal leaders. Their initiation rites are undoubtedly very powerful in their effects, and once the young people have been broken down and indoctrinated to accept the tribal values, religious and social, they remain 'sensitized' to what might be called 'agents of disruption'. If deviation occurs, this may be dealt with by the arousal of fear and the use of drumming and dancing to induce trance, when the deviant is often again 'brought to heel'. He must unquestioningly accept the validity and fairness of tribal ideas and tribal group behaviour. All this resembles the English public school system of indoctrination, in which boys are rapidly broken down and re-indoctrinated to accept the school's values. Similar indoctrination techniques are used in armies, especially in crack regiments. The raw recruit is rapidly changed from a critical individual into a numbered soldier, wearing a special type of costume, loyal to the group and uncritically obedient to commands, sensible or otherwise, for years afterwards. Whether in a 'primitive' tribe or at school or in the army, the process is essentially the same. Severe stress is imposed on the new recruit, by subjecting him to arbitrary and frightening authority, by bewildering him, abusing or ill-treating him, by telling him that his old values and sentiments are childish, and so inducing in him a state of unease and suggestibility in which new values can easily be drummed into him, and he recovers his self-confidence by accepting them. The initial conditioning techniques may have to be reinforced from time to time by further conditioning procedures, and follow-up indoctrination is considered most important in all types of religious or other conversion.

What I wanted most to study among the Samburu was their dancing, which is often carried to the point of trance and collapse. Talking to some of the young Moran through an interpreter, I was told that the effects of their dancing were twofold. Firstly, after dancing themselves into a trance, and especially after the collapse phase, the Moran lost all fear of fighting. Trance and greatly increased suggestibility made them immune from normal fears and doubts about going into battle.

A second, and surprising but extremely important effect was

that trance and collapse freed them from any dangerous resentment which they might have built up against their leaders. These leaders have several wives, and one of the Moran may suddenly lose his girl-friend, who becomes perhaps the fifth or more wife of the elderly head of a neighbouring manyatta. This might naturally cause intense resentment, but the Moran told me that as a result of dancing into trance and collapse, 'the anger leaves our hearts'. In effect, dancing is used specifically to alleviate the resentment and hostility which naturally builds up against the tribal elders and the customs and conventions imposed by society on the young. This is probably effected by recreating the 'conditioning' of the initiation procedures and maintaining a state of suggestibility controlled by the elders.

It was most illuminating to see how the Samburu had found, and for centuries maintained, this method of keeping control in the hands of the few. It seemed to me that civilized men may have to go back and study 'primitive' methods of keeping the majority of people in a state of comparatively cheerful subjection to unequal and often grossly unjust political and social systems. I was now beginning to understand better how Hitler, for instance, had been so successful in using mass rallies, marching and martial music, chanting of slogans and highly emotional oratory and ceremony, to bring even intelligent Germans into a condition of intellectual and emotional subjection. Or how the new 'youth culture' of the West, based on frenzied dancing to the pounding repetitive beat of very simple music played at almost intolerable volume, has helped to create the 'permissive society' and to bring down in ruins a whole structure of beliefs and conventions cherished by the elders of our society. We see in Western countries today, in fact, the same dancing and whirling to a powerful beat, carried sometimes to states of exhaustion and semi-trance, which is little different from what I saw in Africa, though in our society it is not under the control of the elders but ranged on the opposite side.

During our stay with the Samburu we saw four different groups dancing. On each occasion the women began the dancing by themselves, then the men started to dance in their own group, and finally towards the end both sexes joined in the dancing together. When the men danced, they sometimes repeatedly jumped in the air, which seemed to be another way of inducing a mild form of trance. The women were not allowed to go into

Possession by Dionysius 500 B.C.

Dancing to trance among the nomadic
Samburu tribe in Kenya

Casting out possessing spirits in Kenya and Zambia by drumming.
A collapse phase finally supervenes.

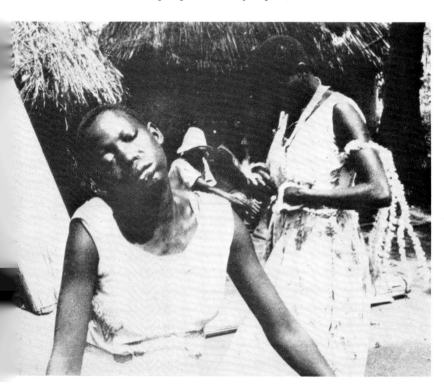

The expulsion of a possessing spirit in Zambia. The patient is in trance, is highly suggestible and has collapsed.

Casting out possessing Pepos by drumming people into trance and 'little death', Kenya

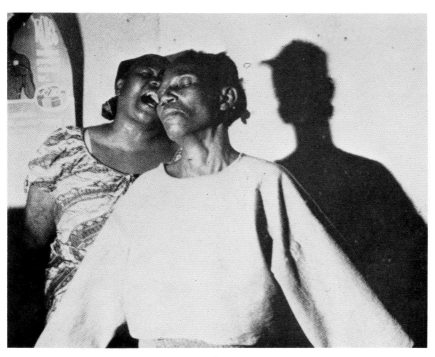

Possessed by the Holy Ghost in Nigeria

Child possession by the Holy Ghost, Nigeria

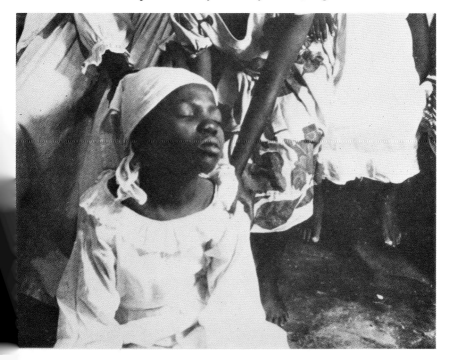

Possessed by the god Shango in Brazil

Possessed by an Indian spirit during Macumba
ceremony in Brazil

Ogoun possession
in Brazil

Shango possession state in
Trinidad

Altar for animal sacrifice which is followed by possession by
Christian Saints in Trinidad

Possessed by Joseph the Carpenter in Trinidad after animal sacrifices

Voodoo possession in Haiti

Voodoo possession in Haiti

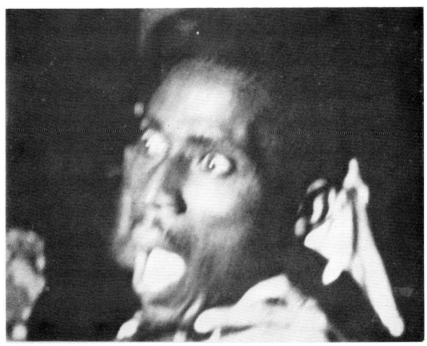

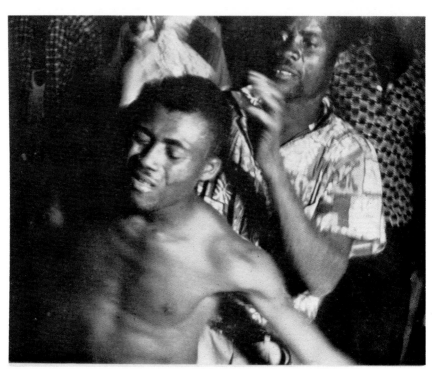

Voodoo possession in Haiti

Terminal collapse phase, Haiti

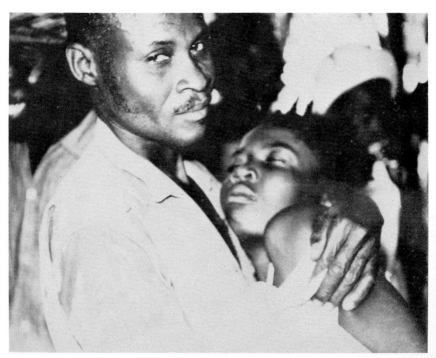

Possessed by the god Babalou in Havana

Entry of Holy Ghost in Barbados

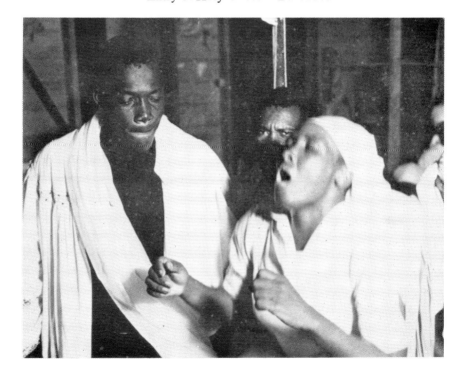

Inducing possession by the Holy Ghost, Clay County, Kentucky

Subsequent collapse state

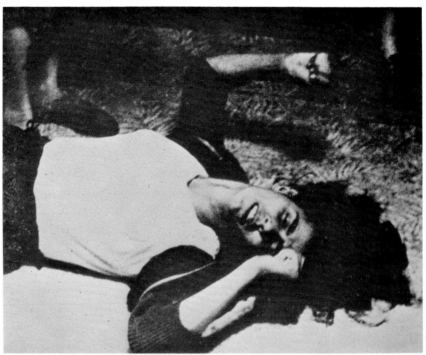

Possession by Holy Ghost in Watts, Los Angeles

'Pop music possession', London

Possession by witch goddess, London

Final collapse state in witchcraft ceremony, London

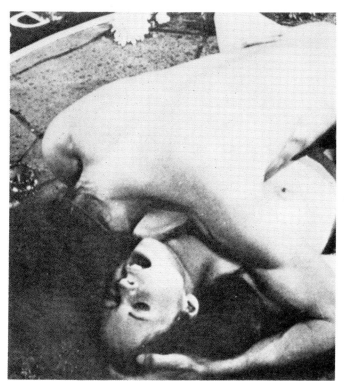

Ritual sex possession in witchcraft ceremony, England

Collapse phase in orgasm

'Beatle possession'

full trance, but some of the photographs taken show them in a highly suggestible and almost ecstatic state. When one woman did go into full trance, the others stopped her and led her away. I got the impression that the reason for not allowing the women to fall into trance was possibly because then the chiefs could not control the situation created. Wives sometime dance with unmarried Moran, and one could see how many emotional transferences could be built up if trance was freely allowed in mixed dancing. Trances were much more common in the male groups. The male dancing was far more energetic and so led on to semi-trance, and full trance in some cases. The men used a form of intensive rhythmic overbreathing with a grunting expiration. I was most interested, a year or two later, to witness the same type of overbreathing in Trinidad in 1964 while studying trance states induced by religious pocomania. It was almost uncanny to see the same type of special overbreathing used to attain similar mental states in both a primitive tribal and a Christian religious setting. A somewhat similar chanting and overbreathing technique also occurs among the Arabs on certain occasions, when they want to go into trance.

While the Samburu were overbreathing and harshly expelling their breath, they were also rhythmically dropping back hard on to their heels. The whole movement required much muscular effort and obviously would soon start to cause bodily and nervous exhaustion. I showed a film of this nomadic dancing to a research bio-chemist, who felt that, if it had been possible to take arterial blood samples, a high degree of blood alkalosis would have been found, leading to brain alkalosis. We know that brain alkalosis tends to produce suggestible behaviour and trance. Undoubtedly the heavy stamping and rhythmic dancing would create more lactic acid in the blood stream, because of the excessive muscular effort involved, which might counteract some of the alkalosis produced by overbreathing. However, the total effect on the biochemistry would still seem to be an increasing tendency to brain alkalosis, which is what is required if a state of trance is to be fairly rapidly induced.

Had these tribal ceremonies been more spontaneous, instead of being specially prepared for us, we might have seen more than one real trance ending in collapse, for we were told that these trance states and collapse phenomena occur much more

frequently when the Moran are dancing in full tribal ceremonies. One man, who did go into trance, left the group and
went away by himself; he was followed by two others who supported him while he continued to overbreathe very rapidly. It
was very similar to what one sees in a state of hysterical hyperventilation in some Western patients. The overbreathing went
on for quite some time and he obviously had lost consciousness
at the end, although he did not drop to the ground as he was
being supported. However, I managed to get photographs of
the final collapse with a dropping to the ground in other Samburu ceremonies. On talking to the man after the attack was
over, he confirmed that when one wakes up there is a loss of all
fear and tension.

Many of the other dancers approached very near trance, and
showed states of increased suggestibility at the end of a long
and intensive period of repetitive and monotonous dancing.
They looked very much like fans of the Beatles or other 'pop
groups' after a long session of dancing.

The Moran took short rest periods between their dancing
sessions. They often joked, and were very friendly. The women
particularly wanted my wife to join in the mixed dancing, so to
please them she did. After some initial difficulty in picking up
the rhythm, she found that the only way to imitate the dancing
was to imitate the movements of sexual intercourse. When she
did this, she found that she was moving in the same way as the
native women. It is important to remember that sexual intercourse itself produces overbreathing, and leads on to states of
excitement, increased suggestibility, feelings of possession of
the loved one, and final collapse.

THE MOLOS

Following our visit to the Samburu, we flew up to Lake Rudolf
near the Kenya–Abyssinia border and there we were able to see
the even more primitive Molo tribal dancing. The Molos are
a very backward tribe. Only about eighty of them are left.
They were living by the side of the lake in very deserted and
arid country. Their diet was mostly fish collected from the lake;
they had not even proper boats but went out fishing on badly
shaped logs of wood. To produce fire they rubbed pieces of

wood together. There was a fishing lodge with an air-strip just near the Molo huts, which were made of fibre. The tribe had recently moved up nearer to the lodge. They could have obtained matches at the lodge but preferred to go on rubbing pieces of wood together to make fire. The health of this small group was on the whole very poor, most of them suffering from malnutrition and the Molo tribal leader had obviously suffered from severe rickets.

When we asked the Molos to arrange a dance for us, they agreed to do so, but being so few in number they had to ask some of the Samburu living near them to join in the dance. The dancing was basically similar to what we had already seen among the Samburu. The men and women again danced separately, and states of trance were quickly induced in the men, though not so much in the women. We saw two sessions of dancing and took some photographs, though at this time my photography was far from good and many films were spoiled by my poor technique. However, enough facial close-ups were obtained to demonstrate the identity between modern and virtually prehistoric methods of achieving the same result.

I also tried to see the trance states that are reported to occur among the Bushmen in the Kalahari Desert and elsewhere. But it proved too difficult to arrange. Richard Lee describes these very well and shows how trance occurs with rhythmic dancing, overbreathing and heavy foot falls in other very primitive people; and where there is trance, ideas of possession may often follow. Lee says that the purpose of these trance states in Kung Bushmen is to 'cure the sick, to influence the supernatural and to provide mystical protection for all members of the group.' This is what this present book is all about. He goes on to say that 'of 131 adult males of a Bushman group, at least 60 were trance performers.' It happens here, as elsewhere, in normal persons and includes an altered state of consciousness. 'The actual entrance into trance may be gradual or sudden. In the first instance, the trancer staggers and almost loses balance . . . (later) falls down in a comatose state, a state called "half death" by the Bushmen.' The sudden entrance on the other hand is characterized by a violent leap or somersault and a later collapse into a state called "little death" in other parts of

Africa. 'While in trance, some rise up and move among the rest trying to cure people by laying on of hands, moaning and sometimes uttering piercing shrieks. After about an hour, the trance healer lies down and sleeps.'[1]

NOTES

1 R. B. Lee, *Kung Bushman Trance Performances. Trance and Possession States.* Edited by Raymond Prince. Bucke Memorial Society, Montreal, 1966, p. 35–54.

10

Tribal Sudan

In 1963 I was fortunate to be able to visit, by a Nile river-boat, some of the tribal areas of the Sudan. Dr Basher, chief psychiatrist of the Sudan, who later became Minister of Health, took me on this journey. First of all we flew down to Malacal, which is 800 miles south of Khartoum, and there we found that the paddle-steamer was an old English one which was used previously by the British administration before handing over the Sudan. Dr Basher, another doctor and myself were accompanied by two non-medically qualified assistants, who sometimes have to treat in the tribal areas owing to the shortage of doctors. Most of the other people on the boat had worked previously in the old British Medical Services of the Sudan and they knew friends of mine. I was impressed by the high standard of intelligence and ability of so many of the Sudanese on board. On the way to Bentui, which is down the Nile towards the border of the Belgian Congo, we stopped at various places for medical purposes. But it was not until we reached Bentui, where a visiting boat is only seen around once a month, that we were able to see and film some primitive tribal dancing, specially arranged for us.

These tribes, such as the Dinkas and the Shilluks, can be called primitive but they have a highly organized social life and customs. Once again we saw the same basic personality types among them as in England or other supposedly more civilized countries. I saw a local judge who was clearly suffering from a typical endogenous depression. He complained of early morning waking, being much worse in the morning and getting better as the day went on, so that he found that it was extremely difficult to pass judgement in the morning, but easier in the afternoon sessions. We treated him in exactly the same way as we would any judge in England. He was prescribed one of the new antidepressants, namely Tofranil, and I learned from Dr Basher later that he had made an initial satisfactory improvement; but then he relapsed, as some patients do, and had to come up to Khartoum for electric shock treatment, when he made a more permanent response. In Bentui we also saw a typical state of anxious depression in a local policeman; he complained of a rapidly beating heart and typical attacks of phobic anxiety in certain specific situations. He was placed on another group of antidepressant drugs which are much more effective in phobic anxiety than in depression, i.e. Nardil, and I have no doubt that he will have responded just as well as similar patients do in England, but I was not able to follow up this particular patient.

The power of the witch-doctor is very great in these regions. The witch-doctor is primarily a healer, but those who really believe in his power can actually die of fear, just as people in the West can die of fear when their basic terrors are aroused. At Bentui the District Commissioner told me how a local witch-doctor had been interfering with the authority of the tribal chief. He was therefore summoned to Bentui, and the District Commissioner locked him up in an open cell next to his office, where he was visible to anyone who cared to come and see him. The witch-doctor was foolish enough to put a public curse on the District Commissioner implying that he would be dead in three days. Three very quiet and tense days ensued, while everybody waited for the dire prophecy to be fulfilled. But the District Commissioner did not die, because he had no fear of the curse. On the fourth day he opened the prison door and released the culprit, who had lost status and credit because it was obvious to everybody that his powers were null and void when put to the test. Witch-doctors frequently try to make their threats come true by using poisons, but such intense faith in the witch-doctor is created by initiation ceremonies in an atmosphere calculated to inspire uncritical belief that a curse can kill by itself. The victim may become so frightened that he goes into a state of acute anxiety, in which most of the bodily secretions and metabolic functions are severely disturbed; secretions essential to life are dried up by fear, and he eventually dies of fright *physiologically*, though not metaphysically, as is believed by some. Similarly, in England, when coloured people believe in spells, it has been found that they, too, may be so frightened that they gradually waste away and die. But if they are given a drug such as Largactil, also used in schizophrenia, it stops the mental fright spreading to the whole bodily organism and thus prevents premature death.

Another cause of death by fear of the witch-doctor's curse is a state of panic, in which the victim runs off into the jungle and may there be eaten by wild animals. In fact, in a true Pavlovian ultraparadoxical reaction, the victim does exactly the opposite of what he would do when well. There is certainly no secret mystery about death by cursing. It is simply a physiological fright process spreading from the brain over the whole body. There were deaths from fright in acute schizophrenia and depressive states before the advent of modern physiological methods of treatment in psychiatry, which are now so successful in preventing them.

While at Malacal, we drove about fifteen miles into the surrounding country and visited the head of a tribal group who ordered some of his men to dance for us. Unfortunately, by the time the dancing began it was becoming dark—too dark for film-making—and a valuable opportunity was lost of recording this. However, some of the photographs I took show the same states of semi-trance being produced in the Sudan by dancing and rhythmic drumming that one sees in all other parts of Africa.

Down in Bentui a tremendous dance was organized for us. Even a group of totally naked convicts, working on a drainage project, danced on request. Most of the other people, male and female, were dressed in colourful tribal costumes. A large military band turned up in our honour, since visitors are a great rarity in these regions. Again we saw the dancing going on and on in the hot sun until the performers became entranced, and there were occasional emotional collapses.

On this trip to Bentui I realized what is perhaps the main function of the dance in primitive society. Along the lush banks of the lower Nile living is very easy; great Nile perch can be caught easily, and food is readily grown in the fertile soil near the river. The tribesmen have very little to do all day and it is obvious that boredom and tension can build up. And so, once or twice a week, groups of tribesmen and women meet and dance together to the point of exhaustion, and thus disperse their built-up tensions and dissatisfactions. All over the world, among 'primitive' peoples, who have learned over thousands of years how to maintain tribal solidarity and social peace in a system whose benefits go mainly to the chiefs and elders at the expense of the younger and more virile members of society, dancing seems to have played an essential part in their stabilization. I would like to point out again that whenever human beings, even in the most advanced societies, are forced to dance to strong and repetitive rhythms, an atmosphere of increased suggestibility is induced which loosens the hold of tensions, hatreds and other emotions on the participants. Belief in religious or political or social leaders or gospels can then be fortified, or can equally be swept away and replaced by some different belief, depending on the attitudes and motives of those who are in control of the proceedings.

11

Expelling Spirits

During my first visit to Kenya in 1962 a meeting was arranged with four of the leading witch-doctors, or traditional healers, in the town of Kisumu where the Luo tribe live. A local Court Judge kindly acted as interpreter. My wife and I spent a fascinating two hours talking to the witch-doctors and discussing their problems of healing in relation to modern medicine. The word 'witch-doctor' is in fact a total misnomer, invented by Europeans. They are the local and often very highly respected medical practitioners of the town or district. Their healing methods are often handed down from father to son, and it would be more appropriate to call them 'traditional healers'. Some have become healers because they have been through a severe illness, have been cured by traditional methods, and so have become interested themselves in curing others. All four of our witch-doctors were extremely interesting and intelligent, and, I gather, were among those earning the most in the town.

I asked them about their methods of diagnosis. One of the methods was to shake several cowrie shells in the hand and then drop them on the ground. Depending on the pattern in which the cowrie shells fell on the ground, so one could make a diagnosis of the patient's illness, even if he was not present. If one special cowrie shell fell in a certain manner, it meant that the patient was going to die, in which case the healer could not charge a fee. I tried throwing the cowrie shells myself several times, and it seemed that the fall indicating impending death very rarely occurred. In other words, it was not very often that the healer could not charge a fee for his services, even if death eventually resulted.

I was told that if the case was obviously organic in nature, due to some definite lesion or infection such as malaria, they would often send the patient straight on to the Western doctor in the town. They realized that their work predominantly concerned the treatment of functional or nervous illness, often thought to be due to spirit possession. These healers showed a remarkable degree of insight. When I asked how they treated a patient suffering from depression, I was in turn asked if I meant a good man who had recently become depressed, or a person who was always depressed. They could heal the good man who was depressed but found it much more difficult to heal the man who was always melancholic. In other words, they have found what we have proved in our psychiatry; that a patient who is nervously ill is fairly easily helped to get well again with modern methods provided the previous personality was adequate. But it is a different matter when the previous personality has always been a poor one. Most illnesses in Africa, unless clearly diagnosed as organic, are thought to be due to spirit possession. The patient has become possessed by a bad spirit and it is the duty of the doctor to cast it out, or in some way to stop the fight going on between the person and the possessing spirit.

Because I was obviously serious in my inquiries and established a good rapport, one of the healers finally asked me whether I would like to go with him to his compound, some miles outside Kisumu in the bush, to see how he treated nervous illness. This was the opportunity I had been waiting for. We quickly got into the Land-Rover and made our way to the compound. There was a hut adjoining the compound. The patients were summoned from near by and we were shown a healing ceremony. Two other people looked on and commented to me on the ceremony, through an interpreter. There was a small number of drummers, and about ten patients to be treated. The 'healer' went to change into his traditional ceremonial robes. The treatment, we were told, would last about a fortnight, and as far as I could gather there would be two curative ceremonies of dancing each day. The patients to whom I spoke through the interpreter were mostly suffering from various forms of neurosis. One described a typical anxiety state, with feelings of tension in the head, another was severely depressed with very severe headaches and was slow and retarded in his movements. The patients were all women, except for the one very depressed man.

When the drumming started, the patients went round and round in a circle and soon several of them started twitching, jerking, performing all sorts of strange bodily movements. They eventually fell to the floor, still jerking and shaking, until the movements gradually ceased. We were seeing, in fact, a repetition of the usual induction of states of excitement leading on to tremendous emotional and muscular discharge, and ending as usual in almost total collapse. While they were jerking and twitching, the 'spirits' possessing them might speak. In the case of one woman an 'ancestral spirit' started to talk when the patient had gone into deep trance. The witch-doctor paid close attention to what the ancestral spirit was saying, but the patient, being in trance, would probably have no recollection of what had been said.

In spite of these abreactive excitatory states, induced twice a day for two weeks, some of the patients were unable to go into the desired trance and collapse. This was true of one patient suffering from severe depression, for instance, who went circling round and round without apparently getting any relief of his symptoms. On the second day we saw him acting as an assistant male nurse, when he could not go into trance himself, helping the other jerking and entranced patients; when they fell to the ground he helped to contain their wilder movements.

At the end of a very exciting session of abreactive discharge and trance states, we were taken into the healer's hut. Here a very impressive ceremony ensued. Some of the patients entered with us. The witch-doctor himself then went into trance and the 'ancestral spirits' started speaking through him instead of his patients. There were two spirits talking, the interpreter told us, one male and one female, although the female was talking in a lower voice than the male. It sounded just like a Punch and Judy show. The ancestral spirits discussed some of the causes of the illnesses of those in the group. It seemed fairly obvious that, during the repeated phases of trance and collapse, and while the possessing spirits were talking through the patient, and being listened to by the healer, a great deal of information had been picked up about the patients.

It was certainly most impressive to hear psychiatric interpretations and advice given by the ancestral spirits through the mouth of the witch-doctor himself. My wife was particularly conscious of the atmosphere of awe and emotional tenseness that was built up in the darkened hut. The ancestral spirits giving their interpretations seemed far more impressive than the modern psychoanalyst giving his interpretations to the patient on the couch! It is a pity that the spirit of Freud cannot be summoned to speak through the mouth of a 'possessed' psychoanalyst, when some really important interpretations are to be given.

However, the whole ceremony became a little unreal when later the ancestral spirits asked, through the witch-doctor, whether the white witch-doctor was going to put a spell on the black witch-doctor. The ancestral spirits also asked the white witch-doctor if he was going to pay the other witch-doctor any-thing for showing him his methods! There were some parts of the ceremony which we did not fully understand, but it seemed clear that the abreactive methods being used were very similar to what we had seen and were going to see elsewhere and were in some ways basically similar to the more advanced methods used in psychiatry today. We learned that the methods used were only applicable to the milder forms of neurosis, such as anxiety states and mild depressions, and were found to be ineffective in severe forms of mental illness, such as schizophrenia and melan-cholia, and in 'mad' people. The healer said that in these latter illnesses much more drastic methods, amounting almost to torture, were necessary. In some cases drugs were put into the patient's ears, probably to try and counteract the hallucinations of schizophrenia. He offered to show us some of these more drastic methods, but we declined as they sounded rather terrible.

Finally one of the other witch-doctors told us that if we would like to come the following day, he would show us a far larger healing compound. But when we arrived there the follow-ing morning, he said there was to be no ceremony because all the patients had been healed and had gone home! We were rather astounded at this, but the interpreter and one or two others present told us that the witch-doctors had become afraid that I would learn their secrets. They had probably discussed among themselves the possible reasons why I was showing such interest in their ceremonies, and appeared so willing to learn from them instead of teaching them the Western methods of healing. Fortunately I had taken films and photographs of the previous day's work.

We were very disappointed and decided to drive back to the compound of the witch-doctor who had been so helpful the day before, but he was not there. We persuaded his deputy to give us another demonstration and this time it was, if anything, even more impressive. The patients' faces were painted with white stripes, the drummers played, and the deputy witch-doctor produced even more severe and exciting trance states. One thing that struck me was the way the patients, having gone into trance, would stand or sit very near the drums and be drummed into what almost looked like epileptic fits. We saw for the first time what we were later to see repeatedly in Africa, that once a patient is in a trance he becomes completely subservient to and dominated by the beating of the drums, in a way paralleled among Mesmer's patients. The effect was as if the patients were experiencing a series of orgasms. The deputy healer himself went into an acute state of trance and 'possession'. He stumbled about the compound, making impulsive but harmless rushes at the camera, and I found myself completely at sea to know what to do. But here the patients came to my aid. They rapidly came out of their own trance states, and one or two took over the drums and drummed the witch-doctor into a more placid quiescence. As his movements became less violent and the drumming continued, we gradually edged him, in trance, towards and into the 'interpretation' hut where he fell down, apparently fast asleep. We were to see many more examples later of the witch-doctor or healer going into a state of trance and possession in the sight of his patients and, so to speak, together with them. On several occasions we saw the patients helping the healer during his own trance, and after he had been safely dealt with they would resume their own trance activity.

I was told that the deputy witch-doctor thought I had put a spell on him. So when he had gone to sleep in his hut and the ceremony ceased we hastily drove away. We had not gone far when we saw the witch-doctor of the day before riding along on his bicycle towards us, and we waved to him. Apparently he had not told his deputy about the decision not to show us any more of their ceremonies. We were fascinated by what we had again seen, though there had been no interpretative session in the hut.

Several years later, in 1966, after I had visited the West Indies and seen healing there, and had also studied Macumba in Brazil, and seen states of possession, supposedly by the Holy Ghost, in the U.S.A., I returned to Kenya.

With the help of the psychiatrist in charge of the main Kenya mental hospital, Dr Mustafa, we went to a village not far away, where a healing ceremony had been arranged for us. The patient had recently been admitted to the mental hospital suffering from schizophrenia and was brought back to the village for this ceremony. For much of the healing session the patient was almost in stupor. There was the usual drumming, and many village people took part in the proceedings. Men and women joined in the dancing and repeated attempts were made to induce the mentally ill girl to get up and dance with the rest of the group. But all efforts were met with stubborn refusal. The dancing continued for a long time even after everybody realized that as the patient would not co-operate in the dance there was no chance of healing her.

Over and over again I found that milder forms of nervous and mental illness can be helped by traditional methods of healing, by dancing and repeatedly going into trance, then talking in states of abreactive excitement and supposed spirit possession, and finally falling to the ground in a collapse, after which the patients may begin to get better. Severe schizophrenic and melancholic cases, however, cannot abreact or dissociate and go into trance and collapse when dancing alone is used, as we saw in the Kisumu male patient who obtained no relief of his severe depression by walking round and round to the sound of the drumming. But it is just these two types of illness that can be helped by our Western methods of electrical shock treatment. This treatment induces an electrical epileptic fit, or a series of such fits at appropriate intervals. It was most interesting to find that both Western and 'primitive' healing methods involved putting the brain into a state of prolonged excitement terminating in final collapse. During the war, as mentioned earlier, we found that abreactive excitement of the brain need not always be aroused about any particular relevant topic in order to be effective. It was producing the brain explosion to the point of collapse that really mattered. And what we saw in Africa and elsewhere confirmed my belief, long held, that there were common factors in many of the new and old effective methods of healing the mind of man.

In Kenya we also watched the casting out of spirits called *Pepos*, at Voi, and visited the Teita tribe in the hills overlooking Voi. The ceremonies for casting out Pepos, said to be the possessing spirits causing illness, were found to be basically the same as those already discussed. The number of people attending the ceremonies was rather larger, the rhythmic drumming was more frantic and overwhelming, and the patients, especially the women, went round and round in a circle until gradually they became entranced; they jumped, jerked, talked in their trance, and finally fell into a collapsed state on the ground. Attendance at these ceremonies for casting out Pepos had been banned by the Government because they occupied so much of the working hours of the people in the district. The new Kenyan Government was tougher than the British Government in this respect. But they allowed a ceremony to take place for this research.

Among the Teita tribes, we found similar ceremonies. I learnt that the Teita tribes, until recently, used to cut off the heads of certain relatives six months after death, and the heads were placed in rock crevices. It was necessary for the families to visit these skulls from time to time to pay their respects to the spirits of their ancestors. It was believed that if they did not do this the ancestors would haunt or possess them and bring about all manner of evil and ills. The ceremonies here, apart from the bringing of gifts to the ancestral skulls, were to cast out possessing spirits and were the same as elsewhere in Africa. One in sixteen of the Teita is said to be mentally ill, and it was interesting to learn that the really mentally ill did not go to these ceremonies; they were only attended by normal people and those with less severe illnesses.

It was at one of these Teita ceremonies that we again saw the tremendously powerful effect of drumming in bringing about complete submission of the individual participant. The girls going round in circles, before going into trance, were often proud and rather intolerant. They tried to avoid being photographed and showed scorn and suspicion at the interest I was taking in them and in what was happening. But as soon as they went into trance they became like malleable zombies. A girl could be led up close to the drums, and then her whole body would jerk and show orgiastic reactions to the drumming. And the drummers themselves often seemed to be trying to produce the maximum effect in a particular participant in front of them. It was almost as if the women were being mentally raped by the drums. It is interesting to note again the relationship existing between orgasm, which is the induction of nervous excitement often leading to a state close to semi-trance, with final nervous collapse and relaxation; the repeated drumming inducing trance and collapse used by primitive tribes to relax tensions and expel the 'spirits' causing neurosis; and the effectiveness of electric shock treatment in severe mental illness in more civilized countries. All these methods appear to have the same purpose and the same sort of results.

12

Experiences in Zambia

When I visited Lusaka, the capital of Zambia, in 1966, Dr Howarth, who is in charge of psychiatry in Zambia, introduced me to various witch-doctors and healers. One of the most interesting of them I met in the market square, where he had a stall containing an extraordinary collection of herbs, plants and skins, including snake skins and the skin of the wild-cat which seems to have particular potency in healing ceremonies. He was an intelligent person in his early thirties. The theory behind his drug practice was that man derived from the earth's surface and so probably had the same chemical constituents in his make-up as the earth. In illness some of these constituents were driven out, or there was a shortage of them, and the giving of drugs derived from the soil helped to replace what had been lost. Not surprisingly, he had herbs and roots which he claimed were of exceptional value in a large variety of sexual troubles. There was a root to make the penis grow larger, but he was anxious to point out that this was only efficacious during the period of puberty, which is the normal time for penile growth. He said it was not effective after puberty. He also had drugs which increased the power of penile erection, and other preparations and herbs to keep the vagina 'moist, dry and warm', as he put it. Other drugs were for bringing out the best in one's personality and allowing a person to show his real potentialities. He also had drugs for various types of mild and severe nervous disturbances. He admitted that if a patient was seriously physically ill he would take him to a Western doctor, and only if the Western doctor said he could do nothing for the case would he be prepared to try his herbal and root remedies. It was much the same in the case of mental illness, and only if Dr Howarth failed would he try his own methods in severe cases. But I got the impression that he did in fact treat many persons without medical supervision. Nevertheless, he was well aware that Western medicine was superior to his own in many serious cases.

One of his methods of healing involved the use of a black doll with a prominent vulva and breasts. The sick patient would be instructed to take the doll to bed with him and to look at it intensively for some time in candle-light, then close his eyes and try to remember the after-image he saw; he also had to try and remember his dreams that night. As if he was a precursor or follower of Freud, the healer was able to find the hidden cause of the patient's illness or problems when the dreams were described to him. Another and even more extraordinary method of healing was later shown to me, which consisted of smoking out any spirits possessing the patient, for along with his other theories he still believed in spirit possession: there were good and evil spirits and one of the common causes of illness, apart from mineral depletion, was possession by evil spirits.

I was able to witness this healer's treatment of an intelligent and educated civil servant who worked in the Finance Department of the Zambian Government in Lusaka. The patient told me that in spite of his education he still believed in possession by evil spirits. He described how he had had a dream that somebody came to him and dropped something harmful into his ear. When he woke up he became giddy, could not always keep his balance, and sometimes fell down. His condition seemed to me to be a typical anxiety state, with rapid heart beat, various fears and phobias of fainting, with perhaps a depressive and hysterical overlay. Dr Howarth had given him some medicine but it only worked for a time and he relapsed. So now the witch-doctor was prepared to treat him. His method was to hold the head and upper part of the patient's body over a brazier which contained a heap of burning herbs and emitted clouds of smoke. Over the patient's head was put a cloth cover, so that he was virtually enclosed by the cloth, and breathing the heavy smoke. I found it difficult to understand how he could stay in this atmosphere of intense smoke for as long as five minutes, but he did. When he was brought out of what would seem severe suffocation, he said he had not lost consciousness but it was an unpleasant experience and the smoke had made him breathe very rapidly and, probably, shallowly; this presumably would help towards the production of states of suggestibility and hysteria. He insisted that he felt very much better immediately after this treatment, and when I saw him half an hour later he had maintained his improvement. The patient was keen to emphasize to me that, although he knew I would not believe him, he was certain he had been got at by an evil spirit, when something was put in his ear while he was asleep, and this had caused his illness. In this instance trance was not induced to the point of collapse, as so often in other healing ceremonies. But putting the patient under a cover in such intense smoke must have caused changes in brain function, if only because of the rapid and shallow overbreathing which probably occurred. As already noted, overbreathing produces a state of brain alkalosis when the carbon, an acid, is blown out of the blood stream, and this often brings about hysterical dissociation and states of increased suggestibility.

I did not see this healer using drumming techniques to bring people to the point of trance and collapse, although I saw it on several other occasions in Zambia. For instance, Dr Howarth took me out to a compound where a man had been ill and had been cured through the casting out of his possessing spirit by drumming. This had so impressed him that he himself had now become a healer and was treating other people by the same method. The patient to be treated was dressed in ceremonial costume and for about half an hour he was made to dance round and round, until finally trance and collapse set in. One of the drummers went off into a trance as well. This was not the first time I had seen the drummers becoming 'possessed', although this is not part of the normal procedure.

Dr Howarth also took us to a healing ceremony in one of the poorer areas of Lusaka. The woman healer had herself been sick for some three years with what sounded like a depressive illness. Having been cured by the casting out of spirits, she had decided to become a healer and use the same methods. I noticed with interest that one of the patients seemed to be much too deeply depressed for it to be possible to excite him with drumming or send him into collapse or make him suggestible. He had a tired melancholic appearance and was sitting listlessly on the ground. We then watched him being drummed and drummed, with a large number of people surrounding him, trying to get him to respond. Finally, after a long delay, he did start to twitch and jerk; he gradually became more and more excited, and ended up in a nervous collapse. In other words, they had been able, by drumming, to induce a state of excitement leading on to a nervous collapse, which I felt would have been much more easily achieved by electric shock treatment. I gathered that this patient would have the same drumming treatment twice a day until he was completely recovered. Two other girls, also being treated, went more quickly into trance and dissociation, and the drumming continued until they fell to the ground.

So again we had seen in Lusaka the widespread belief that much illness, both of body and mind, is caused by possession by evil spirits. These spirits can also be put into you by somebody who has evil intentions towards you. It is the role of the witch-doctor to drive out the evil spirits or to make the patient 'come to terms' with them.

When I was in Zambia there was only one large mental hospital, very much understaffed. There was also, in line with modern treatment ideas, a psychiatric ward which had recently been established in one of the big general hospitals, some distance from the mental hospital. At that time, as there was no psychiatrist available for the mental ward, it was put in charge of a male nurse, with a psychiatrist visiting from time to time. Practically all the patients coming into this ward were being given electric shock treatment because, in the normal course of events, the neuroses and milder depressions do not enter psychiatric wards in Africa. They tend to remain in their huts awaiting spontaneous remission, or treatment from the witch-doctor. It is generally the acutely violent, very agitated and suicidal patients who are finally sent to psychiatric hospitals when they can no longer be controlled and looked after by their families. Many of these patients have probably already been to witch-doctors or traditional healers, and only when these have failed have they been persuaded to go to a psychiatric ward or hospital. Hence it was exciting to learn that of five hundred admissions to the psychiatric beds of the general hospital, no less than four hundred and ninety, after having electric shock treatment, were able to go back to their homes; some were also given antidepressant drugs and the schizophrenics would receive psychotropic drugs.

It is satisfying to know that but for the existence of this psychiatric ward in the general hospital these several hundred patients would have had to go into the mental hospital and perhaps stay there for long periods. I felt I was on the right road to learning why electric shock treatment and drumming and dancing were both so effective in their overlapping treatment spheres with both sophisticated and more primitive patients.

13

Zar Possession

On my first visit to Khartoum in 1963, Dr Basher took me to see a very ancient form of mental treatment called *Zar* healing. Until I persuaded Dr Basher to take me to one of these ceremonies I believe he had never seen one nor had he been particularly interested in this method which is used in large areas of the Middle East. The theory behind it is that the atmosphere is full of Zars, which are good or evil spirits waiting to enter into a person. In Ethiopia, which is a Christian country, the Zars are often called Satans. Elsewhere, as in Kenya, they may be called Pepos. But it does not matter what they are called, they may have the same function of causing illness in the human being. The aim of the practitioner is to find out the particular type of Zar possessing a sick person, and either to drive out the spirit, replace it by a more suitable Zar or to reconcile the patient to having a particular Zar within him; the possessing Zar and the patient may have to learn to live together in harmony rather than disharmony, just as Western man has to learn to live with his personality difficulties.

It is believed that many different Zars can enter the body in various circumstances. These circumstances are often very similar to the circumstances that can precipitate an anxiety neurosis, a depression, or even schizophrenia, in Western cultures. For instance, Zars take possession after a person has committed a breach of moral law, or following childbirth, or after some accident or a severe physical illness. In the Sudan they can be 'doctor' Zars, 'Abyssinian' Zars, 'leopard' Zars and 'child-killing' Zars. They can be good or evil. Generally the possessing spirits are not Sudanese but are Zars from neighbouring countries or districts; and in the Sudan there is even an 'English' Zar!

The first step for a person supposedly possessed by a Zar is to go to a healer. By means of questions and long discussions about the patient's symptoms, the healer gets some hint as to which particular Zar is possessing him. Then there may have to be a period of dancing, and if the patient goes into trance with certain rhythms this will confirm the type of Zar. The ceremony for casting out the Zar may be a long one, perhaps lasting two days, with continued dancing to the point of repeated exhaustion, followed by the ceremonious killing of an animal. If the person is poor it may be a comparatively cheap animal, such as a chicken; but in the case of a wealthy family even a camel may be killed as part of the formal ritual. I was not able to see one of the prolonged rituals, but I learned that when the patient goes into trance, perhaps several times, he is covered with the blood of the killed animal. After trance, dissociation and collapse have occurred, the patient may wake up freed from the possessing Zar, or he may feel in greater harmony with it.

I did have occasion to see Zar healing in three or four different settings. The first was in the Sudan, others were in Cairo and Ethiopia. A patient at Dr Basher's clinic put us in touch with the Zar healer so that we could study his methods. This patient when deeply depressed would come to the clinic for electric shock treatment, but in her milder attacks she found that attendance at the Zar ceremonies was sufficient to relieve her. The tempo and rhythm recorded at the Khartoum drumming ceremony were also found to be effective in putting ordinary people into trance when tested out later in England. When I was playing this recorded music at one meeting, a woman doctor told me that it was very like the old Greek iambic rhythm, a rhythm that was thought to be so powerful in its effects that some say it was forbidden in ancient Greece except under the control of priests.

The Zar ceremony is essentially for women, although men take part in running it. The male leader of the Sudan Zar ceremony told me that he himself had had a special and 'personal' experience around puberty, which made him realize that he was destined to be a healer. So many healers who use these methods have been through trance experiences themselves, either spontaneous or induced by their teachers, which gives them great faith in the methods they are going to practise on others.

We saw women dressed up to represent various Zars which it was thought had or were possessing them. For instance, if it was the English Zar the woman came in smoking a cigarette and brandishing a walking-stick and when in trance spoke in what was meant to be pidgin English. In other parts of Africa the possessing spirit might be a railway train, so much do they try to keep up to date!

Moslem women lead a very shut-off life, often in purdah in their homes where there are few sources of emotional outlet. Weekly or fortnightly discharges of emotion at the Zar ceremonies, together with trance experiences and feelings of reconciliation with the spirits, or having them driven out, often help these emotionally starved or tense wives. The cult is reported to be useful, on occasion, when a woman is afraid of losing her husband. If she suspects him of saving money to take another wife, she may become ill and tell her husband that she has been to a healer and that the only way she can get better is for him to pay for a special ceremony to cast out the possessing Zar. This ceremony will be costly and the wife hopes that the money her husband is saving for the new wife will be spent instead on the Zar ceremony. If the husband refuses her request, he is told that the Zar will probably never leave her and she will become so ill that she will never be fit to work again.

We saw three other Zar healing sessions, at different times in Cairo. On the first occasion in 1963 we were taken to a small, dirty and dingy cellar. There was a very inadequate light, but I was able to take interesting photographs. There was a priestess of Zar with a male attendant. There was the usual music and the gradual induction of trance in several people present. But after a while we were asked to leave as further ceremonies of a more private nature were to take place. In another Zar ceremony we were also asked to leave half-way through. In this instance we saw the chickens the patient had brought for the ceremony. The chicken's throat is cut and the patient is smeared with the blood.

Zar is officially forbidden in Egypt and so the ceremonies are held in secret. The last one we attended, in 1970, was held in a small room on the ground floor. The patient was a man of middle age, suffering from severe pain in his head and noises in his ears. Both the patient and his wife danced twice while I was present, and both went twice into trance and finally collapsed. In trance he spoke, or at least the Zar spirit spoke through him, but his wife was silent. Then the healer went into trance himself and the Zar spirit spoke to me through him. The interpreter told me that he asked if I had any children. When I said I had none, the spirit said, through the healer, that the reason I had no children was because my sister in the Zar spirit world did not get on with my wife's brother who was also in the spirit world. It was necessary, he said, for the Zar brother and sister to be reconciled and then we would be able to have children. These pronouncements were made in an impressive manner, though the atmosphere was not quite so compelling as in some of our other experiences. We had to leave this ceremony early too, because the anthropologist who took us there felt that it was wrong for us to be present when the sacrifices were taking place; though I would very much like to have seen this. The Zar healer seemed quite willing to let us stay, expecting money to be forthcoming, but the anthropologist did not want her long-standing relationship with the healer to be in any way impaired by letting us see what was supposed to be sacred and secret in the ceremony.

The third ceremony was also held in the slums of Cairo. Here, there was a more elaborate band, and the man and woman being treated responded to the Zar music by prolonged excitement, dancing, and much repetitive bodily movement, including head jerking, which ended in almost total collapse.

A Zar ritual we watched in Ethiopia in 1966 was perhaps the most exciting of all. It took place about forty miles outside Addis Ababa, on the estate of Colonel and Mrs Stanford, two English people who have lived in Ethiopia for many years. We went to a very primitive hut on the estate, where the ceremony was held. People and their animals lived in the hut and I had the impression that the ceremonies may well date back thousands of years as the life of these people cannot have altered much during all that time. The healer and chanter was a male. There was no music, as somebody had died in the hut next door and they did not want to disturb them. Instead, rhythmic handclapping was used. The atmosphere was very impressive. Again we saw the usual induction of trance, with the body jerking backwards and forwards and very rapid movements until the final stage of collapse was reached. Children are brought up to accept these ceremonies as an ordinary part of life, and were clapping their hands along with the rest.

Casting-out Devils

Apart from our experience of the Zar cult in a very primitive and ancient form in a hut on a country estate in 1966, where men and their animals all lived together, we were unable to see any more Zar ceremonies in Addis Ababa. Wherever we tried, we were told that they could only be shown at a high price, and everywhere we seemed to be dealing with people who were out to fleece the visitor. Then Professor Critchley, brother of Dr Macdonald Critchley the famous neurologist, who was working in the Medical School at Addis Ababa, said I might like to see an interesting ceremony which he had already visited, some sixty miles outside Addis. He suggested that we went on a Sunday night, to attend the ordinary service and see another special healing service the next morning.

In Ethiopia the air is full of lurking Zars, Satans and other spirits which pounce on and possess human beings and are said to be the cause of a number of nervous illnesses. The number of these demons is legion, just as in popular belief at the time of Christ, and in medieval Europe. The air is so full of them that possession is generally multiple rather than single. Childbirth, accidents, any physical illness, moral offences such as adultery, or feelings of envy, can all give the Satans an opportunity to enter a victim.

In discussing with Professor Critchley what we were about to see, I realized that it was the same exorcism of spirits which was practised by Jesus and other healers of the time, and using the same basic method. This consists in the healer addressing the possessing spirits and commanding them to leave the body of the possessed person.

We arrived at the church in time for the evening service. Outside the door of the church, sitting begging alms, were a number of the 'halt, the maimed and the blind'. I also saw lepers who were 'living among the tombs' in Addis Ababa, just as Jesus had seen in Palestine. Inside the church, which was small and made of wood, was a varied collection of fetters and chains. These were the 'bonds' of lunatics who had come in their fetters and had cast them off when they were healed—just as they did in the days of Christ.

The church was crowded, and there was no doubt about the popularity and influence of the priest. Some high officials of the province attended the service. We heard that he was famous all over Ethiopia, although he had been forced to leave the official Coptic Church because of the methods of healing he used.

He started to preach and intone in a slow monotonous voice. But gradually he worked himself and his audience up to a higher pitch. As he went on, members of the congregation moved down the centre of the church to a square space in front of the pulpit. The priest came down from the pulpit to this space where most of the men and women who had gathered were in trance and started talking through these 'possessed' people. The priest talked directly back to the Satans, commanding them to leave the bodies of their victims. *It is most important to understand that the dialogue was between the priest and the possessing spirits, not between the priest and the patients.* Again and again the priest touched them on the forehead or the shoulder with his cross, at the same time ordering the Satans to leave. In one case several different voices were talking through a possessed woman's mouth in a manner closely resembling the Punch and Judy effect I had observed in the witch-doctor's tent in Kenya. One man was possessed by ten spirits; seven of them left him at the command of the priest but the other three remained, giving various reasons why they had entered his body and intended to stay there. The verbal battle went on until the patient suddenly collapsed and fell exhausted on the floor. Yet again we found that when the final collapse stage had been reached, after the prolonged verbal battle between priest and spirits, the person possessed would wake up sometimes in his right mind again.

After the service we had dinner with the priest. I tried to discuss his methods with him, but he cut me very short and asked me whether or not I believed in the power of God. He believed that he could heal only because he was an agent of God and ordained by God to cast out evil spirits. He was not interested in questions of the necessity of first exciting the patient and then bringing him to a state of final collapse, and would not talk about it. To him the healing was God's doing and nothing else explained it. Naturally, the numerous cures he obtained created intense faith, in the mind of the priest himself, in those who were apparently cured, and in the crowds of people who came to witness the cures.

The meeting the next morning was of a very different type. This time it was as though the priest had read about Pavlov's work and the abolition of previous conditioned patterns of behaviour when the dogs went into a state of inhibitory collapse after being nearly drowned (see Chapter 1). It was fascinating to compare the technique now being used with Pavlov's findings in the Leningrad flood.

A bench was placed near the altar. There were several large tanks of water near by, and a modern bath spray. Holy oil was poured into them, so that they now contained holy water. Then, one by one or in groups of twos and threes, those desiring special healing sat down on the wooden bench. Men and women alike were stripped to the waist and water was sprayed on to their faces and bodies. When they opened their mouths to breathe, they were forced to gulp down water, which gave them a feeling of suffocation and drowning, and their breathing was necessarily rapid and shallow. Later on, I had this done to myself, and a very unpleasant experience it was, although after watching it in others I had learnt how to avoid some of the most unpleasant effects. Through rapid shallow breathing, the patient went into a state of trance and 'possession' while being sprayed. The spirit possessing him would begin to speak and there was again a verbal battle between the priest and the spirit. But with the holy water being sprayed deliberately into the patient's mouth when the Satan was talking, the effects were far more dramatic. Unless you kept your head down and prevented the water from spraying straight into your mouth, you began to feel suffocated. The patients, not realizing this, often put their heads back, only to receive a further mouthful of water, which must have increased the frightening feeling of suffocation. This further increased the overbreathing and the tendency to fall into trance. After a tremendous battle between priest and spirits, and the continued spraying of water on the patient's face and body, the patients finally dropped to the floor in a state of temporary inertia and collapse. It was expected that they would come round healed.

It was noticeable that the priest paid more attention to some patients than to others. He had talked to some of them before the healing ceremony started. A spastic boy received only a cursory spraying; another patient, who seemed to me to be a typical schizophrenic, also received only a token spraying. On the other hand, a handsome, full-breasted girl, who may well have had a reactive depression or an anxiety hysteria, received much attention and repeated spraying, until she went into trance and was finally reduced to total collapse. Case after case was treated, some thoroughly, some cursorily. And I had no doubt that the priest himself had a very clear idea of the type of patient he could help, those suffering from neuroses and milder depressions, and of those he could not help, who seemed to me to be the cases of organic diseases and schizophrenia. And the number of cripples and mentally ill sitting outside the entrance to the church must have convinced the priest that his method must have selective, even if widespread, uses.

On my return to Addis Ababa, while staying with the Dean of the Medical School, I played him some of the tape recordings of the casting out of Satans and the Satanic talking, and the maid waiting at table burst out laughing. She explained to the Dean's wife that her sister had been healed by this priest after a five-year depression following childbirth. The possessing Satan had talked to the priest and said that he had entered the girl because she liked fine clothes and wanted to become a prostitute, and the maid said this was true of her sister. She emphasized that her sister had recovered from her illness and had been better for a year or more after her cure.

There can be little doubt, if one reads about Jesus's miracles and studies the number of successes obtained by this Ethiopian healer, that the method was extremely effective, and in the first ceremony seemed identical with that used by Jesus. The second ceremony, using the spraying of Holy Water, seemed to be a modern modification of the old healing method of repeated immersion in a river. It is known that for centuries immersion in water, which naturally induces fear of drowning, has been used in baptisms and other religious ceremonies, both as a method of healing and as a way of being 'born again', cleansed of your old self, your old worries, troubles and faults. Having seen its effective use by the priest in Ethiopia, I was better able to understand its possible power.

15

Nigeria and Dahomey

During one of my trips to Africa in 1966 I was able to spend a week or two in Nigeria and Dahomey. In Nigeria, Dr Azuni, one of the leading psychiatrists, took me to see two interesting religious ceremonies. The first was a service of the Church of the Cherubim and Seraphim, conducted by a preacher in a small rather dilapidated building in Ibadan. Here again we saw the same pattern of dancing, trance, 'possession' and collapse, but this was a Christian ceremony, in which some of the worshippers became possessed by the Holy Ghost. Many young people took part in this service, which I filmed and photographed. There were young people among the drummers, and most of the dancers were young. I was horrified to see youngsters aged about ten to fourteen going into trance and collapse, and this was taken to be a manifestation, not of tribal ancestral spirits, but of the Holy Spirit and of the same God who is worshipped all over the Christian world. When I asked some of the older members of the congregation what effect the induction of trance and emotional collapse had on the youngsters, they said that the children 'often behaved better' and 'worked better at school' when the Holy Ghost had come upon them. The preacher himself danced and went into a state of near-trance and possession by the Holy Ghost. Although completely collapsed and apparently unconscious, a few of the performers quickly came round again, and in ten minutes or so were helping to take up the collection, which is always a prominent feature of such services.

At a second service in another part of Ibadan, this time in a small house, there were many more adults than children. The same 'possession' by the Holy Ghost took place, while the male preacher led the congregation in hand-clapping and singing, and members of the congregation were dancing, jerking, shaking and obtaining the 'gift of tongues' so prized as a sign of God's presence by the early Christians and since in many parts of the world.

I was extremely fortunate to be taken by Pierre Verger to see the worship of other gods in various parts of Nigeria and Dahomey. Pierre Verger has published a famous book, *Les Dieux d'Afrique*,[1] and it was this book that first made me interested in examining the similarities that seem to exist between African modes of healing and religious worship with the casting out of spirits, and some of the more modern methods of psychiatric healing and Christian worship nearer home.

Verger took me to the home of a local Nigerian king. Next to his palace was a courtyard given over to the worship of the great god Shango, god of thunder. Shango is a very powerful god in this part of Africa and is worshipped by very many thousands of people. We were allowed to look into some of his sacred temples and to see a ceremony which was meant to convey his power to his followers and worshippers. A Shango priest in the courtyard danced himself into trance to the sound of numerous drums and while in a trance he made certain gestures to show that Shango was protecting him from harm. Shango did not speak through the priest (as happened later at a shrine dedicated to the god Ogoun) but the priest put out his tongue and drove a large iron spike through it. The spike was held there for some time and was then withdrawn, without any blood being visible. The spike was then placed against the priest's eye and appeared to be hammered into it. Again when the spike was withdrawn there was no visible damage to the eye. Next the long iron spike was apparently driven into the throat of the priest and when it was withdrawn after a while there was no damage or loss of blood. A fourth feat, which seemed to me to be an old trick, was to hold a stone ball suspended in space on four cords. When the priest loosened the cords the stone tended to fall, and when the cords tightened it stayed in the air. But this was a trick I had learned as a child, and it made me wonder how much of the spiking of the tongue, the eye and the throat was mere trickery. The spike obviously penetrated the tongue, but there might well have been a hole in it. The apparent penetration of the eye and the throat might have been an optical illusion. But the priest was in trance and possessed by the great Shango and the onlookers were duly impressed by the power of the god.

At another shrine in Dahomey, of Ogoun the god of iron, the

temple was entered by the priests while the drumming was going on outside to instil religious fervour in the worshippers who were hand-clapping and singing lustily. The priests of Ogoun eventually came out of the temple in trance, but before entering it they had visited a small shrine of Elegba, the Devil. And here I must digress to say how interested we were to find in Trinidad a Christian sect still offering sacrifices to Elegba before going on to a sacrifice to Christ and the Saints. This is an example of the mixture of Christianity and African religions in the West Indies, partly derived from Nigeria and Dahomey, from which many of the slaves were brought to the New World.

After coming out of the shrine of Ogoun, the priests marched up and down, shaking their iron instruments, which made a clanging noise. The chief priest then went into a trance, and the god Ogoun spoke through him to the people. Ogoun also spoke personally through the high priest to several individuals present, reassuring them, telling them to calm their fears, and giving them messages of hope. There is no doubt that when a religion produces a god who actually speaks direct to his worshippers through the priest, much greater faith is created than in religions where the priest is the representative, not the embodiment, of God, who does not so dramatically manifest himself to the worshippers. The more primitive forms of worship inspire a surer faith, and so does Christianity where it has readopted these forms, as in some of the African Christian Churches or at revival meetings where people are flung to the ground, writhing and groaning, and become possessed by the Holy Spirit.

At an international conference on 'Possession States' in Paris in September 1968, many people spoke who had worked in various parts of Africa, the West Indies and Brazil, and who had spent months or years studying various religious cults involving spirit possession. It struck and surprised me that some of the anthropologists present had acquired a semi-belief in the gods whose cults they had studied. One very famous anthropologist, who shall be nameless, told me that he hoped to go back one day, not merely to film Shango speaking through his priests but actually to film the great god Shango himself!

Certainly, Shango and his like are believed by their worshippers to be just as great and powerful as is the God of the Christians by the millions who worship him; and they are far closer to their followers because they so frequently appear in the person of the possessed priests and talk directly to the people. This is surely relevant to the failure of our own accustomed brand of restrained and respectable Christianity to convey any sense of a deity who is vividly real and alive. Where possession takes place it conveys intense faith because it appears to bring worshippers into the closest possible touch with the divine, just as convinced faith was created among the early Christians when they saw the manifestation of the Holy Spirit at the services. It was this type of experience which sustained the early Church, and still does wherever 'enthusiastic' religious techniques are employed.

In Nigeria and Dahomey we were also able to visit the homes of two healers or witch-doctors, both of whom claimed to have helped patients suffering from neurosis and milder forms of depression by various faith-creating methods. In both places, however, we saw lunatics chained and battened to the floor in irons. Some of these would certainly die of starvation unless they were fed by their relatives. One man, in a virtual cage, told me that he had come back to Africa from England a few months previously. He had been put into the care of the witch-doctor by his relatives and had been shut in there for nine months; he saw no hope of getting out. He was, I think, suffering from schizophrenia, but he was still sufficiently rational to recognize the fate that awaited him.

Another prisoner in the cellar described how he had been there for seven years, with no hope of release. Upstairs in the same house were people, more prominently on view, who had been helped by the laying on of hands, by the expulsion of possessing spirits and by the use of holy oils. In West Africa the *rauwolfia* root is also used in the treatment of severe forms of mental illness, and has been so used for centuries in Africa, and also in India. It has only recently been used in tablet or other form, as Serpasil, to treat the nervously ill and cases of high blood pressure in the Western world.

Finally, Pierre Verger took me to one of the convents of the Orisha cult. People enter the convent to become servants of the gods. Much of what happens within the convent is kept secret; but we saw a girl who was going through the three weeks to three months training which would make her a priestess of Ogoun or Shango or other gods or goddesses in the hierarchy of the Orisha cult. Soon after the postulants enter the convent they are put into a prolonged trance by various techniques. They take part in many ceremonies which lead ultimately to complete nervous collapse. Then, when in a highly suggestible state of mind, they play the role and act out the behaviour of a minor goddess, or a servant of the chief gods and goddesses, and for the whole of the period that they remain in the convent they are treated as, and believe themselves to be, servants of the gods and in union with them.

Pierre Verger himself has become a priest of the Orisha cult, so he could not tell me about many of the secret ceremonies which took place in the convent. But he was able to say that it was a severe brain-washing process in which the normal personality is replaced by a new personality. The postulant is never permitted to remember his normal personality, what he was like and how he behaved as his former self. But when he leaves the convent he is given back his old personality by a special process, and has little memory of what happened during his time in the convent. People go back into the convent from time to time and by the same hypnotic process revert to their god-like personality, to emerge once more with their ordinary personality when they return to the outside world. It will be possible to say more about this dissociation process when we describe Macumba in Brazil, for undoubtedly Macumba is a modification of the Orisha cult in the Old World which has been carried to the New.

Pierre Verger also accompanied me to the seaboard town of Ouidah in Dahomey, which was one of the main African slave-trading ports where slaves for Brazil and the West Indies were brought to be shipped to the New World. Here we saw an out-door ceremony devoted to Voodoo gods. There was the usual drumming, dancing and trance, but no other special ceremony. However, we did see here the worship of the original Voodoo gods with the same symbols which we were to see again during our visits to Haiti, where Voodoo worship has reached its most spectacular development.

NOTES

1 P. Verger, *Les Dieux d'Afrique*. Hartman, Paris, 1954.

16

Macumba in Brazil

I visited Brazil on two occasions, in 1964 and 1968, and, as already mentioned, attended a Congress on 'Possession States' in Paris, where I learned more about the interesting Brazilian possession cults. The so-called Macumba derives from the religions of West Africa, primarily from those of the Yoruba people who number about 5,000,000 and who worship numerous deities. Macumba is still spreading very fast in Brazil and gaining many converts from Christianity. It not only involves the poorer people but also more and more of the rich and the intelligentsia, who are becoming attracted to this form of worship as opposed to the official Roman Catholicism of Brazil. Often people will worship at both forms of service.

On my first visit to Brazil in 1964, while seeing a Macumba ceremony at Recife, I was first tactfully told that the people were supposedly being possessed by the spirits of various Christian saints. When I remarked that although they were given the names of Christian saints, I believed that they also all had equivalent names of African gods, the answer came back: 'Your Christian saints are really dead. Our Macumba gods come all the way over from Africa and show us their living power by entering and taking possession of us.' I may have been in a suggestible state myself during all the drumming, the excitement and the 'possession' I was witnessing, but I felt I was hearing a fundamental truth. For successful religions—those which really grip people's hearts—are those which produce evidence of the actual existence of their gods. The Christian religion, in most of its official forms, rarely now demonstrates the power of its God, and to most worshippers our Christian saints are indeed very dead. The fact of the Macumba gods and goddesses coming all the way from Africa to Brazil to take possession of the worshippers and talk through them is sufficient to create absolute faith in them. In addition they are potential healers of most ills.

Recife is a steamy hot old town in the north of Brazil, and here I met a very famous Brazilian, Gilberto Freyre, who wrote the fascinating book *The Masters and The Slaves*.[1] He arranged for us to see a Macumba ceremony, but it was quite obvious that we saw only what was permitted to non-members of the Orisha cult, which was brought over from Nigeria and Dahomey by the slaves and quickly became established among all classes.

Certain of the Orisha gods and goddesses, and there are at least fifteen of them, were given the additional name of a Catholic saint, but no worshipper, especially a possessed worshipper, had any doubt that he was worshipping not the saints but the Orisha gods and goddesses. Going down to the area where the ceremony was to be held, I noticed outside the door of the building a tree with many decorations on it, obviously connected with the service that we were about to see. In the room there was drumming and dancing, the men and women going round and round to an ever-increasing and exciting crescendo of drums, until they were possessed by a variety of gods and goddesses. It is possible to tell by the behaviour of the dancers which particular deity is possessing them and, often, talking through them. In some ceremonies only one god or goddess, such as Shango, is specifically worshipped and if other deities possess the people then they are removed from the ceremony. But in the one we were watching a number of gods were supposedly present and taking possession of the worshippers, as we saw happen later in the Voodoo ceremonies in Haiti. In the present group, when they were possessed they did not go out and dress up in the special uniform of the particular god or goddess possessing them as in other Orisha ceremonies. This did happen at another ceremony to the god Ogoun, when only those possessed by him went out and came back to dance in the special costume which showed that this god was manifesting himself through them.

The states of possession and trance in Recife were some of the most violent and dramatic we had yet seen anywhere. Extraordinary facial changes occurred, and almost all of the possessed ended up in a state of collapse. Often they fell to the floor and had to be carried out to a special private room. In the intervals we were shown some of the sacrifices that had been performed before the main ceremony began. It was evident that animals had been burnt and offered in sacrifice to the gods of Orisha.

There were other rooms set apart for the Orishas and their servants which visitors were not allowed to enter.

There are hundreds of Macumba groups all over Brazil, especially in the areas where slaves were employed in the eighteenth and nineteenth centuries. Although the Orisha cult still remains secret, one could from various sources obtain quite a lot of information about it. Often entry to the group follows attendance at a ceremony as a spectator, when visitors may suddenly become 'possessed', tremble and shake and fall to the ground, and sometimes even exhibit hysterical cataleptic trance. They are then carried out, stiff and rigid, as happens sometimes in deep states of hypnotic trance.

Dreams also have significance in the Orisha cult. If the dream is disturbing or enigmatic, the candidate for initiation will consult one of the Mothers or Fathers—or priests and priestesses— managing the group. The devotee is put into trance, but quickly taken out of it, and initiation is not proceeded with until after a period during which decisions are made as to whether the person really wants to join the Orisha group, whether money is available, and whether he is fit to take part in what may be a prolonged initiation ceremony. As in Dahomey and Nigeria, initiation into Macumba may last seven days or sometimes even up to three months.

It was difficult to get details of the initiation ceremonies, but we did discover that they include the killing of animals and covering the initiate with the blood, and all sorts of elaborate, and sometimes frightening ceremonies, besides the usual dancing to drumming rhythms. And I was able to obtain a series of photographs of one initiation ceremony which are substantially correct according to some of my informants. These ceremonies usually occur twice a year, when several people are to be initiated. The priest or priestess has to decide which of the gods or goddesses have taken possession and the initiation will vary accordingly. This entails deep hypnotic trance, during which the person to be initiated may show cataleptic phenomena, and then there is the final breaking point. During initiation the person experiences a change of outlook, a change in the way of life, and becomes consciously or subconsciously guided by a particular Orisha. During these sessions lasting two to three weeks, all sorts of suggestions can be made while the initiate is in trance and a new pattern of thought and behaviour can be

implanted in place of the old. There are different initiation ceremonies for different groups, and the cult is also used to heal,
apparently genuinely, various diseases. One person reporting on
these cults says that after initiation some people with a drink
problem have been known to turn teetotal.

It seems that the initiate, when brought back into the outside
world, remembers very little of what happened during his weeks
or months of initiation. Memories are mostly repressed, but the
person's conduct is often materially altered. Whereas in modern
psychotherapy hidden conflicts are brought to the surface with
a view to making the patient understand them better, in
Macumba the implantation of new beliefs and new attitudes to
life during the initiation ceremonies is consciously forgotten, but
continues to influence the way of life, perhaps for years afterwards, supported by return visits to the convent or monastery
for ceremonies and services when the believer is again possessed
and his faith is reinforced.

On speaking to a white woman in 1968 who had been through
weeks of Macumba initiation, and also to a couple of people
who had been present at her ceremony, it emerged that it is
strictly forbidden for people to see themselves, in photographs
or on film, while they are in the process of initiation to
Macumba. For instance, while two of the group had photographs of the third person during her initiation, they dared not
show them to her for fear of driving her mad. She must never
see what a totally different person she is when acting as a goddess. She may see her friends in the group being possessed and
how they behave, but she must never see pictures of herself acting as a vehicle for the manifestation of the gods on earth. The
two separate lives, of course, do still substantially influence each
other subconsciously.

Going to Bahia, lower down the coast of Brazil, in 1964, we
had to wait quite some time to see a ceremony, because a revolution had broken out in Brazil and all drumming was banned as
liable to excite people to riot. However, the Governor of Bahia
finally gave permission for a ceremony to take place, and I took
photographs of what happened. In this particular case only
Ogoun was allowed to manifest himself, and a number of other
people possessed by different Orishas had to leave the room and
were not allowed back during the ceremony. We saw homage
being paid to Ogoun, who was represented by an earthly Mother

of the Orishas sitting on the seat of honour. When a person became possessed by Ogoun he had to go out of the room, to return dressed in Ogoun's ceremonial costume, including a hat and a small dagger.

On a second visit to Bahia a few years later in 1968, through an invitation to attend a meeting of the World Psychiatric Association on Transcultural Psychiatry, I was hoping to see and film more of Macumba. But this was not possible, although I had letters of introduction from Pierre Verger, who spends some time in Bahia as well as in Nigeria and Dahomey, since much of his research work involves tracing the influence of slaves who came to the New World, some later returned to their native land as slave traders themselves. The trouble seemed to be that the Macumba group to which I had obtained an introduction were too high in the social scale to allow themselves to be filmed or photographed while in states of possession and trance. At the end of my visit, while flying down to Rio, feeling thoroughly frustrated, I sat next to a man who had spent the whole of the preceding weekend filming Macumba ceremonies among the poorer communities of Bahia. He said they were not so worried about being photographed and probably more open to receiving money than the group to which I had been introduced. Furthermore, this time there had been no Gilberto Freyre to make my task so much easier, as in Recife.

However, I did see at Bahia on my second visit a formal ceremony dedicated to Shango. Even here I was told that it was doubted whether so many people should be invited to what was essentially an intimate ceremony of a particular group. Nevertheless, the leader agreed that the ceremony should take place, and there were about a hundred or more people present. The same sort of drumming and dancing took place, but possession was very slow in occurring. The next day the leader kindly invited me to lunch and we talked at considerable length about the previous day's ceremony. He said he was disappointed, in spite of all the drumming, that Shango had not presented himself, and he explained that it is forbidden to ask Shango to descend and show himself through one of his worshippers. This must be done voluntarily on the part of the god. However, he had hit upon a device which was not against the rules. He played the particular rhythm used in one of the worshipper's own initiation ceremonies and this proved successful in bringing

Shango down to earth to manifest himself through that dancing worshipper. The man possessed by him, traditionally, went out still in trance and donned the particular robes of Shango before returning to dance, very beautifully, still in trance. None of the members of the cult doubted that Shango was personally now among them.

I was also allowed to see some of the more private rooms and the temple of this mixed white and coloured intellectual group, to whom Shango and other African gods meant so much. Their religion seemed as important to them as to any devout Christian, and their whole lives were influenced by it.

There is no doubt of the hold these cults have on even highly intelligent people. Their belief in the existence and power of these African gods is a very real one. At the meeting in Paris, in 1968, there was a white woman present who had been possessed in a Bahia cult group and had been through a long initiation ceremony lasting three weeks. She was giving an account of her experiences, and I asked her whether as a result she now believed in the existence and power of Shango, Ogoun and other Orisha gods. She was very emphatic in saying that 'of course' she did.

As already emphasized, in these cults the trance life and the ordinary life are different and divorced from each other, and each life is complete. But sometimes there is some memory of what goes on in ordinary life when the person is possessed, and *vice versa*. But as one person described it, all the moral values and all the emotions of the other state disappear. One may intellectually appreciate that one is a different person in trance, but the accompanying feelings and connecting links with the other life are largely destroyed by the hypnotic process used. It was certainly very interesting to see these hypnotic techniques, which have been used for centuries in African religions, now transferred to the New World, when you remember that hypnosis only came into official use in Western medicine less than two hundred years ago.

Undoubtedly, further studies of Macumba and similar religions in Brazil would reveal a vast amount of material on 'possession' and healing by African deities. And what little I saw, and was able to film and photograph, showed me once again the same basic technique of breaking down the nervous system, and so producing states of suggestibility in which quite bizarre beliefs can be devoutly accepted, which we have observed in so many different societies and religious or other contexts in this book. The power of these methods to produce new attitudes and new happiness in living is very great indeed, far greater than most of our modern methods of psychotherapy, or the use of intellectual arguments and persuasion alone. I could not help being again forcibly impressed by the deep and certain faith which this age-old pattern of brain-washing creates.

NOTES

1 Freyre G., *The Masters & The Slaves*. A. Knopf, New York. 1956.

17

Experiences in Trinidad

After my first visit to Brazil in 1964 I went straight on to Trinidad. Here I was fortunate in having the help of Professor Michael Beaubrun, who was then working in Trinidad and is now Professor of Psychiatry in the University of the West Indies in Jamaica.

With the help of friends of Professor Beaubrun's and some of the mental nurses in one of the hospitals in Trinidad, we managed to see very interesting ceremonies and to film and photograph them. At least two of them belonged to what could be called 'transitional religions'; that is, religions which originated in Africa, were brought across to Trinidad by slaves and became established there with a veneer of Christianity on the surface. While the British were in control in Trinidad many of these transitional cults were discouraged as much as possible. But they lived on underground, and have now come more into the open. In some of them bell-ringing, rhythmic overbreathing and hand-clapping had to be substituted for the noisier African drumming, and bell-ringing and rhythmic breathing are still being used as a means of 'bringing down the Holy Ghost', although more drumming is now allowed.

One of these ceremonies took place in the suburban slums of the capital, Port of Spain. It was only through a friend of Michael Beaubrun's who had been brought up in this compound and whose sister was still a worshipper there that we finally prevailed on the leader of this group to let us see the ceremony and even to film it. This particular group of services has been going on for over 100 years and had never before been opened to outside inspection. We were helped in gaining entry by my saying that I was a doctor and had nothing to do with the press, and that I felt that they might have more to teach me, religiously and medically, than I could teach them. I also had to agree to pay quite a considerable sum of money so that a goat and four chickens could be bought for the sacrifice which is an essential part of the ritual.

Although the acting group leader agreed to hold the services for us, no ceremony could take place without the presence of a much older man who was still technically head of the whole group. He had become old and infirm and so had handed on the leadership of the group to his nephew, with whom I had to negotiate.

The services were held in a compound where there was a covered floor for dancing, a small chapel, a burial ground for members of the group, and several houses in which some of the group lived. The buildings were mostly old and decayed, but a few new ones had recently been added.

We had to get up early for the first service, which took place before the worshippers went off to their daily work. For much of the night before, as a goat was to be sacrificed in the morning, preliminary ceremonies were being held which we did not attend; but in the morning we were in time to see the ceremonial killing of the goat. Its throat was cut and the blood collected in a bowl, and then its head was cut off. This sacrifice was made to the great god Ogoun, who was also called St Michael. Four chickens were sacrificed, their heads also being cut off. The first chicken was sacrificed to Elegba. Elegba is the same Elegba as in the Yoruba religion in Dahomey and nominally approximates to the Devil, although he is not really the Satan of Christianity but more in the nature of a mischievous imp who brings chaos into the ceremony and so is always given the first sacrifice, to keep him appeased. When I asked if they had ever omitted this sacrifice to Elegba, to see what happened, they said they would never dare to do this. The relationship between this supposedly Christian ceremony and the Yoruba religion in Dahomey was obvious from the start. We were told that the founder of the group had come from Dahomey more than 100 years ago, but they denied that he came to Trinidad as a slave, though this seems more than likely.

The goat was killed in the open while the worshippers stood around, dressed in white, and some of them started to go into trance and states of possession. The goat was finally cut up and parts of its body were placed on the altar. The group then proceeded to dance in the small dancing hut which had open sides. Three drummers, and the leader, took part, while the old hereditary leader also sat beside the drummers. Before long, several other women went into states of possession, and we were told that they were possessed by Christian saints, though when closely questioned later few of them had any doubt that the Christian saints were also African gods and goddesses. One woman possessed by the Virgin Mary danced with a veil, symbolic of her carrying swaddling clothes. Another, representing St Michael, danced with a wooden sword, a replica of the sword that had been used in beheading the chickens and cutting the throat of the goat. Nobody was harmed, although the sword was waved about by the entranced woman. Another woman was possessed by St Francis, yet another by Joseph the Carpenter; she danced up and down the hut waving a saw. In some cases the people in trances would take up the instruments or symbols which showed who possessed them, in others the instruments were handed to them. We were told that most women were possessed by the same saint, but it was possible for some people to be possessed by various saints at different times. At this ceremony no men became possessed.

After quite a long period of dancing and trances, the ceremony ended and some of the worshippers went off to work. The sacrificial meat was then cooked and served at lunch, which I ate with several of the women who had taken part in the ceremony. I was able to talk to these women about their feelings as they went into trance. All denied having any memory of what they had done in the possessed state. Some confessed that they had felt fearful or had apprehensive feelings in the stomach, but few of them seemed to fear going into trance, and indeed most of them welcomed it as an honour to have been specially chosen by the saint. Again it was believed that the spirits had travelled over from Africa to gain possession of them.

These people's faith in the reality of their saints was absolute because they had personally experienced them; and again one noted the difference between their intense personal experience of possession and our forms of Christian service, in which few now have any real sense that God or Christ or the saints are near or in them. The Christian saints can be prayed to for help, but without any personal contact being achieved. It is the feeling of personally *being possessed* by the saints which creates an *absolute* faith, which can rarely afterwards be destroyed by logical argument and reasoning.

The women told me that on some occasions, when a service was in progress, a woman who had not gone to it but had stayed at home would suddenly feel that she was beginning to be possessed, and later would find herself at the service and just coming round from trance. What had happened was that she had gone into trance at home, had become possessed, and had walked, several miles perhaps, to the service while still in trance, with no memory of it later. One person told me that she had suddenly become possessed while watching one of the ceremonies. As a result, she had been confined to bed for seven days, almost mute and in a condition which sounded very much like hysterical stupor. When she recovered, she became a regular worshipper at the church. She had since experienced possession frequently without any severe after-effects.

What was most impressive about the people we talked to was their normality, though they had been in states of full possession only an hour or two before. We saw the same thing later, in Voodoo. In our culture a person exhibiting repeated hysterical dissociative and trance phenomena would be considered nervously ill, but the same phenomena occurring in normal people in many African cultures leave very little nervous upset behind them; on the contrary, they help to relieve accumulated tension, as well as to create a deep conviction of being important, personally and individually, to the god or gods who are worshipped.

We inquired about the healing functions of these services and were told that depressed people, after a period of possession, would feel very much happier and better than before. But I was told by another man in Trinidad that when he was deeply depressed the services and feelings of possession had no beneficial effect on him. He had to go to the hospital to have electric shock treatment and antidepressant drugs before he was able to benefit at all again from the religious services. In Africa, the West Indies and the U.S.A., I saw several people suffering from depression or schizophrenia who were not amenable to these group abreactive religious techniques, but who could be helped with E.C.T. and drugs, an electrically induced abreactive treatment, which can be repeated up to twenty times if necessary and has beneficial effects on the mentally ill, as opposed to normal people who are less severely depressed and can get relief by repeated dancing and trance with temporary collapse.

That same evening, after working hours, another drumming ceremony with multiple possessions took place. Although there had been so much initial worry about letting non-members witness and photograph the services, when the final decision had been taken several people were invited to come, including the Trinidad Minister of Health. Many of the local visitors were amazed to see what happened, and had been happening for a hundred years, in their midst. Generally you only see such services (which may well be held among black people in England) if you can gain entrance to a depressed social group who, during the week in working hours, may be building up emotional tensions which they have to inhibit at work, but which they can discharge from time to time in sessions of abreactive dancing and emotional release. After epidemics of plague in Europe in the Middle Ages, with the fearful strain which they imposed, abreactive dancing to the point of collapse was common, and there were sporadic groups which used flagellation to stimulate the nervous system to the point of collapse. Hitler animated a depressed and despairing Germany in the 1930s with mass excitatory techniques including rhythmic chanting. This generally resulted in mass hysteria, greatly increased suggestibility and renewed feelings of hope and faith in Hitler as virtually a god. Visitors from other countries could be caught up in the group fervour and some returned home with a similar faith in Hitler as a superman.

On our second visit to Trinidad in 1965 we went to another ceremony, in a purer and more primitive cult of the god Shango. Normally, the worshippers of Shango devote only one week in every year to intensive ceremonies, with persistent dancing leading to states of possession. But other lesser services are held from time to time. The leader of one of these groups arranged a ceremony for us and promised to let us see the type of possession that occurred. The meeting, however, went on for only a short time as several people did not turn up and some of those who did took too much of the rum which we had been asked to provide; the whole affair ended in considerable disaster.

Before the meeting I had a chance to talk to two of the group and was given the same information about possession which I had already received so often elsewhere. They, too, believed that the gods came over from Africa and, under the names of Christian saints, manifested themselves to the group. Ogoun was St Michael and Shango was Christ himself, the Good Shepherd. When they offered sacrifices and worshipped, sometimes all night, they sang hymns to St Michael and St Peter, to Jonah, St Anthony, St Francis, Joseph the Carpenter, St Philomena, Moses, St Teresa and, of course, the Virgin Mary. All these appear to have their equivalents in the Yoruba religion of Dahomey, where the great gods have assistant gods and goddesses. These lesser deities can be called on for help when the great gods are busy or when it is felt that a request is too trivial to bother them with. I was also told that the African gods had been converted, and had now become Christian saints, which I had heard before, at Macumba meetings in Brazil.

When the actual possession occurs, St Michael carries a cross or a sword, the Good Shepherd a crook, and John the Baptist an axe; the Virgin Mary wears a veil or carries swaddling clothes, and Joseph the Carpenter carries a saw. Usually, one saint regularly possesses you, but another saint may substitute for him if your own saint is busy elsewhere. I also learned that the more you try to resist being possessed when you feel that it is beginning to happen, the more certain it is that possession will occur. This suggests that the brain is in an ultraparadoxical phase of activity, as discussed in earlier chapters.

Without meaning to be unduly cynical, the same conclusion is suggested by the impressive amount of love and friendship displayed by those in possession, and the absence of quarrelling. I was told that if you are at odds with someone else at the meeting, the moment you are possessed your saint will go over to that person and smoothe out the disagreements, and you will again feel friendly to him or her. This seems a good way of resolving group difficulties and tensions without loss of face on either side.

In talking to people who take part in these forms of worship, I was repeatedly impressed by the dignity and the evident mental balance which many of them showed. In many cases they were living in dire poverty and yet felt that life was well worth living. They were upheld by their religion and sustained by their African or Christian gods.

One of the women, when initially possessed, remained prostrate and unconscious for nine days in bed. These long trances are called 'travelling' (and we heard of this phenomenon also among other groups). This woman said that while she was lying in bed her spirit left her body and she saw St Michael in a red garment. She then travelled farther on and was told by St Michael to climb a ladder and try to reach the top. This she did, and then realized that she had climbed Jacob's Ladder into Heaven. She saw a beautiful world and felt very happy and pleased that her first attempt to climb the ladder had been successful. Some people apparently may have as many as seven tries in their 'travels' to get to the top of the ladder, and some never succeed. She did not remember coming down the ladder again, but she had also been to Africa in her 'travelling' state. She found she understood the language there, though she had never heard it before. She also went to China and was taken into a shop there. Then she returned and woke up in bed. The parallel with the 'travelling' experiences we discussed in Chapter 3 is clear. This woman not only attended the ceremonies of a Shango group but also went to Mass as a Catholic and she felt that in both she was worshipping the same group of gods, but 'it is the African saints who possess us'.

Another woman had been possessed from time to time by St Francis for the past eight years. She did not need to be at a service or in her bed to become possessed; it could happen at any time, even while she was working. She described her head as 'getting light', and she felt very depressed, but following a period of possession she could 'do everything again'. This particular informant had not 'travelled', but she had had a dream in which she was flying high over the sea and looking down at the water; she had been alone and not with St Francis in her dream. (This incident reminded my typist, a very sane person, of a dream she had had just before the 1939–45 War. She was carried through the air by 'Death' dressed in black, over a vast extent of land where millions of people were lying dead. This gave her a great sense of security during the war although she was living in the heart of London. Death in this instance resembled the figures she had seen many times on Underground posters.)

We were also able to attend Spiritual Baptist services in 1964. Leader John, who ran the Spiritual Baptist group, had a wife who was leader of a Shango group, but they rarely overlapped. The Shango group usually held its ceremony once a year, while Leader John's group of Spiritual Baptists met twice a week, or more frequently, all year round. It was here that I saw one of the congregation being brought back after seven days of 'travelling' and 'mourning'.

If a person has attended this Spiritual Baptist group and wants to become a full member and make a fresh start, he may ask to undergo a period of 'travelling' and 'mourning' so that all his sins may be forgiven. First of all, his heart must be 'reconciled with God', he must make friends with all his enemies, he must confess all his sins, and the congregation are asked whether any person present has anything against the would-be traveller. At the appointed time, after a period of singing, sudden quick bodily movements and head jerking take place, followed by what is virtually the speedy induction of a deep hypnotic trance. The subject is laid on the floor, with a band containing certain secret signs tied round the forehead. The hands and feet are tied together, and the traveller lies in this manner for up to seven days, and maybe more. On the third day the subject is 'raised' and 'put down' again at special services. We saw this happen to a woman who was put into 'mourning' on the Sunday, and on the Wednesday we went to see her 'raised up' as 'from the tomb'; then she was put down to complete her further four days of mourning and travelling. She was brought out on the following Sunday. While lying on the hard floorboards of the chapel, the travellers have an attendant of the same sex with them to attend to their needs, such as giving them a little milk or honey, and to attend to toilet necessities.

While being put into hypnotic trance by Leader John the subject is given a secret word which he must concentrate on and repeat continuously. The word is like a 'mantra' and is known only to the subject and the Leader; it may also become a threatening word. For instance, if in future any trouble occurs, the preacher has only to mention this word, to which the subject is highly sensitized, and it is enough to recreate the feeling of the hypnotic and mourning process and all it entails. Another interesting point is that if the mourning and travelling period goes satisfactorily, God gives the person, during this process, another secret word which is not made known to the preacher. If, when the person is in trouble, the preacher uses his secret word and he does not want to obey it, he can always use the word God has given him to counteract the other. This is reminiscent of the traditional relations between the African patient and the witch-doctor.

During the seven days of mourning and travelling, the soul leaves the body to visit various parts of the world. Travellers generally go to India or to Syria where, one man told me, he was given the job of drawing water. They can travel as far as China or to Africa where, another person told me, he temporarily became the Bishop of a church. I received no account of any-body travelling to England. The travellers may bring home messages to the preacher. It was also said that sometimes souls travel from other countries to this chapel and attend the services in various guises, so that visitors to the services are sometimes suspected of being travellers from another group in a far country.

When the period of mourning and travelling is over, later periods of trance occur in which travellers speak with the 'gift of tongues' in languages of the countries they have visited. Among the congregation, as in St Paul's time, are people who claim to be able to interpret the various strange tongues spoken. One remembers St Paul, when discussing the frequency of ecstatic states, saying that they needed more 'interpreters' of tongues for, wrongly interpreted, the tongues could create confusion among the congregation. St Paul, in his capacity as an administrator, was evidently dubious of too much personal communication between the worshipper and God without administrative intervention. The religious administrator since his day has too often tried to make himself the essential intermediary between each man and his God.

18

Experiences in Jamaica and Barbados

The first of my two visits to Jamaica in 1964 proved the more profitable. What I saw was not as exciting as in Trinidad or Brazil, but it was interesting and informative. Jamaica has its own peculiar mixture of African and Christian religious practices, called Pocomania. Intensive drumming is not used, though a large drum is sometimes employed to mark the beat for singing. The service consists almost entirely of the repeated singing of hymns of a Moody and Sankey type, interspersed with short periods of preaching, prayers and readings from the gospels. There is also a great deal of 'tromping', which means rhythmic overbreathing and the making of peculiar breathing sounds for the purpose of 'bringing down the Holy Ghost', which also makes the worshippers highly suggestible to what is told them by the preacher.

The slums of Kingston, Jamaica, where these services are held, are as bad as any I have seen anywhere, and can be dangerous, especially after dark. The service we attended was run by a black preacher named Karpo. He is also a talented painter and I believe that since our visit his fame as a painter has outstripped his celebrity as a Pocomania 'shepherd' or leader. He told me that he himself had been converted at the age of fifteen; he was now in his thirties. He had been preaching and healing people ever since he was sixteen. During the service he went round laying his hands on those who needed help. He said that he was able to help the mentally ill and to treat some organic diseases as well, and he believed that this was due to the faith created by his preaching and by the services. His congregation looked upon him as the instrument of God, who healed the sick through him.

There cannot be the slightest doubt that among these poverty-stricken people religious services of this sort are of real help, in giving them a sense of dignity and faith in living, despite the appalling circumstances of their lives. We saw the same effects in Africa, where the same techniques are used to smooth away resentments and tensions. I am sure that as the Black Power movement becomes stronger, this type of service will be bitterly attacked, so great is its power to keep people contented with their lot when they possess little or nothing: and indeed they cheerfully praise God for what little they have.

As usual in such services, the preacher dominated the scene. Half-way through he stopped, took us behind the scenes to his room and had a long talk with us, paying little attention to the congregation, which waited patiently for him to resume the service. When he did continue, I was able to sound-record the 'tromping'. It was very similar to what we had heard among the nomadic Samburu tribe in Kenya, who used this same method of inducing trance before battle. The tromping went on practically the whole time that the preacher was talking; this would have the effect of producing a state of greatly increased suggestibility and readiness to accept what he said. There was also rhythmic hand-clapping to the beat of the big drum, while they were singing.

We arranged for a second visit in the same week, to film part of the service, but when we arrived we found the B.B.C. and Alan Whicker there too, for the same purpose. He seemed rather bewildered at what was going on around him at this service. The B.B.C. camera team became very angry with us because, they said, our efforts would impede their own. We tried our best to explain to them that we had arranged to film there before they came along, and that they had been told to come on the same night to 'kill two birds with one stone'. However, their lighting was very useful to us. This was before Alan Whicker left the B.B.C. for I.T.V. and later, at home, we saw an interesting B.B.C. television programme on Pocomania, which contained some of the information I had been able to give him.

When the hymns were being sung, because so many of the congregation were illiterate, the preacher had to give the next line of the hymn as the previous line was being sung. This gave a peculiar chanting effect, with the congregation repeating everything the parson said. Some shouted 'Hallelujah' and 'Amen' after every sentence uttered by the parson in his sermon; there is an agreed body of opinion and no intellectual opposition to any point of view expressed by the preacher. In group worship of this sort, anyone who disagrees with the preacher must leave the church and start his own services elsewhere, or attend some other chapel. There is no room for critical religious discussion or expression of doubt, which would spoil the powerful atmosphere of uncritical faith and mar the happiness and peace of mind of the other worshippers.

At this service there was a notable absence of younger people. While men and women were going into trance and being possessed by the Holy Ghost, the preacher himself started to go into trance, to a lesser extent, no doubt brought on by the repetitive singing and preaching. He identified himself with the congregation in trance and possession, which indicated his personal contact with God. The Holy Ghost would then descend on preacher and congregation alike. At the end of the service, because we had been attacked in the same district earlier in the day, as will be described later, he sent us home in his car as the safest way of getting out of the very tough slum district at night.

There is Indian influence in Pocomania, as well as African, and deities of both continents are mixed up with Christian saints. There is an 'Indian' spirit, another called 'Queen Dove', another 'Bell-Ringer' spirit, and there is the 'River Maid'. According to the spirit present, so the form of 'tromping' changes. A certain East Indian spirit came into Pocomania around 1840, and when one has been possessed by this spirit one grows long hair. In Pocomania they also talk about 'labouring and travelling through the spirit world'.

Sometimes one person in the congregation is delegated to talk with possessing spirits or the Holy Ghost, and then tell the rest of the congregation the content of the conversation. The pastor is known as the Shepherd and the female flock are called 'sisters' or 'mothers'. There is much less identification with African gods, but Indian spirits are identified with Christian saints and the Holy Ghost. Fasting is also frequently used to make people more sensitive to the messages given them by the spirits and the preacher. The fasting usually lasts for about three days, and services go on continually during that time.

On the day of our first visit to a Pocomania service in 1964, we had seen another religious procession going down the street near by, earlier in the day. Foolishly, and it was the only time I did this, I started to film the procession without getting formal permission from the leader. It turned out that they had been out all night, fasting and praying in the country, and were now coming back to their small chapel to complete the service. Some were already entranced, and most of them were in an hysterical and highly excitable condition. Suddenly we were attacked; attempts were made to snatch my camera, and my wife was hit and spat upon. They deeply resented, quite rightly perhaps, that I was endeavouring to film them without their permission. We were rescued by one of the faithful who turned out to be a policeman. He told the rest of the group to leave us alone and that we had as much right to be there as they had. We then asked if we could come to the church with them, and again the policeman suggested to the others that we be allowed to do so since there was 'freedom of worship'. We went along with them, but the atmosphere was still very tense and difficult. When we were in the church, I got up and made a speech explaining that I was a doctor interested in these services, and felt that perhaps they had more to teach us than we had to teach them. I also explained that I had a brother who was a Bishop of the Church of South India. This pacified them as part of the congregation were of Indian origin. Because of the degree of suggestibility and excitement present, quite an ordinary speech on my part was able to switch them completely round to full co-operation, and we were given permission to film and photograph as much as we liked.

Later in the service the policeman gave his own testimony of how he himself once came in to a service, in an official capacity, but suddenly felt the hand of God upon him and from then on had become a believer and a worshipper with them. The preacher and the congregation were all wearing Indian-style clothing, with turbans on their heads. After a while the preacher went off into complete trance and possession; his body was shaking so much and his head moving so quickly that his turban unwound itself and finally fell off. As he went into possession, numerous members of the congregation went in with him and we saw extreme examples of possession-states of the same type as described elsewhere. This was no doubt aided by the long fasting beforehand. Before the end of the service a marriage took place between two of the worshippers, and individual testimonies of conversion were given by several people. Certainly in this service the Indian influence was most marked and there seemed to be little of the African influence which was so prominent in the Trinidad ceremonies we saw.

While in Jamaica we also attended a less excited service at which there were many young people. Two children aged about ten or twelve went into trance, and I saw this again in Nigeria among a Christian sect called the 'Cherubim and Seraphim' (Chapter 15). There was the usual singing and hand-clapping in this service and an intense personal commitment of the congregation, as one by one they rose and gave testimony of their conversion and what it meant to them in their subsequent religious lives. I remarked again how much more religion meant to these people, both personally and emotionally, than it does to most Christians elsewhere.

BARBADOS

In 1967, following a second hurried visit to Jamaica, we spent a week at Barbados attending a Caribbean Psychiatric Congress. I was assured there would be nothing of special interest to me there in the way of the subject I was most interested in. But my informant proved far from right.

Going through the graveyard of one of the older churches I found a funeral procession just starting. A Spiritual Baptist preacher was burying his mother. It was a sight to be seen. The 'mourners' were dancing and jumping with joy around the grave as the coffin was lowered into it, because they were all so certain that the deceased was now very happy in Heaven. Such absolute faith and joy in the face of death was a revelation to me and contrasted severely with the sombre attitudes of most Christians at a funeral service.

I established contact with the preacher concerned at his church the following Sunday. It turned out that he had been trained in the Belmont region of Trinidad and knew Leader John and his group. This church also practised 'mourning' and 'travelling', as Leader John's group did. Of all our experiences in the West Indies, this was one of the most instructive and impressive. There was no drumming, but the loud ringing of a bell 'brought down' the Holy Ghost into the hearts and bodies of the people. The preacher and most of the congregation were in trance, the preacher dancing with individual members of the congregation. Then a succession of people gave evidence of what a change had been wrought in their lives since being saved, after the Holy Ghost had possessed them.

A man with a symbolic sword stood in the doorway, possibly as a defence against the entry of Elegba, the troublesome spirit, and many of the other rituals here showed that the service had partly African origins.

After I had spent some time filming and taking photographs, I joined in the service, as a mark of respect to those present. And here I was nearly 'caught' myself by the surrounding atmosphere. I was struck by their deep fervour and certitude of a heaven hereafter which would free them from their poverty, their tiny slum houses and hovels, their lack of the material blessings enjoyed by their white brothers. Nevertheless, they were beautifully turned out and spotlessly clean, dignified, kindly and humble people, who deserved to enter the Kingdom of Heaven if anybody did. Their religion taught them to help each other and to get rid of all unkindness in their personal relations. This to me was a true religion. The strength of their faith was so obvious that I felt that had they been told to go into the arena and be eaten by lions, they would have done so, trusting in God's help as the Christians did of old.

I soon realized that I was 'co-operating' in the service too much! I had not come to be saved, but to examine the techniques of possession and the creation of faith. So when I returned to a second service I carefully stuck to my camera and recording apparatus, for if you actively take part in, and lend yourself to, these faith-creating techniques, you can easily be influenced and you may come to believe with a firm faith in what may be great truths or utter falsehood.

19

Voodoo in Haiti

Voodoo in Haiti has gained itself a very sinister reputation, though it is doubtful whether the ordinary practices of Voodoo are much different from other Afro-Christian religious practices and beliefs in many of the West Indian islands. However, Voodoo does dominate the life of the poorer classes in Haiti to a much greater extent than elsewhere. There are several reasons for this, one of the most important being that the poverty in this island is so great, the suffering and despair so profound, that some form of religion had to develop which would give ordinary people hope of a better life hereafter and courage to go on living under such miserable conditions. It looks as if Voodoo fulfils this aim better than most other religions. It may be that there are sinister aspects of Voodoo about which little is known and which some books tend to dramatize. But on the surface, at least, and while watching its public ceremonies and talking to some of the people concerned, I never gained the impression that this religion was predominantly sinister and evil, but, on the contrary, that it gave to many of its participants increased dignity, relief from fear and something to live for which was otherwise unattainable in the ordinary circumstances of their lives. So great is its power over the minds of its worshippers, because of the techniques used, that it can of course be put to evil use by some of its leaders. But this is true of other religions too.

I paid two visits to Haiti with my wife in 1964 and 1965 and we were able to see a number of Voodoo ceremonies. As usual, my main interest lay in the phenomena of possession and trance, which are common in Voodoo and form an important part of it. Our first introduction to Voodoo was not the most propitious. We went to see Katherine Dunham's spectacular Voodoo show, especially put on for tourists, which gives a vastly glamorized picture and takes Voodoo right out of its proper village setting.

At the end, however, after the usual dancing and drumming, the participants went into a 'sacred' pool which had stones in the water. Here some very definite states of trance and possession occurred and their intensity made me feel that it was impossible that they were not genuine. As with hypnosis, once a person is accustomed to trance, attaining it becomes increasingly easy and a state of possession and trance can be reached with a less and less intense stimulus, and sometimes at will. In a show like this, it would have been most unwise to let the participants go into trance and possession except at the end. This is what seemed actually to happen. Further examination, the filming and photographing of these phenomena, and a very close inspection of the people concerned—which I was able to make in later visits—showed that they sometimes took half an hour to come fully out of their states of possession after the final pool ceremony was over.

On both our visits to Haiti we stayed at the Hotel Olfson, which was known as the 'Ginger-bread Palace'. It had originally been an old Presidential Residence, and was the setting for Graham Greene's novel *The Comedians*. At the time we went there it was extremely difficult to obtain the visas to enter Haiti. Difficulties had arisen between President Duvalier and the British Government and I only managed to get a visa at the special request of the Minister of Health for Haiti and through the good offices of Dr Douyon, Chief Psychiatrist in Haiti, who was also the nephew of the Chief Justice of that island.

Most people at that time were afraid to visit Haiti for fear of unpleasant consequences. But I could not have been more kindly treated and was given all the facilities and information I needed. At the hotel I fortunately met a Mr Isa. He had important contacts with Voodoo and, after the preliminary visit to Katherine Dunham's show, he was able to introduce us to several genuine Voodoo groups, both in the slums and from two to ten miles outside the capital, Port au Prince. I had no doubt that, as there were so few visitors to Haiti at that time, most of the Voodoo phenomena we saw were genuine and not arranged for tourists. We also had the help of Miss Lavinia Williams, a coloured American of great intelligence who teaches dancing in Haiti, and who was herself very interested in the practices and beliefs of Voodoo. On at least one occasion, she went, inadvertently, into full possession when dancing at one of the ceremonies we attended—a most unwise thing to do unless one desires to get caught up in the religion, with all it entails.

It is not my intention to discuss the full details of the Voodoo religion and its ceremonies. These have been well described in several books, particularly in Maya Deren's *The Divine Horsemen*. Maya Deren was an American who went to Haiti to study and film Voodoo practices; she became possessed herself on several occasions and was able to give a detailed account of the religion from a sympathetic and unsensational angle.

The first proper Voodoo ceremony Mr Isa introduced us to was a very impressive one. We first saw the gods and goddesses being called down with all the complicated ritual involved, and then we saw various participants becoming possessed by the gods and goddesses, or *loa*, and behaving as they would behave. In Voodoo you are described as being 'mounted' by the loa because your foot may suddenly stick to the ground; you then jerk forward on to the other foot and this, too, sticks to the ground while the loa mounts. Gradually you take on the characteristic behaviour of the loa who has taken possession of you. You may talk, eat and drink as a loa, for the loa is a departed spirit who once lived on earth and has been deified. The loa approximate to our Christian saints in Heaven and have human attributes as well as divine ones.

Those possessed have no memory of the possession period, and it is believed in Voodoo that the loa cannot temporarily possess you while your own soul remains in your body. When the loa enters or 'mounts', the worshipper's own soul is temporarily expelled. It was also interesting to find that, as in Macumba in Brazil, the people who watch a person becoming possessed must not reveal to that person how he behaved, although they may tell him which particular loa entered him. Sometimes possessions last for several hours: the possessed person behaves quite rationally but in the way the loa would behave. The loa may ask for food and drink: he or she may talk to other worshippers or to the *hungan*, or priest. The function of the hungan is to intervene between the loa and the possessed person, if necessary. If the loa is apparently behaving too badly or roughly, and making too many demands, the priest may request him to leave the body or to modify his behaviour. In some of the ceremonies we saw a priestess, or *mambo*, also becoming possessed temporarily by one of the loa.

Many of the Haitian loa come from Africa, and the African gods are mostly benevolent deities who will help people if suitably placated. You may also seek their guidance and aid through dreams and through mediumship of adepts. It was when the African slaves in Haiti went up into the mountains to escape from their French masters, and there met and lived with the Indian natives while keeping out of the way of the French, that Voodoo gathered to itself loa who are much more evil, aggressive and angry than the African gods. In Voodoo there are therefore occasional violent possessions by such loa as Ghede (a devil), Dumballah (the snake god), and the various Petro loa, such as Baron Samedi, Legba-Petro, Erszuli Ge-Rogue.

Not all those possessed at the service went on to collapse, though many did, but at the end of their possession, as they came out of it, most of them seemed completely but temporarily exhausted, mentally and physically, as a result of emotional and abreactive release. With such a variety of possessing loa, all sorts of behaviour may be exhibited, which are accepted as coming from the loa and not from the people possessed. The leader does his best to restrain their behaviour, but sometimes the loa get out of control. The spectators do not feel that the possessed are responsible for their actions during possession; they try to help them from falling or hurting themselves, or doing anything dangerous to other members of the group when anger or aggression is being exhibited by the loa.

When the priest himself went into a state of possession, he was looked after by his assistants and standard-bearers, in which case he would be led off into his own small room to rest, and would return a few minutes later to continue the ceremony. When the service was over most of the participants came round fairly quickly, and were soon their normal selves again. It was surprising to see how speedily normal behaviour could return, except for signs of obvious fatigue and a relaxation of tension. These were very normal men and women taking part, not mad or neurotic people. Many of them were most intrigued when I played back to them on the tape-recorder the drumming, and the recordings of the voices of the loa talking through the mouths of the possessed.

The second genuine ceremony we saw was the most exciting of them all. It had been possible to film and photograph the first service because of the presence of a crude electricity supply, which gave just sufficient current to provide lighting. But at the second service, being farther out from Port au Prince, no light was available. We had asked for the ceremony to start early in the day, with the hope of filming it, but the mambo took so long with the preliminary preparations, such as drawing on the floor the symbol of the particular loa she wished to call down, that by the time the dancing and possession began, there was no light left for filming.

The dancing and drumming went on hour after hour and every sort of loa appeared at one time or another. We saw the Dumballah, the snake god, and the person possessed by him behaved like a snake. At a later service at the same place we saw somebody possessed by Dumballah climbing into the rafters of the roof as a snake might do. Some of the possessed women displayed an abounding sexuality. We saw, among others, Erszuli, goddess of love, Baron Samedi, keeper of the graveyard, and Agwe, goddess of the sea. Ogoun also appeared and Ghede, also god of the phallus. When Ghede descends and takes possession, he often exhibits very erotic behaviour as a challenge to the respectability of some of the visitors.

What was perfectly clear from these exciting few hours was that the various possession states provide an outlet for every type of normal and abnormal behaviour among people whose lives are one long struggle against poverty and despair. We saw them becoming gods, behaving like gods, and for a while forgetting all their troubles. After the ceremony was over they were quite convinced that for a time, despite their humility and poverty on earth, they had been one with the gods themselves. Life had regained purpose and dignity for them.

The next ceremony we witnessed was specially arranged for us by the Katherine Dunham group. When we had seen the first public show, I had noted that genuine possessions seemed to take place when the participants went into the sacred pool at the end. We asked for a special repetition of this as I wished to film and tape-record the performers' reactions. It seemed that the drummers and priests could really induce possession at will. As we hoped, some obviously genuine possessions took place among both men and women. The priest also went into a short trance. Then there was a pause and they threatened to stop the ceremony unless more money was forthcoming. They only reluctantly restored the drumming when we complained that we had hardly started the filming and photography.

After this, the leader suddenly became possessed, apparently by a Ghede loa. It was a very fierce possession and he came towards us in a very menacing manner. That he was actually in possession is fairly obvious from the photograph my wife took of him as he came towards her, and while she was falling off a wall as she backed away. My own camera unfortunately went wrong in all the excitement. We were not, however, physically attacked. Apart from the few dramatic photographs we took, the ceremony was not very exciting and ended, as in Trinidad on one occasion, with an argument over money.

I had little doubt that when possession did occur, at both the Dunham shows, they were genuine. They can be facilitated by constant repetition, and it becomes increasingly easy for worshippers to let themselves go into states of possession. Possession may, however, be very agonizing mentally for the first few times when it occurs in a hitherto intact nervous system.

The following year another opportunity arose for us to return to Haiti in 1965 and we stayed at the same hotel. This time I was somewhat more frightened than on my last visit, and we were glad to see Mr Isa waiting for us when we arrived. It turned out that he had been in one of Duvalier's prisons for several weeks, suspected of spying. He had finally been released but was obviously very shaken indeed by his experiences at the hands of the secret police. The Minister of Health was extremely helpful and I was even able to arrange an interview with President Duvalier's secretary at his mansion while the President himself, who was next door, was deciding whether or not he could see me. I had asked him to see me as a fellow doctor and not as a politician. However, he refused.

As soon as I got back to Haiti, I set about trying to arrange a further photographic session with Katherine Dunham's dancers, without being stopped in the middle by further bargaining for money. The matter was finally suitably arranged through Mr Isa. The drumming was tremendous, which facilitated the inducement of possessions in the sacred pool. We expressed the hope that the priest would again become possessed by the Ghede god and, perhaps to oblige us and frighten us again, he did. The photographs and film taken of this possession were most exciting. He did not come round in his hut afterwards for nearly half an hour, and we were able to watch his gradual recovery.

What helped me to know when possessions were genuine or false was my experience during the war in treating fatigue states and hysterical losses of memory in patients, and studying all the hysterical dissociative phenomena occurring in hitherto normal people after being bombed or after long periods of active fighting. During the war, as we have seen, the human nervous system might be bombarded by stimuli of sufficient intensity to produce exactly the same conditions of mental dissociation and trance as are deliberately produced in other parts of the world by drumming, dancing and other excitatory techniques.

Conversely, in Voodoo and other states of possession one again sees very good examples of Pavlovian paradoxical and ultraparadoxical behaviour. Any strong pressure on the possessed person to do something produces immediate resistance and a tendency to do just the opposite. But he can sometimes be persuaded by whispering very quietly in his ear, by blowing gently on his face or by using any *small* stimulus. In other words, a small stimulus may be effective, where a larger stimulus produces a lesser response, or even the opposite response to that desired. This is because the greater stimulus increases states of inhibition in an already overacting nervous system.

We paid a second visit to the group run by the mambo, where there had been no light available for filming. This time the ceremony took place earlier in the day, and again Ghede was particularly active sexually. Two girls both became possessed by Ghede loa and proceeded to have a lesbian encounter with each other. They half stripped each other and one girl symbolically raped the other with a masculine type of pelvic approximation. It ended in the total emotional collapse of both participants. Those of the group looking on were obviously amused by the whole episode. The two girls involved, who were normally quiet and restrained, had no memory of what they had been doing and probably would never be told. The only people who were angry were the boy-friends of the two girls concerned. But they could do nothing about it as these were the gods at work, and the souls of the girls were not in them at the time, being replaced by Ghede himself. As Lewis has stressed about Voodoo, 'Abreaction is the order of the day. Repressed urges and desires, the idiosyncratic as well as the socially conditioned, are given full public rein. No holds are barred. No interests or demands are too unseemly in this setting not to receive sympathetic attention. Each dancer ideally achieves a state of ecstasy, and in stereotyped fashion collapses in a trance from which he emerges purged and refreshed.'[1]

The last ceremony we visited was in the slum area of Port au Prince. On the way to it we say a typical 'wake' for a dead person. Most of the people in the house and those outside were drunk. They were shouting, cheering, laughing, singing and, so to speak, getting the dead man and his soul out of their systems. It reminded me very much of what I had seen in the bush in Zambia when we arrived at a village during a burial service. After a suitable period of mourning and crying around the hut, a vigorous dance was staged in the evening to expel dangerous spirits and break up the prevailing gloom. Death had happened, mourning must take place, but life must then go on. Here again I saw one of the best ways of dealing with some overwhelming and inhibiting mental disaster: a period of deliberately induced excitement, using dancing and alcohol in this case, to break up the previous inhibitory pattern of depression produced by death and mourning.

This last Voodoo ceremony in the slums of Port au Prince was another exciting experience. There was nothing fake or phoney about it and the possessions were numerous and intense. Agwe, goddess of the sea, appeared, and the man possessed by her was miming the rowing of a boat. Erszuli, goddess of love, appeared, behaving most erotically, pulling up her dress and making other sexual gestures. Ghede also came down to show his usual sexual activity. Possession states went on for a long time and here, perhaps more than anywhere else, all participants seemed to end up in a temporary state of profound stupor and inhibition. At all these ceremonies, the beating of the drums controlled the behaviour of all those possessed. The drummers would watch the dancers keenly and when the latter showed signs of becoming possessed they beat their drums in such a way as to increase the depth of possession, so that the dancers fell more and more under the domination of the loa.

It was to this last ceremony that Lavinia Williams came with us and, at my suggestion, started to dance. She had done so at a previous ceremony with no severe sequelae. But this time, very quickly, she went into full possession by one of the loa, ending with an entranced collapse on the floor, which I filmed. She came out of possession fairly soon after her collapse and did not seem unduly upset by the experience. However, I did not feel it was the first time this had happened to her.

Male loa can possess females and female loa males, and most people 'inherit' a particular loa from previous generations of the family. Just as we talk about inheriting certain behaviour patterns from our parents, so in Voodoo it is thought that certain loa possess certain families and influence their behaviour; and these family loa may dominate people's lives. In Voodoo it is also possible to be possessed by different loa at the same time. Like their equivalents in other parts of the West Indies, these loa are identified with Christian saints and may be used for help in people's daily lives. Voodoo worshippers see nothing wrong in going to a Voodoo ceremony and then on to a Catholic Mass. Like the Christian saints, the loa lived on earth before going into the spirit world, and so they are mindful of the needs of human beings: even as loa, they still retain some human characteristics, needs and desires.

Maya Deren's description of her own Voodoo possession must be quoted here, because few people have described so well what happens when a person goes into a state of hysterical dissociation and acts the part of somebody else while in trance. Her account shows the effects that drumming, dancing and the working up of a state of frenzied excitement, added to a lively interest in a religious system, can combine to produce, if you allow yourself to be caught up in the physiological and psychological processes which lead to possession by spirits. I myself was constantly on guard against this, keeping my mind occupied with filming, photographing and recording what was happening around me. To leave your mind blank, or to become emotionally worked up, or angry or frightened, is to make yourself highly vulnerable to the experience which Maya Deren had:

'For now I know that, today, the drums, the singing, the movements—these may catch me also . . . To run away would be cowardice, I could resist; but I must not escape . . . With a great blow the drum unites us once more upon the point of the left leg. The white darkness starts to shoot up; I wrench my foot free but the effect catapults me across what seems a vast, vast distance . . . So it goes: the leg fixed, then wrenched loose, one long fall across space, the rooting of the leg again . . . My skull is a drum; each great beat drives that leg . . . The white darkness moves up the veins of my leg . . . is a great force which I cannot sustain or contain, which surely will burst my skin. It is too much, too bright, too white for me; this is its darkness. "Mercy!" I scream within me. I hear it echoed by the voices, shrill and unearthly: "Erszulie" . . . I am sucked down and exploded upward at once. That is all.'[2]

Finally, I want to quote part of a tape-recording which I made while watching a Voodoo ceremony at night, when I could not film, and perhaps became somewhat suggestible without, to the best of my knowledge, going into trance:

'It really has been an amazing performance. And this is everything one came to Haiti to see—to see this religion where you really do get in contact and live as your god—not just vainly hoping that you will. Your god comes to you, possesses you, mounts you, and you become a god yourself. And these very humble people, with very humble lives, are enabled thereby to live lives of comparative happiness because they have found a religion which does bring down their gods to them. And their gods live in them and they live in their gods. For that reason they are very much happier people than many of us who search for God and never find him, and whose conception of God is some intellectual process conceived in some vague manner in which his God is above, miles and miles away. To them their gods are real.'

NOTES

1 I. M. Lewis, *Ecstatic Religion*. Pelican Books, Harmondsworth, 1971, p. 195.
2 M. Deren, *Divine Horseman*. Thames & Hudson, London, 1953.

20

Revivals in the United States of America

In 1948 I had the honour of being invited to spend a year as Visiting Professor of Psychiatry at Duke University Medical School in Durham, North Carolina. There we were in what had been called the 'Bible Belt' of America, where it is possible to see revival meetings and chapel services which engender tremendous religious enthusiasm and sudden dramatic conversions, such as were seen in England in the time of the Wesleys and the great Victorian evangelists.

Before going to America I had published several accounts of the drug abreactive techniques we had used during the Second World War to help soldiers who had suffered nervous breakdowns in battle and afterwards, and who had become totally preoccupied or 'possessed' by their horrifying war experiences, just as people in earlier days felt themselves possessed by evil spirits. In publications with Dr H. J. Shorvon we had stressed the similarities between some of our findings and the results reported by religious revivalists.[1] In both instances people's emotions were aroused to extreme states of excitement, in one case by preaching and threats of hell fire, in the other by the use of drugs. These emotional states often led to brain inhibition and temporary nervous collapse. In both situations people reported, after collapse, that fear had left their hearts; that they had a sudden feeling of mental peace and a certainty that their sins were forgiven and that by their salvation they would receive their reward in heaven. In the soldiers the result of treatment was that they could remember horrible events of war but without exaggerated emotion, and their fears had left them.

Soon after I arrived at Duke University, I was not altogether surprised to read lurid accounts in a local newspaper of snake-handling services being held at a small chapel in Durham reserved for white people. I was soon inquiring how to get into these snake-handling services, and also how I could attend some of the small active Negro revivalist churches in the neighbourhood. The newspaper reported that live poisonous snakes were being handled by a small group of white worshippers at these chapel meetings—relying on Biblical promises (Mark, xvi: 18: Luke, x: 19) that anyone with sufficient faith could safely handle snakes or drink poison without harm. This was being used to test the faith of the congregation in the power of the Holy Ghost and his ability to protect them from harm.

I called on Mr Bunn, the pastor, and had a long talk with him. He invited my wife and me to one of these meetings and we were allowed to bring a cameraman from the Duke Hospital Photographic Department. I was also able to talk to some of the congregation who had been 'saved' and whose whole lives thereafter had been changed. It would be very foolish to blind oneself to the amount of personal moral and social reform—however shaky the religious premises may be—that revival meetings can produce.

The Zion Tabernacle at Durham was a small hall. The preacher occupied a square space in front of the platform where excited participants could surge towards him as the meeting got under way. Behind him on the platform stood a choir, singing and rhythmically clapping hands. The box containing live poisonous snakes, mostly rattlesnakes and copperheads, stood on the platform. Pastor Bunn and his converts feared to handle these poisonous snakes until certain recognizable signs proved that the Holy Ghost had descended on the meeting and possessed the congregation, so as to protect them from harm. The signs came when some of the people present exhibited what were called 'exercises of the Spirit'. These were in fact hysterical jerkings and twitches of the body and limbs, which usually occurred fairly soon after the harmonium and accordion began playing, and it was only after this that it was considered safe to open the box, take out the snakes and hand them round. As soon as the snakes were produced, the group excitement mounted tremendously, and it was obvious that the pastor could control the excitement by slowing down or accelerating the rate of rhythmic hand-clapping. If he wanted to preach he would temporarily reduce the congregation to awed silence.

At one point in the meeting some students present were

able to take over control of the excitement by leading the hand-clapping and altering its rate according to the degree of excitement shown. Usually this was done by Pastor Bunn and his choir. As the congregation became excited or possessed by the Holy Ghost, they would flock into the pastor's small square and there dance in states of semi-trance or complete trance. The official snake-handler would give the snakes to the pastor, who would then distribute them among the faithful who had handled them before. At this point many of the spectators took fright and left the hall as quickly as they could. But others, especially the women, stayed on, fascinated and becoming more and more affected by the group excitement, and the fear that snakes seem particularly to arouse in women. When Mr Bunn perceived that a person was becoming especially 'vulnerable'—a term used by revivalist sects and, incidentally, in relation to Voodoo by Maya Deren, to describe a change in facial expression which denotes mounting excitement, fear, and the onset of hypnotic states and near-trance—he would approach the person and offer him a poisonous snake to handle. Many of those affected were already showing signs of paradoxical brain activity, so that the snake would often be readily accepted and handled by someone who in his normal state of mind would never have gone near it. Sometimes the handler would then develop acute hysterical symptoms, rapidly followed by stupor and collapse—an effect deliberately induced and intended by the preacher and called 'wiping the slate clean for God'; in Africa this phenomenon is sometimes called 'little death', meaning the death of the old personality and the subsequent birth of a new person. I was seeing here much the same basic technique as we had employed with our Dunkirk and Normandy patients, except that we used drugs to abreact their terrible experiences and restore a more normal nervous system, rather than poisonous snakes, hand-clapping and rhythmic dancing.

Anyone at this meeting who was feeling frightened, bewildered, confused, or who collapsed on the floor, was then reassured: it was quietly whispered in his ear (another example of using the paradoxical phases of brain activity) that it was the Holy Ghost who had brought this about and that he must believe in his power. I found that most revivalist preachers agreed on the folly of expecting sudden dramatic conversions to occur before a suitably excited atmosphere had been built up by personal or group emotional reactions. They know that one must wait for these carefully designed occasions—when the Holy Ghost has descended on the meeting—before making any serious attempt to redeem sinners.

Some of the people who handled snakes for the first time in such a highly charged emotional atmosphere would later join the congregation and indulge in regular snake-handling at later services. None of the people at this meeting died of snake bites, but people have been bitten elsewhere at such meetings, and some die. When this happens it is thought that the person concerned had led a sinful life, or was for some reason being punished by God; the worshippers do not blame the use of poisonous snakes but rather the individual and his past life.

I was also able to obtain a series of close-up photographs of a snake-handling group in Tennessee, and one photograph shows a man sixty seconds before he was bitten by a poisonous snake and died. There was a further photograph of the victim in his coffin several days later at his funeral service, with the worshippers again handling the snake that had bitten and killed him. In this particular group snake-handling services were also used as a means of 'faith healing', so that one patient with severe cancer of the jaw is seen in another photograph, hoping to be healed after handling a snake.

Some years later, on a return trip to America, I witnessed another small snake-handling meeting in Tennessee, but by that time legal measures were being more strongly enforced against the use of poisonous snakes in religious meetings. I was only able to get into this meeting by talking, not to the pastor, but to the person who kept the poisonous snakes in his care; and this was my mistake. This man told me how he had been bitten and was on the point of dying some months previously, and how his wife had procured some snake venom, which had saved his life; but what she had done was quite contrary to his religious principles. It should be left to God to decide whether a worshipper will die, and not to man and the intervention of medical science. He also told me how he had made his peace with God about some of his past attitudes; he felt matters were now all right between himself and his Maker. Later on in the service I saw him handling poisonous snakes, one or two of which had bitten other members of the congregation at previous meetings. Not everybody dies as a result of snake-bite, and some eventually develop an immunity, and endure repeated bites without harm. This is another means of reinforcing faith in God's protective power. But great faith is truly needed to go on handling the same snakes that may have killed fellow worshippers.

Unfortunately, because I had not talked to the pastor first and assured him of my identity and the fact that I had nothing to do with the Press, I was not allowed to take photographs at this exciting meeting. Again I saw a total absence of fear in the participants, once the Holy Ghost had descended upon them with the usual hysterical jerkings and trance-like states. I found myself standing next to somebody who was handling snakes with complete abandon, and they were whipped across my body in a frightening manner. At the meetings of snake-handling I attended I felt that for some reason or other the snakes were not in a biting mood.

We know how Indian snake-handlers, using music, can handle the most poisonous of reptiles, but I became aware that my own personal judgement was at times becoming impaired. At the first meeting in Durham, while in the middle of the milling crowd of hysterical and entranced worshippers, many of them handling snakes, I suddenly had the feeling that I now knew what it felt like to go into battle fearlessly because one was being protected from harm. (This was not long after the end of the war.) This feeling also banished the thought of the possible danger if the snakes fell on the floor and there was a consequent mass panic. Such risks seemed to some extent inhibited by the noise, the excitement and all the possession phenomena that I was studying around me. At both meetings I had a definite feeling that I would have been perfectly safe, even as an unbeliever, in handling the snakes, although I developed no belief that I would be protected by the Holy Ghost. At the Durham meeting I saw two sailors walk straight down the aisle, take the snakes into their hands, give them back, and then walk away. I felt very much like doing the same, but then began to wonder whether my judgement was not being impaired by the whole process. I remember feeling this quite strongly as Pastor Bunn came up to me and tried to make me take a snake myself, which I refused to do. I also remember thinking at the second group I attended that I would handle them if there was any snake venom at hand. However, discretion proved the better part of valour and

I was feeling slightly more nervous at this meeting. But this gave me a very good idea of how one's judgement could become totally confused, and how amid all the noise, enthusiasm and group excitement, normal judgement is impaired.

One of the laboratory assistants from Duke Hospital used to attend the snake-handling in Durham. He told his employer, who was one of the Professors at Durham, that when girls reached the climactic stage of suggestibility, trance and collapse, they appeared to be no less amenable to his sexual suggestions after the meeting was over than they were to Pastor Bunn's message of redemption while the meeting was on. He would follow one of them out from the meeting and found it easy to draw her into immediate sexual abandon. But he said he could not understand why, when he telephoned her a few days later to arrange another meeting, she would say indignantly, 'I am not that kind of girl.' Why had the girls given way so easily immediately after the meeting at which they thought they were 'saved'? The answer must be that the same conversion technique can be employed equally for good or evil ends. This is yet another example of the fact that once the nervous system has had its normal pattern of behaviour disrupted by emotional arousal, all sorts of new beliefs and habits may become acceptable. Nervous illness can be induced or cured. Faith can be created or destroyed, so powerful are these group methods.

According to my wife, I looked just as hypnotized and entranced as the snake-handlers whose photographs I was helping to take. It was certainly a disturbing experience. Most religious groups who use revivalistic methods are accused, by those who prefer a more rational approach in religion, of afterwards indulging in sexual malpractice, and although many of these accusations may be unjustified, I did gain the impression from my conversations with people that those who had been suddenly converted at such meetings often showed greatly heightened sexuality immediately afterwards, especially when it was suggested to them by people who were involved in their breakdown and redemption. I was consulted medically by a woman who kept a brothel in Durham; she assured me that some of her best customers were the pastors and members of the congregation at the revivalist churches.

My wife and I saw further examples of the powerful effects of these meetings at the 'Church of God in Christ Jesus, New

Deal, Incorporated'. This was a small building in an appalling Negro slum area of Durham; there were a few rows of pews, a pastor and again a small dancing space in front of the preaching platform. The Sunday revivalist meetings might last from two to three hours. The congregation were rapidly worked up into states of great excitement and they would then come forward, or be pushed, to the small square in front of the preacher. There they danced singly round and round, most of them in trance, until they reached the point of collapse. When this happened they were helped back to their pews.

At the stage of hysterical suggestibility, when they were supposed to be possessed by the Holy Ghost, the parson would continually remind them of how much they had to thank God for, how merciful he was, and how they must accept their suffering in his name and thank him for his great mercies. The preacher was called 'Bishop Fason'. Towards the end of the meeting he would be rhythmically chanting and shouting with the rest, talking incoherently and what he said no longer seemed to matter. I got the very strong impression that I was again in Africa with the tribal witch-doctor controlling the meeting. At this meeting, however, if the excitement did not mount quickly or strongly enough, six tambourines would be produced and beaten simultaneously instead of tribal drums. On some occasions the Bishop invited us to sit next to him, and having nothing to do but watch I feared I might suddenly be caught up by the rhythm and the enthusiasm, and end up in a state of ecstatic trance myself. Fortunately, both my wife and myself managed to stay in our seats throughout the performances. However, at some of these meetings I gave much larger sums than would be usual for me when the collection box came round!

These meetings meant a great deal to the poor coloured population of Durham, living, as they did, in squalid conditions, down-trodden and exploited by the white population. For one day in the week they would work themselves up into states of excitement and collapse and rid themselves of at least some of the previous week's tensions and frustrations, while the preacher constantly reminded them of God's goodness to them; and this enabled them to face another dreary week. Perhaps, they did sometimes become over-suggestible to the Bishop's exhortations, feeling how important a person he must be, driving around to these churches in his large Cadillac.

During this period I also visited 'God's Bible School' in Cincinnati, where basically the same type of conversion and faith-creating technique was used. Here again all the trance and hysterical phenomena were seen and the people concerned were certain that the Holy Ghost was among them and was possessing them. Several thousands of people would arrive, from time to time, to take part in a week of revival services in a very large hall. Neither rhythmic drumming nor the handling of snakes were needed to bring down the Holy Ghost. Their method consisted of alternate singing and hand-clapping, and sermons about the wrath to come if they persisted in their sinning. This also served to force a mass discharge of guilt among the congregation. Those desiring to be saved and what is called 'sanctified' would come up to a long altar-rail, sometimes weeping and praying. Also on their knees, on the other side of this rail, was a group of people who had already been saved and were able to help the others to achieve the same deliverance. In the background, supervising the scene, stood the group of evangelists, and while the 'saved' talked to the would-be converts, earnestly working upon their emotions, the evangelists would carefully watch for signs of any approaching 'vulnerability'. When this appeared they would converge on their victim and emotionally excite him further until he eventually reached the critical point of total surrender and collapse, and then attained the feelings of sudden conversion.

The individual reactions of people varied greatly. One boy, clearly of schizoid temperament, knelt at the altar-rail amidst the storm of noise, excitement and exhortation, but remained quite detached from it all and simply continued to read a Bible. Near him was a woman who I thought was deeply depressed; she was trying quite ineffectively to break through and reach feelings of possession and salvation. After about half an hour, during which many people on the other side of the rail were constantly exhorting her, to no effect, she stumbled away and walked back down the aisle, seemingly in a state of utter despair, probably thinking that God had found her many sins unpardonable. We have already seen that deeply depressed patients cannot be made to discharge emotion by psychological stimulation alone, but that electric shock treatment, which also works by stimulating the brain to excitement and collapse, is often successful in these cases.

Suicides have been known to result from some of these meetings. Displays of abandoned sexuality were also reported to occur in the evenings, after the meetings, in the grounds surrounding the hall. It was noticed in the mental observation wards in Cincinnati that the number of patients admitted increased considerably after these meetings, when people had been stimulated and excited into states of mental confusion rather than conversion; they settled down again with a few days' sedation and rest. It is always the more normal, as I have already pointed out, and not the mentally ill who can more easily obtain these feelings of salvation and sanctification and of being possessed by a variety of gods, spirits and devils, because they are more suggestible.

It is interesting that while I was at the Duke Medical School a patient came to see me who had had two previous attacks of mental depression. In both these attacks she had gone to religious revival meetings and had attained the feelings of salvation and a relief of her depressive symptoms. But after a third attack the revival meetings had not worked, and she came to the Psychiatric Department at Duke. She was found to be deeply depressed and was given four E.C.T. treatments which greatly helped her. She then went back to the meetings and was now able to attain the desired feelings of salvation and relief at the forgiveness of her depressively exaggerated sins. When I later asked her whether the shock treatment had destroyed her faith, she replied, 'Who sent you three thousand miles to give me this treatment?'

In talking to the people at 'God's Bible School' in Cincinnati who had experienced sudden conversion and sanctification, and had found the strength to maintain their new religious attitudes for long periods, I came to the conclusion that, whatever the explanation for the phenomena seen, it would serve no good purpose to belittle the value of revival meetings in reorientating religiously despairing people. Following conversion, the basic personality may not show any great alteration, but the mind's aims are redirected into other channels.

I talked at considerable length to an obvious psychopath who had spent several years in prison and was finally sent to a chain gang in Georgia, where he went from bad to worse. He developed beri-beri due to vitamin B deficiency in the diet, with the probable additional use of smuggled alcohol. At the lowest stage of his physical and mental condition, he went into the prison church, looked at a perfectly ordinary text on the wall which suddenly became 'alive with meaning'—a phenomenon understandable in terms of Pavlovian physiology and an increased state of suggestibility. On reading this text, 'Believe on the Lord Jesus Christ and thou shalt be saved', he suddenly felt that he understood what this meant—that his sins were forgiven him—and from that moment he underwent a moral and religious reform. On leaving the prison he became an evangelist, taking part in the revivals, though it was noticeable that he was still trying to charge an excessive amount for the pamphlets he was selling. He tended to exaggerate what had happened to him, and I felt he was still a psychopathic personality but that his directions and aims in life had been fundamentally re-orientated in a religious direction rather than towards continuation of his criminal activities. This type of change, with the personality remaining much the same but re-directed, is very commonly reported by revivalists in their memoirs and by those who have written personal accounts of the changes brought about in them.

In the subsequent twenty years, and during further visits to America for lecturing purposes, I was able to visit a variety of other revival and religious meetings. One of the most interesting was in Clay County, Kentucky. This is a truly desolate part of America, in which still live the direct descendants of people who came over from England, Scotland and Ireland in earlier centuries. They might have been prosperous farmers once who had been persuaded to sell the trees on their farms to timber agents. At first there seemed little risk of anything happening as there were no means of carting the logs away. But then the railroad suddenly arrived and all the trees were cut down in accordance with the agreements signed several years previously. Many farmers were also persuaded to sell their rights to the minerals and coal underneath their lands. Then the big corporations came and used open-cast methods of removing large amounts of coal. The land was left treeless, devoid of top soil and totally unworkable for farming purposes. Now, one only sees log huts in a setting of almost total poverty with the population having to live mainly on various forms of relief and charity. The whole place presented a picture of tragic despair and a poverty which I have never seen equalled in any part of the world. It was especially vivid in contrast to the enormous wealth existing in other parts of the States.

I was introduced to a preacher who, with his brother, ran a chapel where the fundamental belief was in the imminent Second Coming of Christ. The congregation were made to understand that unless they had been saved, they might wake up any night to find that the Second Coming had happened. Then, if they had not been saved they were doomed to eternal hell fire. They were also doomed should they leave the meeting and die suddenly of a heart attack before having another chance of achieving salvation through conversion and sanctification.

A series of men in the congregation gave testimonials and short sermons; the hymns were accompanied by a guitar and, as the evening progressed, one saw the same states of excitement, possession, trance and collapse, as were seen in Voodoo meetings in Haiti or in Africa, where quite different gods and spirits were said to enter the worshippers and be responsible for changes in their subsequent behaviour. Many people attending this service appeared to be regular worshippers who came every week to get relief of their pent-up emotions and understandable despair.

During visits to Los Angeles, I attended two meetings at a coloured church in Watts County, where the serious race rioting subsequently took place. In Clay County I had seen what were obviously the church origins of present-day guitar playing and dancing performances. In the coloured churches of Watts County, there was rhythmic jazz singing of hymns, and this has been taken up in recent years with great gusto and swing by groups, both black and white, outside the churches. In my various trips around the States, long before this music had become popular, I had collected a large series of such Negro religious records, which could only then be obtained in the Negro sections of certain towns where rhythm and singing were used to bring about states of mounting excitement, trance and possession by worshippers. Records of Negro sermons are often fascinating to listen to. The sermon is delivered quietly and sedately, to begin with. Every time the preacher makes a positive or a negative statement, a choir of voices cry out, 'Amen. Hallelujah!' In fact, everything the preacher says is continually reinforced by group approval, which is extremely effective in helping to force home to the rest of the audience the truth of what is being said.

At all these meetings, films and close-up photographs were taken, many of which illustrate my point about the probably physiological basis of suggestibility, possession, mental dissociation, trance and other phenomena which occur in old and new religions alike. When studied, these phenomena are seen to be similar in any persons submitting to the same basic techniques, whether they be black or white, sophisticated or primitive.

The reception I received at a Negro Revival church in Harlem was not so friendly, nor were the phenomena seen as intense as in Watts or Clay County. But other similar churches do exist if one looks for them. All over the U.S.A. differing sects of coloured and white people still use methods of procuring salvation which were common in England many years ago, but in the latter country they have been abandoned as the church's impact on the lives of ordinary men and women has steadily diminished.

NOTES

1 Sargant W. and Shorvon H. J., 'Acute War Neuroses', *Arch. Neurol. Psychiat.* LIV, 231; 1945.

Shorvon H. J. & Sargant W., 'Excitatory Abreaction', *J. Ment Sci.* XCIII, 709; 1947.

21

General Conclusions

The material discussed in this book necessarily raises the question of the validity of beliefs which have been cherished by millions of people all through history. We discovered, in treating war-time patients, that battle neuroses could be helped by provoking intense anger or fear in the patient, leading to an emotional explosion and collapse. We found that what mattered in successful treatment was not necessarily the patient's vivid reliving of some traumatic real incident in his past, but the creation of a sufficiently powerful state of emotion about almost anything—a comparatively trivial real incident or even an incident which had never occurred at all. When the patient came round after the collapse, he might find that he felt much better, that he felt a sense of release and calm, that he felt what a revivalist would call 'changed' and 'saved'. When we find that the technique of 'saving' people at revival meetings follows the same pattern and depends on the same brain mechanisms, it is impossible not to wonder about the reality of the divine power supposedly responsible for the 'change'.

As we have seen, it is not just a question of revivalist religious methods but of faith-creating techniques of all sorts. In the preceding chapters I have tried to show that the same physiological processes underlie experiences of 'possession' by gods or spirits or demons, the mystical experience of union with God, the gift of tongues and other phenomena of 'enthusiastic' religious experience, the inspired utterances of oracles and mediums, faith-healing and some aspects of witch-doctoring, and the behaviour of people under hypnosis, under certain drugs, or in states of sexual excitement.

When a man's nervous system is subjected to such a degree of strain that his brain can no longer respond normally—whether this strain is imposed by some single experience or by stresses of less intensity but longer duration—he begins to behave abnormally, in ways which Pavlov and others have charted. He will become very much more suggestible than in his normal state of mind, far more open to ideas and people in his immediate environment and far less able to respond to them with caution, doubt, criticism and scepticism. He may be driven into a condition in which his brain activity, or sometimes one isolated area of it, becomes paradoxical, so that his accustomed outlook and values are reversed. He may reach a condition in which he is as meekly obedient to commands and suggestions as someone under hypnosis, who can be made to behave in ways which, when in command of himself, he would reject as foolish or immoral: and, by post-hypnotic suggestion, he can be made to act in these ways even after he has been brought out of trance and apparently restored to normal waking consciousness. In exactly the same way, psychiatric patients may become so suggestible that they produce in all sincerity the symptoms which suit their psychiatrist's theories: and if they change psychiatrists, they change symptoms.

All this is particularly true, not of the insane, but of the sane, not of the severely mentally ill but of normal, ordinary, average people, who make the best possible material for moulding by those, in religion or out of it, who create faith in themselves and their doctrines by methods which involve the imposition of stress and the working of states of intense emotional excitement (especially, but not limited to, group excitement). Suggestibility is, in fact, one of the essential characteristics of being 'normal'. A normal person is responsive to other people around him, cares about what they think of him and is reasonably open to their influence. If the great majority of people were not normally suggestible, we could not live together in society at all, we could not collaborate in any undertaking, we could not marry and bring up families happily, we could never have in any given society a generally accepted set of values and standards. But if normal people are subjected to the techniques described in this book, it is they who most easily become hysterically suggestible and open to the uncritical and enthusiastic adoption of ideas which may or may not be sensible.

From the Stone Age to Hitler, the Beatles and the modern 'pop culture', the brain of man has been constantly swayed by the same physiological techniques. Reason is dethroned, the normal brain computer is temporarily put out of action, and new ideas and beliefs are uncritically accepted. The mechanism

is so powerful that while conducting this research into possession, trance and faith-healing in various parts of the world, I
myself was sometimes affected by the techniques I was observ-
ing, even though I was on my guard against them. A knowledge
of the mechanism at work may be no safeguard once emotion is
aroused and the brain begins to function abnormally.

On the religious front, one can scarcely help noticing that
against different backgrounds the same process creates convinced belief in different and mutually antagonistic divine
beings. States of possession show this very clearly. In a Christian
context, a person may be 'possessed' by God or by God's opposite and adversary, the Devil. The same mechanism in other
contexts produces possession by the spirits of the ancestors, or
by Allah, Dionysus, Seraphis, Shango, Zars, Pepos, the spirits
of foxes, and an extraordinary variety of other supernatural
agencies. In a mingled context it produces possession by beings
who are half African deities and half Christian saints. Are any
of these beings real at all, and if any, which?

What are we to think, then, about the truth or falsity of the
numerous creeds and faiths that have been physiologically implanted in human beings in different societies and at different
periods? It is sometimes suggested that the proof of the pudding
lies in the eating: that belief in the real god and the right creed
produces good and worth-while results in human behaviour,
while belief in a non-existant god and a wrong creed produces
evil. 'By their fruits ye shall know them.' But unfortunately, the
methods we have been considering are perfectly capable of
making good seem evil and evil seem good. We have also seen
that they are equally effective in maintaining the *status quo* and
keeping people contented with traditional beliefs, conventions
and social systems, or in inducing acceptance of new ideas which
overthrow tradition and orthodoxy. Some people believe that
there is one true God, one great ultimate Reality, behind all
the different faiths of man, and that each of us has a choice
between good and evil. But, unfortunately, there is no question
of man choosing at all, when he can so readily be induced to
adopt beliefs diametrically opposed to those he previously held,
due to the creation by emotional arousal of paradoxical and
ultraparadoxical phases of brain activity.

Again, it may be argued that a great many people never experience possession or states of trance and ecstasy, and so are

not influenced by those means. But the fact is that few, if any, of us go through our lives without experiencing stresses and emotional excitements which cause heightened suggestibility and create states of brain activity in which new ideas and beliefs may be implanted and accepted against our normal judgement. The new faith may fade away again with a return to a calmer state, but in many cases it may persist, secure from criticism in its own niche in the mind.

Our personal vulnerability will depend in part on the type of nervous system and brain that we have inherited. Where obsessional tendencies and compulsive thinking are marked, there is much less tendency to develop states of hysterical suggestibility and mental dissociation or to go into trance and possession. Obsessional people can live much more easily on a basis of rational thought. The difficulty is, however, that if new ideas, whether valuable or not, are finally implanted in the obsessional type of person, the excessive rigidity of his temperament makes subsequent readjustment very difficult to achieve. Many of the great moral reformers of the past, including Wesley, Francis of Assisi, Ignatius Loyola and others, have been people of obsessional temperament. It took a severe illness, a severe physical debilitation, or a prolonged emotional crisis, perhaps occurring all at the same time, to produce fundamental alterations in their patterns of thought and the emergence of new beliefs and modes of living.

The whole process of civilization depends almost entirely on a number of people being born in each new generation who have important new beliefs and ideas, and hold on to them with obsessional tenacity. Most great scientific discoverers, for example, have to cling obstinately to their new ideas and findings, often for years, before they find acceptance. This means that the originators of new ideas and the founders of new systems are rarely themselves 'normal' people; if they were, they would drop their new notions comparatively quickly in the face of the hostility of their fellows.

The person with manic-depressive tendencies, on the other hand, will find himself constantly changing his views and beliefs, in tune with his changing swings of mood. A strong religious faith may be totally lost during a depressive attack and regained in a subsequent elated or normal period. The schizophrenic and the schizoid thinker is the most immune of all to outside influences dominating his ideas. His ideas come much more often from inside himself and may be the product of hallucinations, delusions and other abnormal thought processes which he experiences, and which he tries to explain on the basis of further delusional thinking. During the war, schizophrenics were rarely upset by bombing, for instance, being far too preoccupied with their own inner turmoils and worries.

Anxiety-prone people will change their views fairly frequently unless there are strong obsessive components in their personalities. Anxiety and fear create heightened suggestibility and make them prone to changing states of faith. They may experience periods of wild panic, when an individual starts to clutch at straws and precipitates the ever-present threat of switching into paradoxical and ultraparadoxical modes of thought, resulting in repeated alteration of viewpoint and belief. Persons of hysterical temperament are also highly suggestible. Hysterical behaviour is most commonly the result of normal people breaking down under severe stresses, as was seen again and again during the war and as we have seen repeatedly in this book.

I think I might have to end these long years of research with the conclusion that there are no gods, but only impressions of gods created in man's mind, so varied are the gods and creeds which have been brought into being by playing on emotional arousal, increased suggestibility and abnormal phases of brain activity. Certainly, totally different beliefs can be and are created and maintained by the methods of indoctrination discussed in the previous chapters. Faith-healing, in both simple and sophisticated societies, also depends on the induction of emotional excitement to achieve the breaking up of old behaviour patterns and the emergence of new ones. Faith healing and spirit possession rarely happen in a calm, rational atmosphere, as every witch-doctor and faith-healer knows only too well. Emotion must be aroused for success to be obtained. There is no need for there to be a god to do the healing. Any method which induces states of excitement leading to a suitable degree of exhaustion and consequent alteration in brain function can work miracles on its own.

Perhaps we must therefore conclude that it is man who has created the gods and made them in his image, reflecting his varying imaginings, aspirations and fears, just as he, and not some mysterious fate or necessity or abstract historical dynamic, has created his varying political creeds and moral codes. And yet we need faith. Without faith of some sort living becomes extraordinarily difficult. We do not live by reason alone and we have to take all sorts of people and assumptions on trust. We need confidence in ourselves, in the value of the work we do, in certain people and standards. We cannot, or most of us cannot, for ever be doubting and questioning and withholding final judgement on everything and everyone. Most of us quite evidently need the support of some general religious, political or social framework of faith, however bizarre or dangerous a particular belief-system may be. We need faith and yet, as I have tried to demonstrate, we must suspect it.

This book obviously poses as many problems as it solves. But if it does no more than stimulate fresh thought and help us to be on our guard against beliefs acquired in states of emotional arousal when our brains may be betraying us, then it will have served some purpose. We must equally beware of trying to influence our fellow-men by the methods discussed here. In the future, the conquest and control of man's mind is going to be a far more important matter for us all than the development of bigger and better nuclear weapons, and it is essential that we learn all we can about how the brain works and how human beings can be psychologically coerced.

But the paradoxes remain. We need faith, but must suspect it. We need to be suggestible, but our suggestibility is dangerous. And the last dread paradox is that people's beliefs and behaviour can only be changed radically and swiftly by the methods we have been considering, and very rarely by purely intellectual and rational argument. Man will continue to be possessed by many gods and devils and beliefs. He will continue to reach the sublimest heights of good and the lowest depths of evil, for the range of his normal behaviour patterns, and there-fore his ability to cope with all life's varied stresses, has made him the most successful mammal on earth. But unless the varieties of good and evil behaviour possible to him can some-how be controlled in the future, man and his world will go down to certain destruction by his own hand. Yet how do we control man *rationally*, by appealing to reason rather than by arousing emotion. This is the problem that this book has presented but not solved.

Bibliography

Andrews, E., *The People Called Shakers*, Oxford University Press 1953

Bharati, A., *The Tantric Tradition*, Allen & Unwin, London 1968

Binet, A., and Féré, C., *Animal Magnetism*, Kegan Paul, London 1887

Cavendish, R., *The Black Arts*, Routledge, London 1967

Conway, C., *Magic: An Occult Primer*, Cape, London 1971

Cumont, F., *The Oriental Religions in Roman Paganism*, Kegan Paul, London 1911

Deren, M., *The Divine Horsemen*, Thames & Hudson, London 1953

Dodds, E. R., *The Greeks and the Irrational*, University of California Press 1966

Doughty, W. L., *John Wesley*, Epworth Press, London 1955

Frank, J. D., *Persuasion and Healing*, John Hopkins Press 1961

Freud and Breuer, *Studies in Hysteria*, Avon Library, New York 1966

Grant, K., *The Magical Revival*, Muller, London 1972

Grinker, R. R., and Spiegel, J. P., *Men under Stress*, Blakiston, Philadelphia 1943

Guenther, H. V., *Life and Teaching of Nāropa*, Clarendon Press 1963

Guthrie, W. K. C., *The Greeks and Their Gods*, Methuen, London 1950

Harrer, H., *Seven Years in Tibet*, Rupert Hart-Davis, London 1955

Hooke, S. H., *Babylonian and Assyrian Religion*, Hutchinson, London 1953

Huxley, A., *The Devils of Loudon*, Chatto & Windus 1952

Jones, E., *Sigmund Freud*, Vol 1 and 2, Hogarth Press, London 1955

Kiev, A., *Magic, Faith and Healing*, Collier-Macmillan, London 1964

King, F., *Sexuality, Magic and Perversion*, Spearman, London 1971

Knox, R. A., *Enthusiasm*, Clarendon Press, Oxford 1950

Lanternori, V., *The Religions of the Oppressed*, MacGibbon & Kee, London 1963

Laski, M., *Ecstasy,* Cresset Press, London 1961

Latourette, K. S., *History of Christianity*, Harper, New York 1953

Leary, T., *The Politics of Ecstasy*, MacGibbon & Kee, 1970

Leuba, J. H., *A Psychological Study of Religion*, Macmillan, New York 1912

Leuba, J. H., *Psychology of Religious Mysticism*, London 1929

Lewis, I. M., *Ecstatic Religion*, Pelican Books 1971

Lindblom, J., *Prophecy in Ancient Israel*, Blackwell, Oxford 1962

Lucian, *Satirical Sketches*, Penguin Books 1961

Man, Myth and Magic, Edited Cavendish, R., Parnell, London 1970–72

Maringer, J., *The Gods of Prehistoric Man*, Weidenfeld, London 1960

Mediaeval Mystics of England, Edited Colledge, E., Murray, London 1962

O'Brien, E., *Varieties of Mystic Experiences*, Holt, New York 1964

Oesterreich, T. K., *Possession, Demoniacal and Other*, Kegan Paul, London 1930

Pavlov, I. P., *Lectures on Conditioned Reflexes*, Vol 2, Lawrence & Wishart, London 1941

Podmore, F., *Mediums of the 19th Century,* Vol 1 and 2, University Books, New York 1963

Ross, A. V., *Vice in Bombay*, Tallis Press, London 1969

Sachner, R. C., *Mysticism, Sacred and Profane*, Oxford Press 1961

St. John of the Cross, Poems, Penguin Books 1960
Salmon, G., *A Sermon on the Work of the Holy Spirit*, Hodges, Smith, Dublin 1859
Sargant, W., *Battle for the Mind*, Heinemann 1957
Sargant, W., *The Unquiet Mind*, Heinemann 1967
Shorvon, H. J., 'Abreaction', *Proc. Roy. Soc. Med.* 1953, p 158
Smith, H. W., *Man and his Gods*, Cape, London 1953
Southey, R., *Life of Wesley*, Longmans, London 1820
Spencer, P., *The Samburu*, Routledge, London 1965
Spencer, S., *Mysticism in World Religion*, Penguin Books 1963
Starbuck, E. D., *The Psychology of Religion*, Scott, London 1901

Trance and Possession States, Edited Prince, R., Bucke Society, Montreal 1968

Verger, P., *Dieux d'Afrique*, Hartman, Paris 1954
Virgil, *Aeneid*, Penguin Books 1956

Walker, B., *Hindu World*, Allen & Unwin, London 1968
Wasson, R. G., *Soma*, Harcourt Brace, New York 1968
Wesley, J., *Journal of John Wesley*, Charles Kelly, London 1909–16

Youssoupoff, F., *Lost Splendour*, Cape, London 1953

Articles and Books published by author on subjects discussed in this book

N.B. *BMJ* refers to the *British Medical Journal*.

1938 'Hyperventilation Attacks'. Fraser, R. and Sargant, W., *BMJ*, p 378.
1940 'Acute War Neuroses'. Sargant, W. and Slater, E., *Lancet*, p 1.
1940 'The Hyperventilation Syndrome'. Sargant, W., *Lancet*, p 314.
1941 'The Treatment of War Neuroses'. Debenham, G., Sargant, W., Hill, D. and Slater, E., *Lancet*, p 107.
1941 'Amnesic Syndromes in War'. Sargant, W. and Slater E., *Proc. Roy. Soc. Med.*, p 47.

1941 'Modified Insulin Therapy in War Neuroses'. Sargant, W. and Craske, N., *Lancet*, p 212.

1942 'The Treatment of Depression in Later Life'. Sargant, W. and Sands, D. E., *BMJ*, p 520.

1942 'Physical Treatment of Acute War Neuroses'. Sargant, W., *BMJ*, p 574.

1944–72 *Physical Methods of Treatment in Psychiatry.* edns. 1–5. Sargant, W., Slater, E., and S. Livingstone, Edinburgh.

1945 'Acute War Neuroses'. Special Reference to Abreaction. Sargant, W. and Shorvon, H. J., *Arch. Neurol. Psychiat.*, p 231.

1947 'Chronic Battle Neurosis treated with Leucotomy'. Sargant, W. and Stewart, O. M., *BMJ*, p 866.

1947 'Treatment by Insulin in Sub-shock Doses'. Sargant, W. and Slater, E., *J. Mental and Nervous Dis.*, p 493.

1947 'Excitatory Abreaction: with special reference to its Mechanism and the Use of Ether'. Shorvon, H. J. and Sargant, W., *J. Mental Sci.*, p 709.

1948 'Some Observations on Abreaction with Drugs'. Sargant, W., *Digest of Neurol. and Psychiatry*, p 193.

1949 'Some Cultural Group Abreactive Techniques and their Relation to Modern Treatment'. Sargant, W., *Proc. Roy. Soc. Med.*, p 367.

1951 'The Mechanism of Conversion'. Sargant, W., *BMJ*, p 311.

1957 *Battle for the Mind*. Sargant, W., Wm. Heinemann, London, and Pan Books, London.

1957 'Aim and Method in Treatment: Twenty Years of British and American Psychiatry'. *J. Mental Sci.*, p 699.

1961 'Drugs in the Treatment of Depression'. Sargant, W., *BMJ*, p 225.

1962 'Treatment of Anxiety States by Antidepressant Drugs'. Sargant, W. and Dally, P., *BMJ*, p 6.

1967 'Witch Doctoring, Zar and Voodoo: Their Relation to Modern Psychiatric Treatments'. *Proc. Roy. Soc. Med.*, p 47.

1969 'The Physiology of Faith' (Maudsley Lecture). *Brit. Jour. Psychiat.*, p 505.

Index